The Mystic Life of
Alfred Deakin

For Cherry

The Mystic Life of Alfred Deakin

Al Gabay

Department of Humanities
La Trobe University College of Northern Victoria

CAMBRIDGE
UNIVERSITY PRESS

Published by the Press Syndicate of the University of Cambridge
The Pitt Building, Trumpington Street, Cambridge CB2 1RP, UK
40 West 20th Street, New York, NY 10011-4211, USA
10 Stamford Road, Oakleigh, Melbourne, Victoria 3166, Australia

© Cambridge University Press 1992
First published 1992

Printed in Hong Kong by Colorcraft

National Library of Australia cataloguing-in-publication data
Gabay, Al, 1946–
The mystic life of Alfred Deakin.
Bibliography.
Includes index.
ISBN 0 521 41494 6.
ISBN 0 521 44681 3 (pbk.).
1. Deakin, Alfred, 1856–1919—Religion. 2. Prime ministers—
Australia—Religious life. I. Title.
994.032092

Library of Congress cataloging-in-publication data
Gabay, Al, 1946–
The mystic life of Alfred Deakin/Al Gabay.
Includes bibliographical references and index.
ISBN 0 521 41494 6 (hardback)
1. Deakin, Alfred, 1856–1919—Religion. 2. Statesmen—Australia—
Biography. I. Title.
DU116.2.D4G35   1992
994.04′1′092—dc20
[B]   91-45554
                                                                CIP

A catalogue record for this book is available from the British Library

ISBN 0 521 41494 6 hardback

Contents

Acknowledgements

In the course of this study, I have received both intellectual guidance and personal encouragement. I owe more than I can express to my supervisors, Dr John Hirst, Mrs Inga Clendinnen and Professor Rhys Isaac; to Dr F. B. Smith for his pioneering study of Freethought; and to the late Professor J. A. La Nauze, who granted me access to his restricted collection of papers and thus enriched my own research immeasurably. I am grateful also to Mrs Judith Harley for permission to use the Deakin papers, and to Mr Graeme Powell and his capable staff at the Manuscript Section, Australian National Library. Among those others upon whom I have depended for friendship and assistance in a variety of ways, I mention in particular Ms Kaye Bignell, Ms Carole Gabay, Mr Rodney Sharp, Mr Peter Sharp, and Dr Roger Sworder. My deepest thanks go to my wife Cherry, for her patience and support at crucial points in the lengthy process of revision.

Introduction

The only existing film footage of Alfred Deakin survives in a short pictorial record of the inauguration of the Commonwealth of Australia at Sydney's Centennial Park on 1 January 1901, the first day of the new century. Attired in tophat and tails, Deakin descends the octagonal pavilion where he had just been sworn in as Attorney-General in Edmund Barton's government.[1] In this brief glimpse of the living man, self-consciously doffing his hat to the crowd as he descends alone after taking the oath of office, we note first the slight stoop and lean physical stature, a certain fatigue described on his face, and a truly enigmatic smile. It is the smile of a public man accustomed to ceremonial, but there is something besides.

At the bottom of the stairs Deakin sees the camera and gazes into it for a moment, then in the remaining seconds as he passes by, the hat somehow comes between his face and the lens of posterity. In another, this gesture might easily be passed over or be put down to natural shyness; but in this unusual man, it is a gesture that might well have carried a meaning, even if half-conscious and impromptu. With a profound sense of history and destiny, a penchant for 'signs' and significant dates, and with an abiding Faith in the All-Seeing Providence, perhaps to Deakin this action signified humility at this triumphant moment they had been working toward for over a decade. At any rate that smile and fixed gaze, however fleeting, are not easily forgotten.

Alfred Deakin had been 'whirled into' politics early, and became a legend during his own lifetime. One historian has aptly described him as 'the great phenomenon of Australian political history, even of Australian experience', not only for that long and illustrious career, but because Deakin was unusual among Australian intellectuals in his association with the 'Occult', in a lifelong quest for 'spiritual enlightenment and discipleship'.[2] On the public stage Deakin was an adept at parliamentary tactics, yet widely respected for his brilliant capacities and trusted even by political opponents. He was admired as a masterful orator whose 'burning, bristling and commanding' eloquence[3] could on occasion subdue an unruly Parliament. Deakin's political significance rests in his status as key member of that small educated elite which Pember-Reeves called the 'barrister politicians' of the prosperous generation after the gold rushes.[4] Rising to power first in the colonial legislatures, they exercised considerable influence on the political processes of Australia in framing the Constitution and establishing the political and judicial institutions of the Commonwealth.

This book is not intended as a full biography of a master politician. Deakin's enormous contribution to these political labours of nation-building has been documented and sagely analysed in Professor J. A. La Nauze's biography, and to a lesser extent by Walter Murdoch, author in 1923 of the first sketch of Deakin's life. Rather, it is intended as a corrective, for although each author illuminated aspects of this complex man and his political milieu, neither in my view succeeded in integrating Deakin's public exertions to what was unquestionably their motive power: a profound, almost pietistic, private religious faith.

Deakin always took pains to obscure the creative and spiritual dimensions of his being from the gaze of others, yet he did leave an enormous volume of private writings, spanning a range of genres. It is principally through this body of writings that occupied his diminishing leisure over some forty years, that the substance of his personal faith and its relation to the well known public life and persona are disclosed, however opaquely. That fecund inner life can be glimpsed also, I shall argue, in his public life and even in his public writings.

At this triumphant moment of the inauguration of the Commonwealth fleetingly captured by the camera, Deakin could look back in thankfulness at the workings of Providence as he believed it had touched his career: a meteoric rise in the Victorian Parliament, when he became the voice of the Australian-born, radical reformer of factories legislation and 'father' of irrigation; and before the age of thirty Liberal leader and co-leader of a coalition government. That Providence had now brought them to nationhood, against what seemed at times insurmountable obstacles. But had Deakin been gifted with true prevision of the events to follow the brief elation of a federated Australia, he would have been less sanguine. He would remain the dominating figure, in or out of office, during the first decade of the Commonwealth, and the three ministries he led would put into place foundational legislation like the Judiciary Act establishing the High Court, and advanced social legislation such as pensions and an arbitration system that would earn Australia a reputation in this era as the 'social laboratory' of the world. But that final decade of his public service would entail great compromises in his political ideas, particularly in the 'Fusion' in 1909 with his former Conservative opponents, exacting an enormous personal cost in diminished faculties and broken health, which by the end of the decade would finish Deakin's effectiveness as a political leader.

This book endeavours to look behind the 'affable' exterior to another Alfred Deakin given intimate expression through his private writings: the 'silent student', the seeker for Providential 'signs', the fervent believer in prophecy and inspiration, the would-be poet, preacher and mystic, whose insights and experiences gradually convinced him that his political labours were mandated by the Divine will, and that the fate of his beloved nation was somehow linked to his own capacity for spiritual gnosis and moral improvement.

Notes

1 Two versions exist of the inauguration of the Commonwealth. I have seen both, but have been able to document only this one, NA 1009, which is reproduced in a 1966 A.B.C. documentary 'Mr Prime Minister', NC 211; National Film and Sound Archives, Canberra.

2 M. Roe, *Nine Australian Progressives, Vitalism in Bourgeois Social Thought 1890–1960*, St Lucia, 1984, p. 18.

3 W. H. Watt, Obituary Testimonial, 23/74, 22 October 1919.

4 W. Pember-Reeves, *State Experiments in Australia and New Zealand* (1902), Melbourne, 1969, 2 vols, vol. 1, pp. 54–5.

1

A Sense of Mystery

In the seventies I was bearing in my breast,
Penned tight,
Certain starry thoughts that threw a magic light
On the worktimes and the soundless hours of rest
In the seventies; aye, I bore them in my breast
Penned tight

Thomas Hardy,
'Moments of Vision'

Extraordinary powers of imagination, a love of mystery and a preoccupation with heroism and death, along with a precocious philosophical seriousness, were apparent early in the character of Alfred Deakin. His parents were English migrants, nominally Church of England members and tolerant in their attitudes, devoted to Alfred and his older sister Catherine, who practised considerable self-denial to give their talented children a good education.[1] William Deakin came from Northamptonshire where he had been a commercial traveller, and Sarah Bill was the daughter of a Shropshire farmer. In 1849 they married and emigrated to Australia where, with help from relatives, William first became a partner in a mail run from Serpentine to Swan Hill; then, moving to Melbourne, he was accountant to Cobb & Co. for the rest of his working life.[2]

In a handwritten note self-effacingly entitled 'Parents of Alfred Deakin', Catherine describes the characters and the middle-class values of these 'refined, simple people with a strong thrall of duty'. They were 'broadminded and unconventional', yet also 'great believers in good manners and the customs of well-bred English folk'. They were 'lovers of home and children'. William was impressionable, enthusiastic and talkative, with great powers of description and a fondness for literature, especially for the English classics which he would read aloud to the family. He was very regular in his habits and 'most particular as to dress'. Sarah was modest and, though less talkative, 'when she spoke it was to the point'. She is described as full of shrewd common sense, often witty and humorous, and her influence is characterised as 'all pervading in the home life but never dominating'. In this environment Alfred and Catherine, although allowed absolute freedom, '[n]ever undertook anything without the influence of their unspoken principles of life guiding the decision.'[3]

In his youth Alfred was enjoined to attend services, probably by Catherine, which he found boring. Half a century later he recalled how during the sermon he had preferred to read the Old Testament, describing himself at age eight as 'a curious compound ... highly nervous, slender, overgrown, sensitive, sympathetic, variable, emotional, apprehensive & dreamy.'[4] Though normal in every respect, in these early years he suffered from frail health, a stigma of girlishness and awkward physical development.

Suddenly at age thirteen, probably from 'an impulse of reading' as he remembered, Alfred took up Sunday school where he taught during 1869–70. However, when confirmation was made compulsory for all teachers he refused, since as he understood it, 'Christianity ... was wider than any & all of the Churches, & therefore acceptance of any formal limitations impossible', and also because of his father's 'feeling against conformity'.[5] When Alfred turned to spiritistic investigations in late adolescence, his parents displayed neither great interest nor antagonism.

The lessons at the Melbourne Church of England Grammar School were a drudgery 'lived through without interest or aim'.[6] His delight was to hurry home to storybooks, whose magic unlocked a treasure of gallant dreams and faraway places. *Robinson Crusoe, Pilgrim's Progress* and the *Arabian Nights* became his real friends, along with books by Dumas, Fenimore Cooper, Dickens and other classics. Fed by a habit of constant reading acquired from his father, these dreams increased in intensity, so that escape to literature became for a time the dominating feature of Deakin's adolescent life. Many years later he wondered whether he had not 'lived more, & more intensely, in & through books';[7] for the moment literature became a fertile mental playground. He would spin romances in his mind where he was 'the culmination of all heroes, & in turn every kind of noble being', engaged in 'winning a long line of peerless beauties under the most desperate & amazing circumstances'.[8]

In order to collect 'fresh knowledge & inspiration' for these reveries, from around 1865 when he was nine Alfred began to visit public libraries most Saturdays and holidays, reading on occasion from 10 a.m. to 6 p.m., with a short interval for pocket lunch. His schoolmasters thought him unpromising, but this was due to a lack of interest and application, which he reserved for his copious private reading and daydreaming. A new world opened in which he regularly worked out each career, involving 'a geography of an extensive character, peoples of different complexions, cities & seaports, navies & armies, courts & industries'. Thus he undertook in turn 'the labour of Hercules, campaigns à la Napoleon, seafights à la Nelson, & statesmanship à la Louis XIV':

> Often in school I continued to dream at my desk—walked home rapt in its development— remained for hours in its varied responsibilities—always those of the explorer & conqueror who devoted himself to the elevation of his people & the enrichment of his country. These grew longer as I became possessed of more material & might last for a week or two. At this time ... I lived in these creations more than in that in which I moved, an often silent, absent & contented visionary—& of all this, neither friend, or companion, or relative ever heard a single word.[9]

What seems unusual, as Deakin's first biographer Walter Murdoch noted, is not the fact of adolescent fantasy but the intensity and sophistication of his imagination, a detachment of his inner world and private thoughts from the gaze of others, and the 'steady and glowing persistence with which he went his own way', a singular trait of character becoming more marked with maturity.[10]

The year 1872 marks an important watershed in Deakin's intellectual development, as his thoughts were gradually turning to ponder deeper questions concerning the human condition. In this year his reading tastes began to mature, and he commenced writing. Shortly after entering the senior school, encouraged by J. H. Thompson who alone among his teachers had earned his almost worshipful admiration, he embarked upon more serious reading. Always a rapid reader, the sixteen-year-old Alfred raced through Macaulay's *History*, Buckle's *History of Civilisation*, Bacon's *Essays* and other worthy tomes, increasing all the while his acquaintance with the English literary classics—Shakespeare, Milton, Byron, and Coleridge among them. It was also in 1872 that Deakin was introduced to the two dominating influences in his early adult life, through two older friends then employed at the Post Office. By Edward Mickle he was introduced to the philosophy of Herbert Spencer, who would remain 'an authority on practical affairs' until after Deakin had entered the Victorian Parliament. In 1873, together with Arthur Patchett Martin, later editor of that self-confident testament to 'Marvellous Melbourne' *Victoria & Her Metropolis* and a biographer of Robert Lowe, they formed a 'home circle' in his parents' home to investigate the phenomena of Spiritualism.[11] For a time these two seemed encyclopaedic and omniscient, but as the sincere enthusiast embarked upon six months of 'hard & happy work', his reading eventually 'raced up to & even ahead of them'. Of this exhilarating period Deakin wrote many years later, and without a trace of irony, that he was then seeking 'a system of philosophy, an interpretation of the universe, & a key to all the mysteries of life & being'.[12] This search for system and for a 'key' to the perennial mysteries of life was an enterprise that, in diverse ways, would continue to occupy him throughout his life.

By the early 1870s Melbourne was no longer the frontier town on the banks of the sluggish Yarra surrounded by a 'tent city' of canvas and calico, that had served as port and entrepôt to the thousands of miners eager to reach the goldfields in the interior. The wealth torn out of the ancient earth had tangibly transformed Melbourne within two generations into a budding metropolis of two hundred thousand population. A secular university, a public library which was 'a monument to received good taste', largely Redmond Barry's, and a museum had all been established in the 1850s.[13] An English gentleman writing in 1869 could recommend to his countrymen its 'fine and fashionable suburbs; its noble public institutions ... [and] ample mathematically-appointed streets, resplendent with the gaiety of amply-furnished shops'.[14] The city had also acquired an active cultural life of its own though, with a large migrant population, still derivative of English mores. In colonial Melbourne as in London, the platform and the pulpit, along with pamphlets and newspapers, were the principal means of communicating ideas. Through the many societies that sprang up, serious public debate was thriving not only on political questions like land reform, 'free, compulsory, and secular' education and the all-important protective tariff, but also on wider social issues and on the perennial questions of religion and the nature of human existence.

The first major forum for the colonial intelligentsia on religious and social topics was the Eclectic Association, founded in 1867 by the atheist and rationalist H. K. Rusden. Its membership included E. W. Cole the bookseller, B. S. Naylor the Spiritist and Socialist, and the journalist Charles Bright, as well as the ubiquitous James Smith, also a journalist for the *Argus*, trustee of the Public Gallery, and general social gadfly, best remembered as severe critic of the '9 X 5' exhibition of the Heidelberg school in 1889.[15] At the Sunday Free Discussion Society, also founded by the energetic Rusden in 1870, political and secular subjects predominated. The meetings in the 'Turn Verein' Hall on La Trobe Street, leased from the Spiritualists, were to remain a feature of Sunday night life in Melbourne until the early years of the new century. Like the Democratic Association, which took its name and much of its co-operative programme from later Chartism, a general atmosphere of Reform, a 'scientific' enthusiasm and a definite anti-Christian feeling prevailed. Following English trends, especially the 1869 London Dialectical Society debates, 'spiritualistic' (or spiritistic) phenomena became topics of controversy in Melbourne's public forums. In the same year, a celebrated Eclectic Association debate between W. H. Terry and H. G. Turner, the Unitarian banker and future historian of Victoria, generated a good deal of publicity and several pamphlets for and against, leading to the establishment of the Victorian Association of Progressive Spiritualists (V.A.P.S.) the following year.[16]

Spiritualism was a largely working-class religious movement, originating in 1848 in the 'burnt over' districts of upper New York State, when two adolescent girls were reported to have established contact with the spirit of a departed individual.[17] Their experiences were publicised widely, and soon seances (literally: sittings) purporting to contact the dead via 'mediums' were being conducted in drawing rooms all over the eastern seaboard of the United States. Throughout the 1850s decade the movement spread rapidly via England to Europe, and then to the settler societies, including the Australian colonies. It attracted public men like Horace Greeley, Judge W. Edmonds of the United States Supreme Court and Robert Owen to its beliefs, and even eminent persons like Napoleon III and the Russian Czar, but also many powerful detractors, especially among positivist scientists like Michael Faraday.[18] While never reaching the proportions of hysteria it had in the United States, the Spiritualist movement, carried along with other progressive ideas by many among the gold-rush generation, attracted a strong following in Victoria.

In Spiritualism the prevailing atmosphere of religious doubt, exacerbated by the popularised Darwinian thought, found expression in a peculiar amalgam of Swedenborgianism, mesmerism and popular freethought, especially in its ideas about 'science' and 'progress'. In essence, this produced a religion which sought to prove the continued existence of the human personality beyond the grave, and claimed to receive deeper teachings from more exalted spiritual 'guides'.

Many persons, while not completely losing their religious faith, were rejecting doctrinal Christianity. Marcus Clarke writing in the *Victorian Review* reflected upon the dilemma of many of the educated among his generation who could no longer accept 'the dogmas of the priesthood . . . they would fain believe, but for their reason; they are compelled to reason, despite their belief'.[19] During these years, many strands of Freethought flourished, and there were calls for many kinds of Reform. The theist Judge Williams denied that Jesus was God, but a great man, and he denounced much of the Old Testament as 'unsuitable and filthy'. Charles Bradlaugh's secularism was to arrive in the colony first with Thomas Walker, a spiritist medium converted to Secularism, later a prominent Western Australian politician, even before the vulgar Joseph Symes came in 1884 to found the *Liberator* and to bait and insult the established religions.[20] When the *Harbinger of Light*, the organ of the Spiritualists, in September 1872 advertised 'Agricola', a co-operative to be formed under the Free Selection Act, the editor W. H. Terry wished them God-speed, for 'we look upon the organisation of labour as the remedy for all the sufferings of humanity'. Even a stalwart of the establishment like Dr Bromby, the liberal Anglican theologian who had been Deakin's headmaster at Melbourne Grammar, outraged listeners to an 1870 sermon by denying the reality of a theological Hell. In the 1880s he would be instrumental in having women admitted to the university, and during the celebrated 'trial' of Dr Charles Strong, he would again inflame conservative opinion by trading pulpits with that 'heretic'.[21]

The disaffected in Victoria generally turned either to the Unitarian church, to the Secularists, those 'brave witnesses to unbelief', or to the largest heterodox religious organisation in the colonies, the Victorian Association of Progressive Spiritualists (V.A.P.S.), whose optimistic, if ponderously declared, aims were:

> to extend the domain of science to the realms of the invisible, the impalpable, and the imponderable, and to supersede the supernatural by proving that the occult mysteries of human nature heretofore deemed beyond the reach of human intellect, are destined to be revealed to the truth-seeker, to the unspeakable advantage of humanity.[22]

This stentorian declaration fairly reflects Deakin's own early views: an Enlightenment faith in Reason and in the possibility of its extension to higher spheres, and 'scientific' objectives in an optimistic quest for religious Truth. Public opinion on these 'strange things' ranged from indifference to scorn. Some ascribed the phenomena to the devil, or like the Anglican Bishop Perry, denounced Spiritualism as 'a recrudescence of the ancient divination of Egypt and Chaldea'.[23] In January 1871, a debate extending over three weeks was conducted through the pages of the *Argus*. James Smith, publicly declaring his faith in 'Spiritualism Defended', was responded to by eminent sceptics such as H. G. Turner, Marcus Clarke and David Blair.[24] When it was asked why, if spirit phenomena were the work of the devil, Melbourne Spiritualists were men of such high moral stature, the Anglican Dean of Melbourne, H. B. Macartney, responded that 'the Devil was too shrewd to use inferior agents.'[25] Deakin's early interest was sparked by such controversies, and grew with his reading. Huxley, then other detractors of Christianity such as the Spiritualists, were using the new scholarship of the higher Biblical criticism, which challenged the authority of the Bible as 'verbal inspiration', and the triumphs of science, especially geological evidence for the earth's antiquity and the evolution theory of Darwin and Wallace, as potent weapons against the sacred domain of organised religion. In this atmosphere Deakin like many others of his generation, imbibed the spirit of Reform.[26]

The lively discussions with Mickle and Martin, usually after Sunday dinner at the Deakin home in Adam Street, South Yarra, centred on 'moral evolution' and other Spencerian doctrines, and on the phenomena. Articles published in 1872 by two eminent scientists were important not only to the young Alfred, but to the movement as a whole, in lending it some measure of scientific respectability.[27] Upon reading Sir William Crookes' startling accounts of 'materialisations' occurring in his own home under 'test' conditions in the *Quarterly Journal of Science*, of which he was then editor, and the *Fortnightly* article by Alfred Russell Wallace, co-originator of the theory of the evolution of species by natural selection, on the evolutionary implications of a continued existence after death, Deakin 'at once took up the theme' of investigating these matters personally.[28]

Deakin had seen juvenile attempts at mesmerism (hypnotism), and years before he had witnessed planchette writing; it was all very odd and mysterious.[29] At one improvised drawing-room performance then in vogue, Alfred was staging a feat of mesmerism for the mixed company, where his 'keen interest was intended to be ridiculed'. Instead, to everyone's amazement the young subject found herself 'speechless & helpless, falling into a kind of a swoon'.[30] While on holidays with his family in Dromana at the end of the same year, Alfred took his damp boots to the hotel kitchen to be dried. There he found a young man delighting a group of maidservants at the expense of a lanky stableboy whom he had under a mesmeric trance, inducing him thereby to perform various ridiculous feats with eyes closed. After watching these antics for a few minutes, Alfred obtained permission to apply a test. Taking a watch from his pocket, he placed it at the back of the subject's head with the watchface towards himself, and ensuring there was no clock in the room, he asked for the time. Without hesitation he received an answer that was entirely wrong. But as he was returning the watch to his pocket, Alfred observed that he had been holding it upside down, and that the time given was correct if the dial were held upright. He reversed the watch and repeated his question without explanation, whereupon the youth gave the correct time.[31]

The 'plunge into Spiritism' was chiefly consequent upon the Dromana test, and the articles by Wallace and Crookes. Deakin remembered also that Newman's *Phases of Faith* was another cause for his gradual departure from Spencer.[32] With Mickle and Martin he visited two 'medical clairvoyants', William H. Terry and George Stow, who enjoyed a considerable clientele in Melbourne. They were founding members of both Dr Motherwell's famous home circle in 1869, then the best-known assembly of the kind in the colonies, and of the V.A.P.S. the following year.[33] Terry, a draper by trade, was a gold-rush migrant, listed in the *Cyclopaedia of Victoria* as a 'chemist and medical botanist'. Avuncular in manner and unswerving in his dedication to the movement, he was for forty years perennial secretary of the V.A.S. ('Progressive' was now dropped from the title) and the Sunday Lyceum, founding editor of the *Harbinger of Light*, as well as being a healing medium and bookshop proprietor.[34] In this, the first instance of 'mediumship' Deakin had witnessed, Terry readily submitted to questions relating to the cure of physical complaints, and permitted Deakin to 'test the results obtained under his guidance'.[35] Terry would remain conscious while he diagnosed visitors' ailments, for whom he prescribed herbal remedies stocked in his herbal emporium and bookshop in Russell Street, Melbourne. Stow performed the same diagnostic task, though in a condition of complete unconsciousness or 'deep trance', when a 'control' calling himself 'Martin' would diagnose and prescribe.[36] Deakin was greatly impressed by these healing mediums; thirty-five years later he could still judge their diagnoses 'remarkable for the general success attending them, even in difficult cases'; and of these two, he insisted, 'I never heard of a single mistake in their prescription.'[37] Deakin's current interests are indicated by a small book of press cuttings, which includes an 1872 lecture given by James Smith on 'the world beyond the grave', another by the visiting American Spiritualist J. M. Peebles, along with accounts of the death of Lord Lytton, and an article on the admission of ladies to the university.[38]

Around August 1873, together with Mickle, Martin and three young women (to provide an equal polarity of 'magnetism') Deakin formed a 'circle' to meet twice weekly in his parents' home. It included his sister Catherine and Martin's sister Letty, who was to become the 'medium'. The parents took no part, and Mr Stow attended the first few meetings to launch the venture. Young, enthusiastic, and anxious to be convinced as they were, their ardour abated considerably after three fruitless months of sitting in the dark round a table with fingers touching. Then at one session the table began to oscillate, and after a time to move with a vigour wholly inexplicable, since the members were 'resolute not to lend any conscious assistance'.[39] It commenced rapping out 'messages' purporting to come from various deceased persons, none of them very 'evidential', nor very important. In full light the table would lift and perform other curious feats, at times with a force that was capricious and utterly wilful. After a further six months, when the group's initial excitement waned as it became clear that the intelligence(s) controlling these manifestations—whatever they were—had 'nothing to say & said it very badly', the circle closed. The net results of their enquiries were 'a little aimless purposeless & inconsistent chatter, & some inexplicable motions'.[40] Nevertheless the mature Deakin remained mystified by these exhibitions, when he had personally witnessed the table dancing, swaying, or moving around the room with no discernible assistance.

There was another and more important reason why Deakin disbanded that circle: 'It was May 21, 1874, when I learned that I had been chosen as a member of Dr Motherwell's circle.'[41] For over twenty years from 1869 this seance circle met in the doctor's consulting room in Collins Street, Melbourne. Dr James Bridgnorth Motherwell, educated at Glasgow, was a respected physician and early pioneer who had come to Victoria via Port Arthur, where he had been medical officer. He was honorary physician at the Melbourne Hospital, one of the 'progressives' on the University Council, and a member of the influential Medical School Committee which determined the medical curriculum.[42] Deakin remembered him as 'the most kindly amiable & considerate of men', that 'his faith in the message received was absolute' and that 'he died without renouncing it'. This circle had a religious character, and included stalwarts like Terry and Stow, and Dr W. L. Richardson, father of the novelist and first president of the V.A.P.S., among its membership. They also met twice weekly, once to listen to 'trance speaking' and once to obtain 'inspirational writing'. At the speaking sessions, following a prayer and invocation, the doctor would make a few mesmeric passes over the medium George Stow who would fall into an unconscious trance, and 'Martin' or other deceased and sometimes distinguished persons would speak.[43]

The writing sessions were conducted around a large table by five persons with pencils poised for the forthcoming inspiration. In this virtual factory of inspirational writing the methods varied. Deakin recalled two elderly women conversing with almost bored indifference and looking around while 'communications' were procured, as each rested one hand lightly upon a planchette attached to a roll of paper on which 'spirits' laboriously inscribed their messages, which came in different orthography and with no spaces between the words. These were separated, and obscure passages were referred back to the spirits, who would obligingly write them out again. He remembered how the older woman would occasionally indulge in '40 winks', and still the planchette continued writing. One 'elderly gentleman' (William Terry) wrote as if normally but, as he always declared, without his will or consciousness obtruding. Deakin judged the writing thus obtained as good, but not noticeably superior to what this 'thoughtful & well informed man was himself qualified to produce'.[44] With their personal messages, little sermonettes and pious exhortations, the spiritual communicators taught 'a gospel respectful of Christianity as the first of revealed religions, & sympathetic with the best in all faiths'; its tone was not dictatorial but 'grave, kindly, sympathetic & relatively simple', disclosing no new revelation but illustrating, explaining, and elaborating the main themes of all lofty creeds.[45] Honoured to have been chosen into this older and select company of 'scientific' mystics, attracted to the mystery of it all, and impressed by the 'evidences' of the phenomena, Deakin became for a time, as he phrased it, 'a Spiritualist of sorts'.[46]

In that hallmark year 1872 Deakin also began to write. He produced first an essay on religion based on the 'Solar Explanation', then essays on 'Skepticism' and 'Morality and its Development' read before the Eclectic Association where from 1873 he was member, then librarian. Four notebooks in a large student hand contain outlines of the works of Herbert Spencer, the omnimath and social evolutionist whose positivism exerted a profound influence on many in Deakin's generation. His *First Principles* and *Principles of Biology* are critiqued, as are his thoughts on *Education*, where he urges physical education, since the first aim of man is 'to be a good animal'. Another notebook, on Land Reform, has selections from J. S. Mill on *Political Economy* and Carlyle's *Chartism*. On the basis of his Spencerian studies, Deakin informed the Eclectic Association that 'the civilized is organically superior to the savage at his birth' since he has '20 to 30 cubic inches more brain than the Papuan'.[47]

Deakin became a lifelong Temperance man and until 1879, a rigid vegetarian. In what he later described as 'a pathetic effort to "find" myself', he visited a steady stream of astrologers, chiromancers, graphologists and clairvoyants. An attempt to cultivate mnemonics led indirectly to a phrenologist who 'read my head with curious correctness', advising that such a head indicated he was best suited for the legal and literary professions.[48] From 1875 Deakin's writing turned to creative channels; he penned a number of short dramatic pieces, historical romances with heroic Carlylean themes bearing titles like 'Maternus', 'Jeanne D'Arc', and 'Three Partings'. Five years later a more mature Deakin, now embarked on a political career, remarked that these juvenile efforts were 'often ponderously mystically didactic'. He was right.[49]

Alfred's current ambition was to devote himself to the elevation of the stage, starting from the bottom as actor and playwright. 'Cross & Crescent' is typical, a cloying tale of three acts set after the Moorish conquest concerning an ascetic Muslim priest and magician who falls in love with a young Christian virgin. In one scene we witness 'the emaciated Moor, on his knees, clad in white, absorbed in prayer to the power of powers'. In due course he is rewarded for 'his prolonged abstinences, sacrifices, solitary studies, obedience & aspirations' with a vision of the spirit of Mohammed who descends, drawn by the ascetic's 'pure potency of soul'. At this point the Prophet gravely soliloquises on the descent of the soul and, incredibly, on the 'primacy & superiority of Christ', while exulting in 'the status so rapidly achieved by Islam'.[50] 'Three Prayers' could almost serve as a prescient outline of Deakin's future life: the first prayer of the aspirant was for 'universal fame & power'; in manhood he was 'champion of right & deliverer of the natives', and in old age, he became 'humbled & penitent'.[51]

These early literary ventures were blatant didactic vehicles for Deakin's current opinions, owing much to works like Draper's *Conflict of Religion and Science* and to Gibbon, yet Deakin believed some of them at least to have been 'inspired'. On New Year's day 1876 he recorded:

This year opens with verses at 5 am on January 1, the result of one of those inexplicable visitations of verse, arriving without warning as if from without me, though needing revision & sometimes additions ... This was a 'New Year Carol'.[52]

It is impossible to say whether Deakin believed all his literary efforts during these years to have been inspired. *A New Pilgrim's Progress*, to be considered later, was dictated in 1877 purportedly by the spirit of John Bunyan as an 'allegory for modern times'; and scattered writings like one from March 1876, no longer extant, which was attributed to the deceased historian H. T. Buckle, were claimed as inspirational, that is, originating from deceased and always eminent persons.[53]

Deakin's only published creative work is an 1875 play written in an Elizabethan style about the fifteenth-century artist *Quentin Massys*. The hopeful Alfred published it at his own expense and sent a copy to Andrew Harwood, a famous theatre owner and critic, who panned it mercilessly. In what must have been a disheartening critique but was probably altogether objective and fair criticism, Harwood judged the play as 'too devoid of action', its style 'loose and turgid', with too many colloquialisms and 'quasi-philosophical utterances which are at least questionable ...', adding that he had 'rarely seen the printer's art so disgraced'.[54] Since with one or two exceptions he thereafter ceased writing drama altogether, it is hard to escape the conclusion that this episode had a devastating effect on Deakin's perception of himself as budding artist. The sting was still there in notes made nearly forty years later: Harwood had received him grudgingly, obviously bored, and had 'barely glanced at the cheaply printed little blue covered copy which then meant so much to me'.[55] Privately Deakin continued writing volumes, but never again did he attempt to publish the considerable body of verse and prose which he was to produce over the next thirty-five years.

After matriculating from Melbourne Grammar School, a brief interlude as a teacher, and a short and unhappy career as bookkeeper, Deakin decided on the advice of classmate and future law partner Theodore Fink, on the legal profession. In 1873 he enrolled at the University of Melbourne. But Deakin never had a real interest in the law, nor did the legal profession appeal to him as a vehicle for gaining wealth. H. B. Higgins, fellow student and later independent Arbitration Court judge, believed that 'Deakin's mind and a lawyer's mind traveled in different directions.'[56] It makes curious comment upon the first, and some would say the best, Attorney-General of the Commonwealth, that though his student life was fairly exploding with the most varied interests, as Murdoch put it, Deakin 'seems to have been extremely keen about everything—except law.'[57]

Literary attempts already display wide reading and real, if eclectic, learning. Another 1875 play 'Before the Inquisition' has Giordano Bruno redeclaring with scorn for his persecutors his doctrine of the plurality of worlds.[58] With Fink and four others Deakin formed the short-lived 'Nouthetic Association' (a word they coined from the Neo-Platonic *nous* or intelligence) for the 'unrestricted temperate investigation and discussion of any subject whatever of general social interest and importance'.[59] Higgins also remembered Deakin in the university quadrangle telling four or five students, one of whom was Richard Hodgson (soon to conduct a celebrated debate with T. H. Green on the subject) that with the arrival of Spencer's philosophy all studies of mathematics, logic and history were utterly useless.[60]

Deakin's political career had its germinal beginnings at the university also, through one of his lecturers C. H. Pearson, politician, former Cambridge historian, and the most important intellectual of the radical Liberal Party. Pearson was founder of the Presbyterian Ladies' College, whose first matriculant was Deakin's sister Catherine, and as part of the 'schoolmaster group' was instrumental in having women admitted to the university for all but the medicine course.[61] Pearson exerted considerable influence upon the mind of the young Deakin, and was later to serve with him as Minister of Education in the 1880s in a coalition government. Deakin was greatly impressed in 1877 on seeing Pearson and the firebrand Graham Berry together at a political meeting. Perhaps it was a symbol of democracy for the young radical that night at the Princess Theatre, when he saw the Cambridge don and the former grocer espousing the same Liberal ideals on a common platform.[62]

The University Debating Club, inaugurated by Pearson, was a virtual incubation chamber for prominent public figures, including H. B. Higgins; William Shiels, future Premier of Victoria; the journalist Alexander Sutherland; and Theodore Fink, Deakin's future law partner and Royal Commissioner on technical education. In debates Deakin was for female education, for scientific rather than classical studies, for universal suffrage, cremation, evolution and Temperance; he became 'in brief, a radical of radicals'.[63]

Deakin's law course, or rather his relative indifference to it, left him considerable leisure, and a remarkable memory allowed him to get by with minimum effort. Like most Victorian intellectuals, Deakin read prodigiously; among the titles listed for 1877 are Cervantes' *Don Quixote*, Goethe's *Faust*, Schiller's *Wallenstein* and *Don Carlos*, Motley on the Dutch Republic and *Cornelius Agrippa*, as well as other works by Virgil, Matthew Arnold, the Brownings, Swinburne, Rossetti, Molière, George Sand, Victor Hugo, and Montaigne.[64] The activities of the young student-at-law were many and varied: with great enthusiasm and boundless energy, he was debating the great issues of the era, first at the Eclectic Association, then under Pearson's guidance at the University Debating Club; composing verse and drama heavily laced with reformist and spiritist ideas; attending twice-weekly sessions at Dr Motherwell's; and teaching on Sundays at the Lyceum, all the while participating in 'test' seances, consulting astrologers, phrenologists and clairvoyants and, of course, reading everything he could lay hands on. At one session the 'sibyl', a Madame Siècle (literally: Madame Century) upon asking his deepest wish, was surprised when the young Alfred, Solomon-like, responded: 'to be wise'. About this frenzied period he wrote:

> Student life rarely occupied half of my waking hours—the rest were filled with visions, dreams, poems & prophecies. The real world was transfigured by these not seldom, while the ideal, wavering in its detail, absorbed the greater portion of my waking life.[65]

For a short time Deakin even believed, or half believed, himself to be an 'impressional writing' medium. His transient career as 'medium' remained a bewildering and inexplicable interlude, a role in which he was never comfortable and which he was to renounce within two or three years, although the historical evidence for this period is sketchy.[66] In a manuscript written some time in the 1890s, Deakin attempts to look back detachedly on his 'mediumship' and his other 'Personal Experiences in Spiritism'.[67] Its alternative title 'Spiritism & After' confirms its retrospective character, but he had by no means abandoned a supernatural explanation of the universe. The opening passage contrasts a 'spiritism' that means 'belief in bogeys, in raps, in sheeted figures masquerading at dark seances—a recrudescence of ancient superstition figuring in a modern dress & making prey of the weak minded', and Spiritism:

> that implies spirit—a denial of materialism, a denial that death is the end of life & more than that, a hope of communion with those who have gone before, a brighter reading of the present & the future, more hope, more faith, more evidence of God & God's goodness.[68]

To the reader familiar with Deakin's outlook, it is everywhere clear in 'Personal Experiences ...' that the events recounted were perceived by the author as a significant and interconnected series, implicitly telling the story of a personal development of awareness. Intended as a series of publishable articles, this manuscript belongs in Deakin's own parlance to his 'outer' expression. There are omissions in this twenty-year retrospective relating to the private significances of events, where in a playful, not to say gnomic manner, Deakin only hinted at the 'inner' meanings of the events he was recounting.

The splendid manifestations achieved in the first circle, and the pronouncements of the spirits, convinced the older members of Dr Motherwell's circle that Deakin was destined to become a great medium, and much subtle pressure was exerted on him. In 'Personal Experiences ...' he relates how finally after many months, and because Mr Stow the regular medium was in England, 'I spoke in his stead, impromptu, without preparation or consideration, upon some theme that rose to my lips.'[69] His 'mediumship' seemed to please the doctor and his circle, yet for all his doubts about his own role, during these years at least, Deakin believed absolutely in the operation of spirits upon the human world.

An enthusiasm for the 'Cause' and already visible qualities of leadership were channelled into other areas, mostly by Terry, the virtual workhorse of the movement in Victoria, who had founded the Progressive Lyceum in 1872 and served as its first conductor. Deakin became Corresponding Secretary of the association, then Conductor of the Lyceum for which, together with Terry he edited the *Lyceum Leader* manual. This Spiritualist Sunday school, though not limited to children, was predicated on the Wordsworthian notion of their supposed remembrance of things Divine. It is doubtful whether Terry, a man of great dedication but little formal learning, was conversant like his young co-editor with erudite authors like Swedenborg, Marcus Aurelius, Whittier, Bacon, Schiller, Dante, Carlyle and Spinoza, whose noblest sentiments were appropriated in its 'Golden Chain Recitations' for the guidance of young Spiritualists. Deakin also composed pieces on 'Liberty Equality Fraternity', and on 'the Higher Pantheism'.[70]

Fifty children attended the Lyceum in 1872, and by 1884 when it reached its heyday it attracted some 1200 members and visitors. A newspaper account from that year describes the incredibly regimented proceedings, then held in the Horticultural Hall. A typical format of one and a half hours included sacred songs and responses, followed by a fifteen-minute address on the progress of religious thought, simple calisthenics, and a five-minute address on the significance of the colours of flowers. They were then split into twelve groups from the 'fountain group' for small children to the 'summer group' which included grey-haired adults, to hear a twenty-minute discourse. The finale was a marching order, with all twelve groups waving flags and bearing shields.[71]

In September 1878 Deakin was elected president of the association after one of its numerous schisms. Aged barely twenty-two, he discharged his responsibilities with thoroughness and diplomacy.[72] When the American medium Emma Hardinge Britten, whom he described as being 'of large proportions, excellent appetite, & unshakeable self-confidence', gave a series of lectures, Deakin insisted on taking a small percentage of the proceeds for the association which had sponsored her, much to her consternation.[73] He remained on the committee until 1882 when from a combination of increasing political work and a flagging faith, he ceased attending. A letter from four of his female students at the Lyceum in April 1879, upon his resignation as Conductor, expressed appreciation for his interest, 'knowing, as we do, the great prejudice which exists against women sharing in any discussion which does not treat of dress or amusement'.[74]

Deakin describes himself during this period as 'very young & enthusiastically devoted to the study of the unseen'. From 1876 his interest turned for a time to research on the 'physical' phenomena such as the alleged materialisation of spirits and 'apports'.[75] One series in this exhaustive round of 'test' seances was held at St Paul's, in the manse of Dr Bromby. They brought no striking occurrences, and for his part Bromby confided to his journal that they were 'palpable humbug'.[76] Another test held the same year with a Mrs Purton produced more impressive phenomena, solemnly attested to by a committee comprising, besides Deakin, William Terry, Dr Richardson and Thomas Stanford, a wealthy American immigrant. Several 'apports' (from the French *apporter*: to carry) were allegedly transported by spirit agency into an hermetically sealed seance room in Russell Street, among them seaweed, 'sea insectivores' and large stones from St Kilda beach![77]

Deakin's absorption is evident in the sheer time and energy he devoted to these puzzling pursuits. His reading increased and broadened. It was around this time that Deakin plunged—the metaphor is apposite—into the heavy volumes of the Swedish mystic Emanuel Swedenborg. He even approached Margaret Turner, minister of the Unitarian church in Eastern Hill who was to retire, regarding his suitability to replace her in the post. 'Fortunately', Deakin writes, 'as it proved, none of my attempts were encouraged.' A poem composed on his twenty-first birthday vowed, in an unusually pious mood, to:

> *Seek simply for the light, content, not sad,*
> *While the path inward winds and upward tends*
> *For my trespasses I make amends.*[78]

The most baffling of Deakin's spiritistic experiences were the prophecies he received through three mediums between 1877 and 1881, designated in 'Personal Experiences...' as 'A', 'B', and 'C', elsewhere identified respectively as Mrs Armstrong, Mrs Cohen and Mrs Stirling. A current advertisement for the latter reads:

> Mrs Stirling, Trance Medium and Clairvoyant, at the request of her friends will hold a Seance every MONDAY EVENING at 8 o'clock, at her residence Crayke Cottage, Stanley street, Richmond. Twelvth house on the right from Swan street. Admission, ONE SHILLING.[79]

At least three accounts of these significant events survive: in a 'Spiritual Diary—Personal & Mundane', maintained between 1880 and 1882, which records in meticulous detail his attendances at seances; in 'Personal Experiences ...' dating from the late 1890s, where Deakin gives a vivid account of these experiences with the intention of publishing them as articles; and in autobiographical notes made in 1910, when he again commented in considerable detail upon these now distant experiences. Of the numerous seances attended between his sixteenth and twenty-first years, three series of prophetic readings stand out for their continued, even increasing, significance to Deakin's inner life: the first given in 1877–8 were predictions of a personal nature, while the two subsequent series dealt with political events; one prophecy was received in 1880 before the final phase in a lengthy electoral contest, predicting his immediate political success; the other, what I have termed the Grand Prophecy recorded in 1881, relates to Deakin's distant political future.

The three mediums, apart from their clairvoyance, were, according to Deakin, remarkably similar in being average; they were each 'thoroughly domesticated, decorous members of the lower middle class', more than middle-aged, married with families, and engaged in household duties.[80] In the seance room, however, these ordinary women were transformed into modern seers, who described what they claimed to see or hear. To the young radical, eager to be convinced of a grand future, their very ordinariness served as counterpoint and confirmation of their ethereal role. On occasion they would recount visions of scenery and symbolism, and messages would appear as 'letters of fire'.[81] Usually they uttered, or were caused to utter, personal messages 'evidential' of an afterlife, and predictions about the future. Invariably these were received in piecemeal fashion (hence a 'series'), and would begin to make sense only after his eager cross-examination of the medium. Deakin was particularly impressed by the occasional corroboration, when the same prophecy was conveyed independently through two mediums, or when one would appear to continue a prophecy commenced through another medium. He was of course aware of the possibility of collusion, but had great confidence in his own powers of observation, and in the weight of accuracy of readings given over long periods and through different persons. Moreover to the mature Deakin, prophecy was superior to other phenomena as an item of scientific enquiry, for not only did it considerably simplify verification, but it also precluded possible fraud or mind reading on the part of the medium. Most importantly, as he explained in 'Personal Experiences ...':

> To describe in anticipation the details of what is not but is yet to be is an evidence not only of powers of prophecy, but of a fixity in the order of the apparently casual incidents of our existence pregnant with suggestions of far reaching significance.[82]

As an unemployed barrister, Deakin was at this time 'by no means lacking in eagerness to forecast a very uncertain future'. He never invited, though he carefully noted and sometimes followed financial predictions, usually with disappointing results.[83] When the political prophecies suddenly commenced, unsolicited, in October 1878 and he learned through Mrs Cohen that 'within two years I should be ushered into active public life in spite of myself, & forced into prominence', Deakin received the statement with 'smiling incredulity', for he had then 'neither the desire nor the anticipation' of entering politics.[84]

On 11 February 1878 Deakin took chambers at 29 Temple Court, shared with W. K. Vale, an association that would have important, and to Deakin providential, consequences for his political future. A democratic temper was proclaimed with the omission of the title 'Mr' from his door, his being the only office door so unadorned.[85] Immediately upon installing himself in chambers, Deakin inaugurated his professional career by 'consulting Chaucer on prospects', randomly opening in a version of the *sortes virgilianae* at these lines in the 'Merchant's Tale':

> *But weet ye what? In counsel be it said,*
> *Me reweth sore I am unto her tied.*[86]

Whatever unconscious process it might suggest to the reader, the future Attorney-General and founder of the High Court took this divination as an inauspicious omen, from which he concluded that his nascent legal career, to which he already felt 'tied', was 'not at all hopeful on prospect'.[87] One need not have been clairvoyant to prophesy that a 21-year-old Spiritualist with Liberal leanings, and without family connections, would face less than hopeful prospects in the staid profession of barrister.

Even 'wholesale reading' and his responsibilities as V.A.S. president and Lyceum Conductor left the young barrister with few briefs, and a great deal of time on his hands. Currently engrossed in Ruskin's works, he embarked on an ambitious aesthetic treatise. 'Poets & Poetry' sought 'standards & methods by which we could systematize the inexhaustible treasures of our most cherished muse'. With its leading motif the Spencerian idea of the evolution of aesthetic instincts, it was to be a monumental oeuvre of five parts, but other events intervened and only the first section of around 200 manuscript pages was completed on a 'General Philosophy of Poetry'.[88] It was as though, having failed in his own eyes as creative artist, Deakin turned for a time to criticism.

On 23 May 1878 Deakin met David Syme of the *Age* via a Mr Dempster, through their common interest in Spiritualism.[89] His lasting friendship, with some rough patches, with the usually distant and irascible Syme was to be of supreme importance to his political career, but its immediate fruit was a badly needed income. Within a month Syme engaged Deakin as a leader writer. There is a certain prophetic irony in that his first assignment, a review of an English article on 'Politics in Australia', spoke rather lightly of 'the Downing Street hobby of federation'.[90] The next, on the 'Wreck of the *Loch Ard*', was about a current maritime disaster and a number of unrecovered bodies. In a short sub-leader he managed to parade a wide learning and, amidst several literary allusions, to introduce ideas on burial from the ancient Greeks to the Elizabethans. Continuing the Greek ambience, he urged in vaguely mysterious tones that the rites of burial be accorded soon to the shipwrecked, 'lest disgrace should come upon us unawares'.[91]

Over the next five years Deakin worked variously as leader and special writer for the *Age* and the *Fortnightly*; for a time he edited the *Leader*, and took over the 'Verandah' column on Marcus Clarke's retirement. David Syme, who had earlier served on the committee of the Spiritualist Association, always took a cool, intellectual and distant interest in the phenomena, and he enjoyed debating the well-read, enthusiastic and voluble young Deakin on these and other matters.[92] But politics and power were Syme's real interests, and here he had considerable influence upon Deakin, converting him almost immediately from Freetrader to lifelong Protectionist. As the older Deakin noted, 'In journalism, my Spencerian laisserie-faire, including Free trade & individualism in excelcis, crumbled away almost at once'.[93] Deakin was rapidly outgrowing one world and entering another. Under the influence of radicals like Syme, Graham Berry and Charles Pearson, and of more distant role models like that unrepentant radical Liberal George Higinbotham, and in the reportage of political events Deakin, already a 'radical of radicals' in social and metaphysical matters, in time naturally aligned himself with the radical political party of the day.

It was during this period that the first of the three prophecies to have a lasting significance was apparently fulfilled. As early as May 1876 'A' (Mrs Armstrong) had emphatically predicted that Alfred would travel and commune with nature. At about three-monthly intervals thereafter, and under his eager questioning, she expanded and refined the prophecy. A trip to the United States was mentioned, whose purpose was described at various times for educational purposes and to help recuperate his health. Finally in January 1878 she said the trip, for which no time scale was given, was to be for health reasons, and that his companion would be a white-haired gentleman, insisting that Alfred 'was to be at no expense or trouble in arranging for or executing the plan'.[94] He tried to learn how to assure himself of this delightful prospect, but to no avail, and soon forgot about it. Then on 30 September of the following year, 1879, Mr Sidney Watson, an elderly (and white-haired) Spiritualist whom Deakin scarcely knew, stopped him in Collins Street and asked him to be his companion on a forthcoming business trip to Fiji. The astounded Deakin gladly accepted, for at this time his health, always indifferent, had been affected by the rigours of his first two electoral campaigns.[95]

Deakin wrote that the accuracy of this prediction remained for him 'unimpeachable & inexplicable'.[96] If there remains room for reasonable doubt as to the spontaneity of the invitation, it was their mutual interest in Spiritualism, and especially the fact that Watson's three daughters were friends of his future wife Pattie, and with her attended the Lyceum where Alfred was already entertaining secret hopes of winning the hand of the young Sunday-school scholar. The handsome Conductor could hardly have missed being discussed in the homes of these admiring adolescents. Moreover his first political battles in February and August, and his dramatic resignation in July of that year 1879, had already brought him an unusual degree of notoriety. Yet for Deakin the significant fact was that the event had been perfectly predicted at least eighteen months earlier.

The events which led to Deakin being 'whirled' into politics have been recounted by Professor La Nauze in all the atmosphere of breathless intrigue and reformist zeal which the Berry forces generated during the heady years of the late 1870s. Under the fiery leadership of Graham Berry, the Liberals had become a real political force in Victoria. 'Berry's men' were radicals like the Minister for Lands J. M. Grant, a student of the French revolution, J. L. Woods the Chartist, the Irish baronet Sir Bryan O'Loghlen who spoke of 'Saxon oppressors', and Peter Lalor the hero of Eureka; they were accused of 'wild and communistic attacks on property'.[97] Many believed that revolution was imminent, as the grinding struggle between classes became manifest in the clashes between the Liberals in the Assembly and the 'obstructables', the squatters and big business interests who dominated the Legislative Council, then at the height of their power to retard Reform.

In retaliation for the passage of a mild land tax, the reactionary Council had avenged itself by rejecting a Payment of Members Bill tacked onto an Appropriation Bill. On 8 January 1878, 'Black Wednesday', the government responded by sacking the upper civil service, police magistrates, and County Court judges, many of whom were Conservative supporters. The subsequent 'Embassy' to London by Berry and Pearson seeking the help of the imperial government in resolving the deadlock between the two chambers brought no solution, but 'peace with honour'.[98] The government then revealed its strength by winning the election in West Bourke, but the incumbent died in office, and the Liberals were left with no viable candidate to stand against the Conservative Robert Harper.

This was when Deakin was thrown headlong into the fray as a strange, and to him providential, chain of events resulted in his contesting and winning the seat of West Bourke, one of the centres of this controversy. A small deputation from the local Reform Leagues came to Melbourne to approach potential candidates, among them W. K. Vale. According to Deakin it was by the accident of Vale's absence from chambers that out of desperation they 'pressed me to undertake the forlorn hope of winning the seat'.[99] With the recklessness of youth (and the advice of spirits) he accepted the challenge and, having never made a political speech nor entered a polling booth, against all odds Deakin won the seat in February 1879. In the dramatic entrance of the young 'radical' on the public stage, an event which has passed into Australian political lore, we see vivid illustration of tensions apparent even in this hour of Deakin's political baptism, a fondness for power set against a high personal moral standard.

The opening session of the Victorian Parliament on 8 July 1879 was proceeding with the usual pomp. After the Governor's customary address to the two assembled chambers outlining the proposed schedule of legislation, a member of the newly elected governing party would respond. Yet as these ceremonial duties were discharged for the first time in the new Queen's Hall, there was an unusual tension over the two issues of great moment: constitutional reform, and the so-called Newham incident.

Alfred Deakin, an overgrown, pale and slender young man of twenty-two, was called to deliver the address in reply. He duly thanked the Governor in tedious detail, as convention required, for each measure listed in the address. The young speaker paused, then offered some personal observations on a variety of topics. The Member for West Bourke of barely four months, having never addressed a Parliament nor a gathering of this size before, now lectured with great composure, delivering what James Service later called a 'philosophical dissertation upon constitutional reform and the right of the majority to rule'.[100] Journalism had already versed Deakin in the issues, and the language, of politics. Gaining heart from Pattie's presence in the gallery, and from his own rhetoric, Deakin now invoked Herbert Spencer, J.S. Mill and other authorities to defend the 'plebiscitium'; he railed against the obstructionism of the Legislative Council, which ensured that 'the majority does not rule, but the minority at present in its name.'[101]

The benign indulgence of members at this eloquent if naive disquisition turned to surprise and, among the Liberals, to horror as the young radical informed the Speaker that, before sitting down, he wished to bring up a personal matter. He recounted first the unfortunate incidents surrounding the Newham affair, when a shortage of ballot papers meant that a few persons in the small village of Newham had been unable to cast their votes, and the poll was called into question. He described his subsequent attempts to resign (when he had been told it was doubtful whether he was a member of the Assembly before being sworn in, and hence could not resign until then). Without discussing the matter further with anyone, he had resolved to resign his seat at the first available opportunity, and had this day brought his letter of resignation with him. A sudden hush fell over the House as the Speaker, incredulous, asked: 'Am I to understand the honorable member wishes to resign his seat immediately?', to which Deakin quietly replied: 'Immediately.' Pattie recalled many years later that it was 'a very stirring scene'.[102]

The confusing chronology of Deakin's troubled and 'miraculous' entry into politics, of which these dramatic events form a part, is as follows: after the alleged irregularity in the polling at Newham and his resignation at the first sitting of Parliament, the election was fought over again in August, and Deakin lost. It was during this period that he accompanied Sidney Watson to Fiji, returning in time to fight the general election of February 1880, which he and the Liberals also lost. Finally, an unexpected dissolution of Parliament was granted to the Conservatives in June 1880 and on 14 July, Bastille Day, on his fourth attempt, Deakin was finally successful in securing the seat. Hence Deakin did enter politics 'within two years', and under highly unusual circumstances. The saga of this lengthy electoral struggle, seen through the perspective of an apprehensive Deakin commuting between party meeting, seance room and the hustings, is irresistible in its suggestion of his current state of mind and belief.

With this dramatic gesture Deakin did what certainly no veteran politician would have done. The spirit of the reformer was in the ascendancy in him. Probably he had been asked to deliver the address to dissuade him from the resignation he had threatened, and perhaps too, with the ebullience of youth and the advice of the 'spirits', he was confident that having won unexpectedly he could win the seat again. Yet whatever histrionic sense or precocious political timing the new M.L.A. showed, his primary motivation was a simple sense of justice and fair play. In this maiden political experience he showed an independence of thinking, a tendency to go his own way and to differ without fear from colleagues, following his own conscience. For his part, Dr Bromby observed in his journal that 'the election is going against the party of order', and with his success that he was 'the first of my Grammar School pupils to rise to Legislative Honours; would that it had been in a better cause!'[103] James Service, the Conservative leader (perhaps with some glee), congratulated both sides of the House for introducing a member 'so eminently qualified to adorn a chamber of legislation', his only regret being that Deakin 'should do so on the wrong side'. With the shifting alliances of the 1880s, it would not be long before they were both on the same side.[104]

Walter Murdoch remarked that to one who could view Deakin's whole life, it seems a natural and inevitable step for him to have taken. There is great insight in this comment, despite Murdoch's panegyric tone. However, Deakin's letter to the returning officer was anything but idealistic, demanding that he immediately declare the poll valid.[105] Perhaps as a lawyer he wished to see the letter of the law respected, although there were conflicting legal opinions on the propriety of adjourning a poll. Yet, having won that victory, he resigned according to his highest principles. As with other episodes in his life, higher and nobler principles coexisted in Deakin with a keen ambition for power.

It was a quixotic and futile gesture, or so it must have seemed to his exasperated colleagues when over the next eighteen months two further electoral fights were successively lost. The sole encouragement came from transcendental realms, cold comfort even for the young 'mystic' after the third unsuccessful attempt in February 1880. The defeat of the Liberals by Service was still fresh in his mind when shortly after the election Mrs Cohen ('B'), who had earlier predicted his entry into politics within two years, told him casually that he would be in Parliament again within six months.[106] This was before the newly elected Parliament had even assembled. We can imagine that Deakin, disheartened by failure after three exhausting campaigns, was seeking solace and guidance regarding an uncertain future (he did not receive a substantial legal brief until 1882). On 10 May 1880, to his amazement, the same prediction was given through Mrs Stirling ('C').[107] What followed in this second series was a remarkable exercise in political forecasting. A sceptic might wonder why the irregularities in the first poll at Newham were not foreseen, and whether the medium might not have inferred a fourth attempt from Deakin's communicated anxiety to win. In any case, as we have seen, on 14 July 1880 Deakin was finally elected M.L.A. for the seat of West Bourke. As political events they were remarkable enough, but for Deakin they assumed a lasting transcendental significance. He was positively animated by the apparent accuracy of these prophecies, as he would be seven years later by the Grand Prophecy.

Deakin had no illusions about the vulgarity and triviality of some phenomena, and the gullibility associated with Spiritualism in the popular imagination. The common impression that his participation in such happenings had been restricted to his youth was on his part wholly intentional. In this fourth and final campaign he learned an important political lesson. The conservative Melbourne *Daily Telegraph* launched a vituperative personal attack, accusing Deakin of mocking the Catholic calendar with his 'Calendar of Saints' in the *Lyceum Leader* (which it turned out was itself a parody of Comte's 'Positivist Calendar'). The intellectual quality of *A New Pilgrim's Progress* was judged 'beneath contempt', a record of 'the delirious dreams of an illiterate, ignorant and impure mind'.[108] Henceforth Deakin closely guarded his metaphysical opinions. In a newspaper interview in 1903 Deakin, now Attorney-General of the Commonwealth, when asked about Spiritualism responded:

> There were many people interested in the subject at that time, and as a searcher after knowledge, it possessed considerable attractiveness for me. Unfortunately, the Psychical Research Societies did not then exist, and besides, time did not permit me to follow the questions with the assiduity of my earlier days. As soon as I attained my majority, professional and political work became all absorbing.[109]

With characteristic adroitness the master politician evaded the point and managed not to lie. As a man Deakin had great respect for the truth, while as a lawyer and politician he knew how to use facts to best advantage. His statement is both true and false, depending on the terms employed. While his formal connection with Spiritualism did cease around the age of twenty-six, 'Spiritism', later referred to as the 'Occult', was to remain an absorbing and lifelong interest.

Almost immediately following his successful bid for West Bourke Deakin commenced his 'Spiritual Diary—Personal & Mundane' (after Swedenborg who had also kept a journal bearing that title). On 1 August 1880 he wrote:

> I am induced to commence this diary by the extraordinary prophetic information given me this year, & since proved perfectly accurate & by a desire to ensure the absolute correctness of all details which I may hereafter wish to refer to or reason upon.[110]

'To reason upon'—that was Deakin's principal interest in these phenomena, beyond any momentary advantage of prevision. Elated after a frustrating period when only the spirits had been certain of his eventual triumph, he remembered how at his lowest ebb in February he had been assured that he would be in Parliament 'within six months'; what had then seemed absolutely incredible had come to pass.

The third series of prophecies, concerning his then distant political future, remained for Deakin the most impressive, the most definite, and the most inexplicable of his encounters with the 'unseen'; indeed, he regarded the Grand Prophecy as the crown of all such experiences. That he plays it down in 'Personal Experiences...' intended for publication, mentioning it almost in passing as 'an extraordinarily persistent effort of hers to describe the Imperial Conference in London in 1887', rather confirms its private significance.[111] The Grand Prophecy was revealed to Deakin over several successive sittings with Mrs Armstrong. Through this 'elderly, timid, & silent mother of four children', whose 'circle of acquaintance was the smallest, whose interests were of the simplest, whose book knowledge was nil, & whose education had been of the plainest', Deakin learned that:

> ...before long, I should be officially sent to London to appear for Victoria before a tribunal which was not a court of law but a gathering like a court, that would deal with the interest of Victoria, of Australia, & of the whole Empire—I was to attend, to belong to, & to address a tribunal which she described as the highest in the land— It was to sit in London, & its consequences were to be very great.[112]

Could she (or he) have taken a lead from the current furore over the London 'Embassy'? The entranced medium could get no closer to describing this improbable event than by negatives. Deakin cross-examined her eagerly over the next few seances, but he could not shake her confidence in the prophecy. At any rate, the precognition of these events in London and their relation to the path of his political career remained among his most deeply cherished convictions, and became the object of a great deal of private speculation.

The 'Spiritual Diary' fairly reflects Deakin's beliefs and assumptions in the early 1880s, in the 'prophetic information' recorded by the now 'Honorable' Alfred Deakin. The record of a typical seance attended on Friday morning, 6 August 1880, evidently the second for that day and probably with Mrs Cohen, reads in part:

> What RH said as to coalition & new ministry had proved true—described old man, bald, drawn to me ... desiring to help in literary direction ... BS Naylor & wife ... saw interior Parliament House ... must study ... be reserved, cautious, self-contained, shall be impressed ... I am the boy ... change of sphere ... want of errors in communications by intervention of undeveloped spirits ... the female Justice ... herald of the spirits are one & the same, an embodiment of the principle of reform—... The fourth sphere of active knowledge, teaching & being taught, John Bunyan not with me at the moment, not my activity, I only a small unit ... the fifth sphere, inspired to be a reformer both in Church & State, have done something in the first, now do same in the State. Almost too spiritual for politics ...[113]

'I am the boy', he was assured. Whatever was envisaged for his present work, it surely had something to do with the two most divisive issues in the politics of the time: reform of the Legislative Council, and the defence of the secular Education Act. Probably this was why the deceased reformer B. S. Naylor, an early advocate of Spiritualism and Socialism, and Richard Heales (RH) the radical Liberal politician, were assisting from the 'other side'.[114]

We see the extent to which Deakin was then under the thrall of the predictions, for if they reflect his own opinions, as they almost certainly do, they suggest that he still harboured literary aspirations, but now saw himself first as a reformer. He was in the process of 'changing spheres'. These it can be inferred were spiritual or mental spheres somehow related to stages of spiritual evolution and mundane activity, spheres of consciousness as well as parameters of spiritual influence. With the new focus of his activities John Bunyan was not 'with' him because the 'fourth sphere' of active knowledge was now abandoned for the 'fifth sphere' activity as reformer in Church and State. Having already 'done something' in the 'Church', presumably through his work for the Spiritualist Association, the Lyceum, and as the reference to Bunyan suggests, as amanuensis for *A New Pilgrim's Progress*, he must now do the same in the 'State'. We note that fully three years after abandoning 'mediumship', Deakin still believed he enjoyed a spiritual link with the great Nonconformist.

If he was 'almost too spiritual for politics', Deakin adapted admirably to his handicap. Within two weeks of the election on 14 July 1880 he was involved in an effort to end the continuing deadlock over reform of the Legislative Council that had precipitated the dissolution of the Assembly and the premature election. The kernel of the problem was that the Council was organised along exclusive rather than democratic lines; its narrow electoral base and steep property qualifications for both members and electors ensured that substantial property holders dominated, and the Victorian Constitution, with no provisions for the resolution of deadlocks, was framed so that any reform required its unlikely agreement. With another Liberal Deakin took a stand against his radical colleagues, seeking a compromise Reform Bill rather than having it rejected once again. We might wonder how far this courageous stand reflected the advice of Heales, Naylor and co.

Deakin's resignation gesture the previous year had earned him the respect of Service and Berry, and unusual notoriety for a backbencher, and his power of oratory was already acknowledged. On 30 July 1880 Berry sent for Deakin to act as conciliator between the Liberals and Conservatives on the terms of a compromise Bill, a role that would engage him frequently during his political career. The Council did not give much, and the Liberals did not gain much, but it was enough for the matter to be resolved for the moment.[115] Hence in considering the shaping of this episode in Australia's political history, we must acknowledge at least the possibility that the early intervention of 'spirits' was instrumental, at least in the mind of one of its key participants, in the partial resolution of what had been a thorny issue in colonial politics since the achievement of responsible government in the 1850s.

Two weeks later Deakin, still flushed by his precocious political coup, was confidently informed at a seance through Mrs Stirling that he would 'hold the reins of power' within three years.[116] If he had an insatiable appetite for 'signs' at this time it was not, or not solely, for personal or political advantage. In his reflective writing, drawing on his current reading of Martineau, Plato and Crozier, and especially of Swedenborg, he was beginning to 'weave an idea of Deity'. A current journal 'Impromptus' first sounds a theme that would figure prominently in his mature meditations, of a universe in essence moral and teleological:

> 'A wicked & adulterous generation seeketh after a sign' but so also do the souls of those who aspire to do right & who believe that the universe is full of great but invisible beings sympathising with them & governed by an Almighty Spirit whom they are anxious to obey if only these finite & infinite forms of good could manifest themselves.[117]

Increasingly dissatisfied with the phenomenal aspects of Spiritualism, Deakin now yearned for sure and direct knowledge of his Duty. In this deepening commitment to moral religion, he seemed to be searching for the signs of that Mission even now manifesting in his mind. In 'Impromptus' he bemoaned the fact that Spiritualism taught only 'in a frail degree' the Divine truth that should be taught with 'irresistible potency & in daylight', voicing a lament where even the imagery of light serves to condemn dark seance rooms. How strange it was 'that we should be left to stumble altogether among contradictions, absurdities, doubts ... moving but in a realm of mists & twilights, overshadowed by everlasting depths of night'.

And with evident frustration, he could envisage how 'a revelation direct, personal & prophetic of a kind easy to be pictured would make millions of saints & martyrs even in everyday life.' His greatest fear was self-delusion but alas, everything was left to the self, there was nothing in the universe that 'replies to us—shows sympathy with us or encourages us with the idea that our life, deeds or duty are of none than self interest.'[118]

Except for his uncomfortable role as 'medium', Deakin's experiences with Spiritism had been largely vicarious. The teachings of the eighteenth-century Swedish mystic Emanuel Swedenborg, especially his claim to sudden Revelation in the opening of his 'inner sight', kindled Deakin's hope for an unfolding of his own spiritual gifts. Of arguably greater importance, as we shall see later, were his teachings on morality. Deakin was already contemplating an article or small volume, written in 1889 as two large volumes, that would give a 'modern rendering of the vital teaching' of Swedenborg.[119]

Efforts to reconcile past insights with a growing religious sentiment also brought Deakin into long-term association with Theosophy, although he was formally a member for only one year, following the lecture tour in 1894 by Annie Besant, champion of the London matchgirls, former Secularist and Fabian Socialist, and now president of the society, when she suggested he join for a trial period.[120] The Theosophical Society was attracting many like Deakin who could accept neither orthodoxy nor simply the 'bare facts' of Spiritualism. Founded in 1875, Theosophy had by 1882 reached the height of its popular appeal, and it was still three years before the 'miracles' attributed to the society's principal founder, the ineffable Madame H. P. Blavatsky, would be discredited by Deakin's friend Dr Richard Hodgson, when he was sent to its headquarters in India to investigate her for the British Society for Psychical Research. Theosophists disdained Spiritualism's proletarian interpretations for the higher phenomena. While they accepted the manifestations, they rejected the spirit survival theory, substituting a complex spiritual hierarchy, and providing more in the way of 'occult' theory for many among the Victorian heterodoxy. At the top of the hierarchy, according to Blavatsky, were two 'Masters' (Koot Hoome and Morya) who directed the efforts of a Great White Brotherhood toward the further evolution of humankind through the recovery of an original Wisdom Religion. A powerful and dogmatic leader, she expounded this system in her massive rambling works *Isis Unveiled* and *The Secret Doctrine*. After her death, a letter to Deakin from her co-founder, the American Colonel H. J. Olcott, spoke of her in mixed terms. She was an enigma, the 'most baffling personality I ever met'. He referred to the danger of the growth of an 'H.P.B.' cult, which he had recently moved to circumvent, for he was not ready to worship any idol, 'let alone one whose clay feet I had so often seen beneath the Magian robes'.[121]

If it appealed to his nature to believe in evolved beings, actuated by the purest universal love and working for the benefit of humankind, Deakin was benignly ambivalent to theosophical claims regarding 'Invisible Masters'. As he noted in one journal in 1882 while reading the two-volume tome *Isis Unveiled*, if it were untrue 'it is so harmonious with my conception of what ought to be true that I feel bound to give it acceptance'.[122] While it provided more in the way of theory, Theosophy also taught reincarnation, a doctrine (at this time) rejected by Spiritualists that appealed to Deakin's sense of cosmic justice, and even to his political Liberalism. If man has but one life, he reasoned, then the 'disparities of condition under which it is passed are certainly unjust', for then heaven seems 'easily won' and hell 'hardly merited by a few years of earth life'.[123]

An implicitly elitist evolutionism, a legacy of his Spencerian days, and a deepening religious morality were also leading Deakin to search for the rudiments of an Idealist philosophy which gives primacy to mind, conscience and reason. 'Impromptus' for 29 January 1881 cautions against the 'current materialistic philosophy', whose tendency it was to 'sap the highest morality & the best religion of which we can conceive human nature to be capable'. To doubt mind by making it a 'metaphysical shadow' is to exalt matter, leading inexorably to 'the debasement of intelligence, of morals, the individuality, & finally affection'.[124] These early concerns at the evil consequences to flow from a renunciation of morality and mind may seem overstated, and while they reveal a naive intellectualism that supposes moral choices to be made from intellectual considerations, they formed an integral part of his philosophy. This Idealism was to be considerably refined over the years, but it remained, like his religious morality, a cornerstone of Deakin's belief. In the atmosphere of smug scientism and positivism of his day, Deakin's antagonism to a materialist world view, like that of Cardinal Newman, was heartfelt and lifelong.

Deakin had entered public life with a flourish, but he was determined to learn all he could on the backbench. In September 1881 he presented his first Bill as private member. The Protection of Animals Bill was apposite as an introductory measure, for Deakin still adhered to some Spiritualist beliefs, such as animals possessing both individuality and a future existence. His love for all forms of life is conveyed in a tender passage from a somewhat later journal:

My own eye in street or park is generally turned inward, but the gravity of a basking dog stretched at full length upon the sward, the blinking dignity of a nodding cat on a sunny doorstep, or the happy song of a free bird, are light arrows winged to my heart.[125]

In introducing the measure, Deakin was not taken altogether seriously. One member had delayed bringing forward another Bill because 'so much sympathy had been generally evinced with regard to dumb animals that he now felt certain that he would receive the support of honorable members when he brought forward his measure dealing with human beings.' Another suggested that the Chinese should be provided for either in this or another Bill. But the Act did make important changes, especially in the treatment of work animals.[126] Deakin was to remain associated with the work of the R.S.P.C.A. for most of his adult life. During debate he had his first serious clash since entering Parliament, with the aggressive Francis Longmore, former commissioner for Crown lands, since dropped by Berry. Deakin would remember him as 'a bitter, tenacious & intemperate temperance man'. Longmore accused Deakin 'of being a young man without enthusiasm, rather glib with his tongue, but [with] no fixed principles'.[127]

Another, and a most intimate, prophecy appeared to be fulfilled on 6 July 1881, when at the Lyceum Ball Pattie accepted Alfred's proposal of marriage; she was eighteen, he was twenty-four. It had been predicted that he would wed an 'auburn haired girl'; against great odds he had nourished the hope over some four years that he could win the hand of this beautiful daughter of a wealthy Spiritualist. Though it was omitted from 'Personal Experiences ...' as being too personal, it was among his most cherished predictions. During their courtship he wrote volumes of poetry for her in 'Song Sonatas', since destroyed. The intensity of his ardour is indicated by their extent. The sonatas were written in three parts: 900 lines were written in 1876 and 600 lines in 1877, and a further 600 lines in 1878.

There were also 1000 lines of a 'Song Symphony of Love' written for Pattie between 1878 and 1882.[128] She remembered him as a beautiful dancer and a great entertainer, very tall and slim but with a slight stoop, a pale complexion and suffering with weak eyes from overstudy. He was too garrulous for the boys and 'gave them the pip' and, she added, with his 'eternal tongue' no-one else was heard when he was about.[129]

Alfred and Pattie were engaged against her parents' wishes, who thought him 'rather delicate and too masterful for a strong willed girl' like herself, so that their future was unlikely to be successful. Deakin's class origins, and something of his radicalism, are indicated by the reception he received from her father. Hugh Junor Browne was a Scotsman who had arrived with the gold rush and, meeting with some success, made a return voyage to Natal bringing back a cargo of sugar, and selling both ship and cargo. He established the Australian Distillery Works. From spirits he gravitated to spirit return, first becoming interested in the subject on the death of a child. He became a convinced believer, and wrote numerous books and pamphlets on the subject. Despite their similar metaphysical views, the conservative and very wealthy Mr Browne thought Alfred beneath their status. They argued about the Bible, plural voting and education.[130] To a Temperance man, the fact that Mr Browne had made his fortune from a distillery must have rankled. The romantic aura was further augmented by the fact that their marriage so displeased the Brownes that Pattie alone among her sisters was cut out of a share in the considerable family fortune.[131] She came to him, as he remembered warmly 'without dower, peerless and priceless'.[132]

Alfred and Pattie were married on 3 April 1882, leaving the next day for a ten-day wedding tour in Tasmania. With his young bride he visited the Port Arthur settlement and other historical sites, giving her all the while a running narrative on the penal history of Van Diemen's Land. During long walks, perhaps showing off, Alfred would quote Wordsworth, Emerson or another favourite poet at length, exhibiting a remarkable memory. He also took her to two Salvation Army meetings; when she commented that few people would attend such events on their wedding tours, he replied gravely: 'they would go anywhere to get nearer to God.' He never relaxed; when not lecturing or quoting poetry, he would read or discuss the deepest subjects. 'What an old mind for such a young man', she recalled in later years.[133]

On 5 February 1883, the Deakins had a 'sitting' with J. Milner Stephen, the South Australian healing medium, and two days later, they attended a materialisation circle along with David Syme.[134] Pattie had been raised as a Spiritualist, and her continuing interest is illustrated by the psychic experiment with Professor William Denton, a geologist whose occult specialty was psychometry, the reading of past events through the vibrations retained in objects. On a lecture tour for the V.A.S. he had left a fragment of stone with the Deakins, and from New Zealand he wrote: 'I think Mrs Deakin did uncommonly well ... I wish you would induce her to go back in time and see the country, when the igneous activity is at its greatest ... the people she saw were in all probability the Maori ori'. This was followed a few days later by another letter containing a meteoric fragment, along with the ambitious wish that 'you and Mrs Deakin should get the position in space of the world of which the specimen formed a part and follow if you can its career'.[135]

With growing Parliamentary and family responsibilities, Deakin's involvement with the Spiritualist Association was now less frequent, but the change was due mainly to what he perceived as Spiritualism's deficiencies as a system of belief. Around the time he was writing about the 'Invisible Masters' he had made a symbolic break, crossing out a list made earlier in his 'Spiritual Diary' of supposed communicators—Richard Heales, Sophocles, J. S. Mill, Giordano Bruno, Thomas Macaulay and Edmund Burke among them—which he annotated alongside as 'Rubbish'.[136] It was not, as Deakin's principal biographer Professor La Nauze allows us to infer, that Deakin with this action forever rejected the phenomena, which he links to his severance of formal ties with the association. Nor can I concur in La Nauze's judgment that though Deakin recorded political predictions 'he was not concerned with them in practical conduct.'[137] For the moment Deakin's action may indeed have meant a wholesale rejection, yet later in the same year, commenting on Seeley's *Ecce Homo* he observed: 'Strange what such a man misses by a want of knowledge of Spiritualism. All he knows must be added to it to make its facts serve true religion.'[138] Deakin's momentary revulsion was neither against the movement, nor against the prophecies he had sedulously recorded; rather, he was railing against his own pretension and egotism in the credulous assumption that the mighty dead were concerned with his personal fortunes. He added: 'Instead of the arrant nonsense with which I have filled the first part of this book, I will now try to put the remaining pages to better use, recording thoughts in the place of superstitions.'[139] The remaining pages of the diary were devoted to literary criticism conspicuously devoid of religious or metaphysical subject matter.

On the same page, below the excision of the names of the famous, he continued this ritual cleavage with the past, inscribing a quotation from Augustine which proclaims a new beginning:

> What is now called the Christian religion has existed among the ancients & was not absent from the beginning of the human race until Christ came in the flesh, from which time the true religion which existed already, began to be called Christian.[140]

Doubtless his interpretation of this passage would have differed dramatically from that of the Bishop of Hippo, for having 'once & for always' rejected past creeds, Deakin was not now embracing doctrinal Christianity. His eclectic disposition cherished the insights of the Bible, especially the prophets and what he called 'the pristine Christianity of Jesus',[141] and he believed always that their lives had been permeated with superphysical phenomena. It was perhaps in this sense, as a fact of experience that for him Christianity had always existed, as the Ideal of the Christ Spirit, of which Jesus was one corporeal expression.

On that same day in January 1882, writing on 'Ideal Satisfaction' in another journal, Deakin observed that 'the horizon of ideal content advances with us', and asked rhetorically 'what it is that does utterly and wholly satisfy', to which he responded: 'It is well doing ... [w]hat we give we have forever.'[142] And another entry a week later raises for the first time directly the subject of Providential guidance:

> Canst thou by searching find out God? Yes! After long watching & long weariness— The day is coming to me, the knowledge for which I have waited several years, have felt the ... imperative need of, for myself & all mankind.[143]

It seems a rather grandiose thought for a 26-year-old, its depth and sonorous resonance augmented, as with all his supplications to God, by its expression in archaic language. This is the first recorded instance where his personal endeavours are linked to 'all mankind'. He added that his experiences had been such that 'I could almost believe looking back, that my guidance has been from the first providential & to this end.'[144] It is here, if anywhere, that one can sense a 'turning', the germ of a 'higher' interpretation for those mysterious occurrences that had characterised his life, and especially the manner in which, as he would put it, he had been 'whirled into' politics.

Deakin would have a great deal to say on this head in years to come, when the conditional tone would disappear altogether. For the moment he launched into a deep and absorbing study of Jesus and the Bible. He was also beginning seriously to consider politics as a full career, under the renewed influence of Carlyle and other writers, and to reflect on his career to date: the miraculous ambience of his entry into politics against all odds; the trip to Fiji; his marriage to Pattie; and a growing political stature within the Parliament. Taken together and reflected upon in his deeply introspective self, they were changing the 'tone & temper' of his mind. The 'reformer for Church & State' was now directly soliciting a revelation so far hinted by his experience, not only for himself, but for 'all mankind'. Here then was the inner dynamic of both Deakin's private faith and his public actions, the seedbed for that profound sense of Mission.

In June 1882 Deakin inaugurated 'Clues', a series of numbered and dated entries of varying lengths, comprising a mélange of philosophic speculation and literary criticism, of aphorisms, personal memoranda, and stories and sketches, maintained for some twenty-five years.[145] The title is suggestive of a search for answers to life's riddles, just as 'Impromptus', now almost at the end of its term, suggests spontaneity and spirit assistance. The 'Clues' are the longest-running of Deakin's journals, apart from the books of prayers, and their subject matter speaks with a different voice; they were notes kept for their intrinsic interest, and so that he might some day 'note the direction & measure the curve' of his mind.[146] As was now his custom, 'Clues' opens with quotations. The first of these, quoted in French from St Martin, taken together with the quantity and regularity of his reflections, speaks in its brevity of Deakin's deepening religious orientation: 'There is my God, I have a soul, I need nothing more to be wise.'[147]

Notes

The principal manuscript sources for this study are the Deakin papers, series 1540, National Library of Australia (N.L.A.). All end-note references are to this series unless otherwise specified. Some N.L.A. reference numbers relate to entire volumes, while in other manuscripts, each page has been given a separate reference number. In each case, the N.L.A. system has been adopted. Pagination reference has not been practicable in some instances. Typescript compilations from several of Deakin's journals and prayer books were made by Ivy and Herbert Brookes, and where the originals are still held by the family, or because of difficulty with Deakin's handwriting, these have been employed.

1 Catherine Deakin, 'Parents of Alfred Deakin', 19/370, undated.

2 See *Bendigo Advertiser*, 24 March and 18 May 1859, advertising Deakin & Bill coach service.

3 Catherine Deakin, 'Parents ...', undated; see also interview with Alfred Deakin, *Sunday Times*, 2 August 1903.

4 Autobiographical Notes for 1864, typescript, 3/300, 5 June 1910.

5 Autobiographical Notes for 1866–7, typescript, 3/300, 9 June 1910.

6 Walter Murdoch, *Alfred Deakin: A Sketch*, Sydney, 1923, p. 9.

7 Autobiographical Notes, typescript, 3/300, 12 January 1908.

8 Autobiographical Notes for 1865–6, typescript, 3/300, 5 June 1910.

9 Ibid., June 1910.

10 Murdoch, *Alfred Deakin* . . ., p. 15.

11 Ibid., p. 20.

12 Autobiographical Notes for 1873, typescript, 3/300, June 1910.

13 S. MacIntyre, *A Colonial Liberalism: The Lost World of Three Victorian Visionaries*, Melbourne, 1991, p. 64. Redmond Barry, judge of the Victorian Supreme Court from 1852, was highly influential in the cultural life of Melbourne, serving as first Chancellor of the University, and chief trustee of the Melbourne Public Library and Art Gallery, where he had a strong hand in the choosing of the holdings; *Australian Dictionary of Biography* (*A.B.D.*), vol. 3, 1851–90.

14 J. Rattray, *Round and Round and In the World*, London, 1870, p. 227.

15 L. Stuart, *James Smith, The Making of a Colonial Culture*, Sydney, 1989; Mary Eagle, 'Painting an Australian Culture', in J. Carroll (ed.), *Intruders in the Bush*, Melbourne, 1982.

16 On the Dialectical Society debates, see W. D. C. Denovan, *The Evidences of Spiritualism*, Melbourne, 1882, pp. 84–5; on the Eclectic Association and other societies, see S. Merrifield, 'George Leonard Vogt', *Labour History*, no. 7, November 1964, and no. 8, May 1965; and I. Selby, *The Old Pioneers' Memorial History of Melbourne*, Melbourne, 1924; see also H. G. Turner, 'Spiritualism', and W. H. Terry, 'The Reality of Spirit Communion with Man—A Reply to H. G. Turner', Melbourne, 1869, La Trobe section, S.L.V., Spiritualist Pamphlets, vol. 1; and H. G. Turner papers, MS ll68, La Trobe section, S.L.V.

17 G. K. Nelson, *Spiritualism and Society*, London, 1969, p. 3.

18 It is estimated that by the 1850s there were 100 mediums in New York City, and some 50 to 60 private circles in Philadelphia; Ruth Brandon, *The Spiritualists: The Passion for the Occult in the Nineteenth and Twentieth Centuries*, London, 1983, p. 42.

19 Marcus Clarke, *Victorian Review*, vol. 1, 3, 1879.

20 On Judge Williams, see G. H. Stephens, 'Syon Angitur A Babylone—or the Rise of Secularism and Heterodoxy During the Episcopate of Bishop Moorhouse', unpublished B.A. (Hons) thesis, University of Melbourne, 1961, p. 20; the close links between the secular and spiritualist movements in Melbourne, united only in their opposition to the 'sacerdotalism' of established Christianity, are evident in the rupture in 1884, when Thomas Walker broke away, denouncing Spiritualism, and taking half the membership with him; see F. B. Smith, 'Joseph Symes and the Australasian Secular Association', *Labour History*, no. 5, November 1963, and Janet Courtney, *Freethinkers of the Nineteenth Century*, London, 1920.

21 W. H. Terry in the *Harbinger of Light*, September 1872; the metropolitan V.A.P.S. derived much of its support from the country. The regional centres, where much gold was still being mined, were populous, and even the smallest settlements had literary societies and the ubiquitous mechanics' institutes where earnest debate on all manner of issues took place. Close links were maintained between organisations like the Stawell Psychological Association and the Sandhurst (Bendigo) Spiritualist Association, and the V.A.P.S.: Minutes, 1872, La Trobe section, S.L.V. see note 66 below.

22 *Harbinger of Light*, June 1874. For a discussion of Freethought and its relation to Spiritualism and Secularism in Melbourne, see F. B. Smith, 'Religion and Freethought in Melbourne 1870–1890', unpublished M.A. thesis, University of Melbourne, 1960, pp. 158–60; G. Serle, *The Rush To Be Rich*, Melbourne, 1971, p. 128, on the V.A.P.S.

23 Bishop Perry's Pastoral Letter was reported in the *Harbinger of Light*, December 1871.

24 Stuart, *James Smith...*, pp. 141–3.

25 Smith, 'Religion...', p. 153.

26 On the theory of evolution and the higher criticism and their effects in Australia, see W. W. Phillips, *Defending a Christian Country*, St Lucia, 1981.

27 J. Oppenheim, *The Other World: Spiritualism and Psychical Research in England 1850–1914*, Melbourne, 1985, especially chapter 4, 'Psychical Research and Agnosticism'.

28 'Personal Experiences in Spiritism', alternatively 'Spiritism & After', 5/1175–1452.

29 The planchette was the precursor of the 'ouija board', a little tray on wheels to which a pencil is attached and upon which sitters place their hands until it moves and thus allegedly writes without their conscious effort. Deakin had seen it at the home of American friends of his parents, and later at the home of a suburban medical man, who might have been Dr Walter Lindesay Richardson, father of the novelist H. H. Richardson, who was for a time in practice in Hawthorn: 'Personal Experiences...', 5/1202, section II, p. 1.

30 Autobiographical Notes for 1872, typescript, 3/300, June 1910.

31 'Personal Experiences ...', 5/1203–6, section II, pp. 2–5.

32 Autobiographical Notes, typescript, 3/300, 1910.

33 Autobiographical Notes for 1873, typescript, 3/300, June 1910; V.A.P.S. Minutes, October 1870.

34 J. Smith, *Cyclopaedia of Victoria*, Melbourne, 1904, 2 vols, vol. 2, p. 224; E. H. Britten, *Nineteenth Century Miracles*, New York, 1884, p. 231; 'W. H. Terry', *A.D.B.*, vol. 6, 1851–90.

35 'Personal Experiences...', 5/1208, section II, p. 7; repeated in Autobiographical Notes for 1873, typescript, 3/300, June 1910.

36 Autobiographical Notes for 1873, typescript, 3/300, June 1910.

37 Autobiographical Notes for 1874, typescript, 3/300, June 1910.

38 22/4, press cuttings for 1872.

39 Autobiographical Notes for 1873, typescript, 3/300, June 1910.

40 'Personal Experiences ...', 5/1210, section II, p. 9; 5/1216, section II, p. 15.

41 Autobiographical Notes for 1874, typescript, 3/300, June 1910.

42 Dr James Bridgnorth Motherwell was a medical graduate of Glasgow University, an early pioneer and a leader in his profession. He was for 25 years honorary physician to the Melbourne Hospital, an original member of the Medical Board of Victoria and the Medical School Committee. See J. A. Neild, 'The Medical Profession in Victoria', in A. Sutherland *et al.* (eds), *Victoria and Her Metropolis Past and Present*, 1888, 2 vols, vol. 2, p. 785; see also K. F. Russell, *The Melbourne Medical School 1862–1962*, Melbourne, 1977, pp. 20, 56; and G. Blainey, *A Centenary History of the University of Melbourne*, Melbourne, 1957, p. 89.

43 Autobiographical Notes for 1874, typescript, 3/300, June 1910.

44 'Personal Experiences...', 5/1272–5, section V, pp. 9–12; 5/1278, section V, p. 15.

45 Autobiographical Notes for 1874, typescript, 3/300, June 1910.

46 Counsel Fees, 3/290, circa June 1910.

47 Blue notebooks, 3/88-91, 1873; 'Morality', 5/139, 29 March 1874.

48 Autobiographical Notes for 1875, typescript, 3/300, June 1910; e.g., phrenological reading, 5/33, 25 April 1875; chiromantic and astrological reading, 5/34, 11 November 1876.

49 'First Fruits', vol. II, 4/861, 1876; all pages in this notebook were destroyed but one, to which this note was added on 13 February 1880.

50 Ledger, 3/292, precis of 'Cross & Crescent' (November 1876), 19 July 1911.

51 Ibid., 'Three Prayers' (1874), p. 9, undated, circa 1911, when Deakin wrote precis of many of his early dramatic pieces.

52 A3 Ledger, 3/292-A3, 1 January 1876.

53 Events from 1876 were noted after the rediscovery in 1913 of an old notebook, 'March 1876 'Impressional Writings' credited to H. T. Buckle pp. 19-26'; followed by a list of seventeen articles on Spiritualism written by Deakin covering some 130 pages of this now extinct notebook: 'Medley', 3/296, 21 November 1913, p. 326.

54 Andrew Harwood, criticism of *Quentin Massys*, 4/110, 1875.

55 Counsel Fees, 3/290, 19 October 1913, p. 140.

56 Murdoch, *Alfred Deakin...*, p. 176.

57 Ibid., p. 17.

58 Ledger, 3/292, precis of 'Before the Inquisition' (1875), 1910, p. 14.

59 5/1, circa June 1873; the membership was Theodore Fink, J. Kelly, J. Martin, M. Cohen, and Deakin as secretary and treasurer.

60 Higgins added that Deakin lived up to his principles by not working for the degree, and taking only the law subjects: Murdoch, *Alfred Deakin...*, p. 39. Hodgson's article defending Spencer against T. H. Green was published in *Contemporary Review*, XXXVIII (1880), pp. 898-912.

61 Macintyre, *A Colonial Liberalism*, p. 148; E. Scott, *A History of the University of Melbourne*, Melbourne, 1936, p. 100.

62 19 February 1877; cited in J. Tregenza, *Professor of Democracy: Life of C. H. Pearson*, Melbourne, 1968, p. 102.

63 Tregenza, *Professor...*, p. 69.

64 Autobiographical Notes for 1877, typescript, 3/300, 1910.

65 Tregenza, *Professor ...*, p. 69; Mme Siècle reading, 5/36, 27 August 1877; Autobiographical Notes, typescript, 3/300, June 1910.

66 There is some confusion about which organisations existed between February 1873 and July 1877, and during 1878. The Victorian Association of Progressive Spiritualists (V.A.P.S.) minute books survive for 1870-3; in the mid-1870s they dropped the 'Progressive' from the title of the association. V.A.S. minute books exist for part of 1877, and from 1879 to 1896. The V.A.S. minute book commenced on 6 July 1877 bears a pencilled notation on the front leaf: 'Following dissolution of the Amalgamated Spiritualistic and Freethought Association'; F. B. Smith states that a group of materialists infiltrated the V.A.S. in 1875, which led to another schism in 1877-8 when they opposed the second visit of the American Spiritualist lecturer Dr J. M. Peebles. Deakin was elected president of the V.A.S. in September 1878: V.A.S. minutes, 6 July 1877; Smith, 'Religion ...', p. 140.

67 'Personal Experiences in Spiritism', alternatively 'Spiritism & After', 5/1175–1452. The most accurate dating for this manuscript is derived from the writing surface; Deakin was in the habit of recycling old letters and circulars, and writing some of his private prose on the backs. Among these is a 1901 calendar, and he speaks of the 'remorseless ridicule' to which Spiritualism, founded in 1848, had been subjected for 40 years; together they give limits to the probable date of composition as between 1888 and 1901.

68 'Personal Experiences...', 5/1175, section I, p. 1.

69 Autobiographical Notes for 1874–5, typescript, 3/300, June 1910.

70 W. H. Terry and A. Deakin (eds), *Lyceum Leader*, Melbourne, 1877; copy in Deakin Papers, 5/1056; see also Louisa Shepard, *Dialogues and Recitations Adapted to the Children's Progressive Lyceums*, Cleveland, 1871.

71 Melbourne *Herald*, 9 January 1884.

72 Autobiographical Notes for 1878, typescript, 3/300, June 1910.

73 Ibid.; Smith 'Religion ...', p. 253.

74 Nellie Bowley, Alice Hyslop, Alice Brotherton and Mary Balmain to Deakin, 1 April 1879.

75 'Personal Experiences ...', 5/1417, section XIII, p. 3; in general terms these were of two sorts, 'physical' and 'mental'. The former included 'apports' (from the French *apporter*: to carry) where objects were said to be dematerialised and carried through solid matter; and 'materialisations', whereby spirits employed 'ectoplasm', a substance produced by the medium and sitters in a seance circle, to clothe themselves temporarily so as to be visible to the naked eye. 'Mental' phenomena included 'clairvoyance' and 'clairaudience' (French: clear seeing and hearing), psychometry, prophecy and inspiration, the last connoting to Deakin both 'inspired' speech and writing such as he experienced in his early life, and that Higher inspiration originating from Deity which he later believed to be transmitted directly through the Higher Self. For definitions of these phenomena and their putative occurrence in the Australian colonies, in England, and the United States, see W. D. C. Denovan, *The Evidences of Spiritualism*, Melbourne, 1882, especially 'Spirit Materialisation in Melbourne', pp. 650–60; and Paul Miller, *Science in the Seance Room*, London, 1945; for another view of Spiritualism and its phenomena, see Ruth Brandon, *The Spiritualists*....

76 J. E. Bromby, journal, 22 February 1878; copy in La Nauze papers, series 5248, N.L.A.

77 A. J. Gabay, 'The Seance in Melbourne of the 1870s: Experience and Meanings', *Journal of Religious History*, December 1984.

78 Autobiographical Notes for 1877–8, typescript, 3/300, 1910; Foolscap A3 Notebook, 3/294, 3 August 1877.

79 *Harbinger of Light*, 1 March 1876, p. 985; inconsistencies as to the identities of the mediums emerge in Deakin's record, comparing this manuscript against the several reminiscences Deakin produced between 1909 and 1915, and his 'Crude Indexes'. Regarding the Grand Prophecy, the principal source is Deakin's June 1910 reminiscences, but also 'Personal Experiences ...', 5/1358, section X, p. 4. In the 'Crude Index to the Diaries' covering the years 1878–1916, he lists Mrs Cohen predicting on 15 August 1880 that he would hold the reins of power in three years, Mrs Stirling predicting on 11 March 1880 that he would go to England within many months, and on 10 May that he would be in Parliament in six months. In the 'Spiritual Diary' he lists under 'Preliminary record' no less than three mediums, Mrs Fielden, Mrs Stellard, and Mrs Stirling, as predicting his entry into Parliament within six months: 'Spiritual Diary Personal & Mundane', 5/1453.

80 'Personal Experiences ...', 5/1283, section VI, p. 4; Janet Oppenheim has called attention to the number of middle-class housewives who became mediums in the 1850s through the 1870s; she suggests part of the explanation lies in the paucity of opportunities for women in Victorian society and the role of medium as one avenue of expression: Oppenheim, *The Other World ...*, pp. 9–10.

81 'Personal Experiences ...', 5/1285, section VI, p. 6.

82 Ibid., 5/1305, section VII, p. 5.

83 'Dixon gas' is one such venture Deakin did follow; in a late reminiscence he mentioned that his father had lost in this venture, which must have been urged on him by his son, based on the predictions of success he had received in seances: Autobiographical Notes, typescript, 3/300, 12 November 1913.

84 'Personal Experiences ...', 5/1313–14, section VII, pp. 13–14.

85 Interview with Alfred Deakin, *Sunday Times*, 2 August 1903.

86 Diary notes for 1878, in 'Medley', 3/296, 21 November 1913, p. 327.

87 Ibid.

88 Autobiographical Notes for 1878, Counsel Fees, 3/290, 8 June 1911; there are three volumes in 'Poets & Poetry': 4/862, commenced 12 March and completed 13 April 1878; 4/859, commenced 18 April and completed 29 June 1878, consisting of 373 quarto pages penned in one month; and an incomplete volume, 4/858, was commenced 8 July 1878.

89 Autobiographical Notes for 1878, typescript, 3/300, June 1910.

90 Review, 'Politics in Australia', *Age*, 8 June 1878.

91 *Age*, 25 June 1878.

92 V.A.P.S. minutes 1872–3; Syme joined the V.A.P.S. committee on 20 November 1872 for twelve months, and he served during 1873, and his wife and daughters were active in the association for many years.

93 Red Spine Book, 3/281, 6 May 1911.

94 'Personal Experiences ...', 5/1310–11, section VII, pp. 10–11.

95 Ibid.

96 Ibid., 5/1319, section VII, p. 18.

97 B. Mansfield, *Australian Democrat: The Career of E. W. O'Sullivan 1846–1910*, Sydney, 1965, p. 28.

98 Theodore Fink is quoted by Murdoch: 'Class feeling ran high, and for a young man of education to announce [himself] a Liberal was, at that day, in the minds of the comfortable classes, an admission that he was a scoundrel who was certainly selling his convictions for a mess of pottage in the shape of salary': Murdoch, *Alfred Deakin ...*, footnote, p. 53. La Nauze, *Alfred Deakin*, vol. 1, Chapter 2, 'Whirled into Politics', discusses the almost revolutionary temper which the events of 1877–79 had given to Victorian politics, and the tense atmosphere following 'Black Wednesday' and the unsuccessful 'Embassy' to London of Berry and Pearson, pp. 45–6. See G. Serle, 'The Victorian Legislative Council, 1856–1950', *Historical Studies*, vol. 6, no. 22, May 1954.

99 'Personal Experiences ...', 5/1322, section VIII, p. 2; another version is given by Murdoch and repeated by La Nauze, that the deputation had called on David Syme who gave them Deakin's name as a last resort: Murdoch, *Alfred Deakin ...*, p. 50; La Nauze, *Alfred Deakin*, vol. 1, p. 41.

100 *Victorian Parliamentary Debates* (*V.P.D.*), vol. 30, 8 July 1879, p. 31.

101 Ibid., p. 27.

102 La Nauze, *Alfred Deakin*, vol. 1, p. 43.

103 J. E. Bromby, Journal, 18 and 19 February 1879.

104 *V.P.D.*, vol. 30, 8 July 1879, p. 31; see G. Bartlett, 'The Political Orders of Victoria and New South Wales 1856-1890', *Australian Economic History Review*, vol. 8, no. 1, March 1968, pp. 49-53.

105 Murdoch, *Alfred Deakin* ..., p. 3; a letter dated 20 February 1879, dictated by O'Loghlen, acting Premier and Attorney-General in the Berry ministry, to the returning officer, was tabled: *V.P.D.*, vol. 30, pp. 12-13.

106 'Personal Experiences ...', 5/1314-15, section VII, pp. 14-15.

107 Ibid., 5/1325, section VIII, p. 5; 'Spiritual Diary', 5/1453, lists three mediums responsible for this prophecy: Mrs Fielden, Mrs Stellard and Mrs Stirling. See note 79 above.

108 Melbourne *Daily Telegraph*, 7 and 14 July 1880.

109 Interview with Alfred Deakin, *Sunday Times*, 2 August 1903.

110 'Spiritual Diary...', 5/1453, 1 August 1880.

111 'Personal Experiences ...', 5/1358, section X, p. 4.

112 Counsel Fees, 3/290, 12 November 1913.

113 'Spiritual Diary ...', 5/1453, 6 August 1880. Most of the seances Deakin attended were in the 1870s, with a gradual diminution through the early 1880s. But contrary to Professor La Nauze's statement, he attended such events into the 1890s and he occasionally had home circles in the Federal period: La Nauze, *Alfred Deakin*, vol. 1, p. 64. See Diary, 16 April 1894, 15 March and 28 September 1897, for careful records of alleged psychic phenomena occurring in his home.

114 B. S. Naylor edited the *Glowworm*, a Spiritualist journal with strong ties to Socialism, during 1869; S. Merrifield, 'George Leonard Vogt', *Labour History*, no. 7, November 1964, p. 15; Richard Heales, a coach builder by trade, was Premier of Victoria during the struggle to 'unlock the land'; see G. Serle, *The Golden Age*, Melbourne, 1963, pp. 301-2; A. W. Martin, *Henry Parkes*, Melbourne, 1980, p. 63.

115 The Victorian Constitution is framed so that the Legislative Council has to agree to any reform in its tenure or electoral base. Deakin and another new M.L.A. stood against David Syme, Pearson and Berry, and the Liberal caucus. Syme wanted 'no surrender', but their stand caused Berry and others to waver. The reforms agreed to were: a change of electoral base from 30,000 to 100,000; property qualifications reduced to £100; tenure reduced from ten to six years; and membership in the Legislative Council increased from 30 to 42: J. Tregenza, *Professor* ..., p. 157; C. E. Sayers, *David Syme: A Life*, Melbourne, 1965, pp. 140-1.

116 'Personal Experiences ...', 5/1316, section VII, p. 16. The prophecy was given on 15 August 1880, and Deakin became minister in March 1883.

117 'Impromptus', 5/1508, 19 December 1880, p. 93.

118 Ibid.

119 Ibid., note 17, 16 October 1881, p. 115.

120 5/3, Certificate of Membership of the Theosophical Society, dated 21 February 1895; see J. Roe, *Beyond Belief: Theosophy in Australia 1879-1939*, Kensington, 1986.

121 H. J. Olcott to Deakin, 20 March 1895.

122 Literary Memoranda, typescript, 3/302, 3 February 1882.

123 Ibid., 6 October 1883.

124 'Impromptus', 5/1508, 29 January 1881, p. 95.

125 'Clues', vol. 1, 3/283, no. 146, 28 November 1886.

126 *V.P.D.*, vol. 37, 5 October 1881, p. 243. This included prohibiting anyone driving a dray to which a horse was tied by the neck pulling another dray, a common practice of the day, so as to prevent stumbling and choking; Deakin was a lifelong member of the R.S.P.C.A., later serving as its president.

127 *V.P.D.*, vol. 37, 5 October 1881, p. 243; 'Francis Longmore', *A.D.B.*, vol. 5, 1851–90.

128 'Song Sonatas', Foolscap A3 Notebook, 3/294.

129 Pattie Deakin, Reminiscences, 19/276, undated.

130 La Nauze, *Alfred Deakin*, vol. 1, p. 50; see a letter from H. J. Browne to Deakin, 10 September 1891, which relates a vision where he claimed to have seen his recently deceased daughter.

131 'Hugh Junor Browne', *A.D.B.*, vol. 3, 1851–90; each of the Browne girls was left ten thousand pounds, with the exception of Pattie. For evidence of her 'mediumship' during adolescence, see H. J. Browne, *The Grand Reality*, Melbourne, 1888, pp. 15–16, p. 506.

132 A4 notebook, 3/290, 12 November 1913.

133 Pattie Deakin, Reminiscences, 19/277, undated.

134 'Crude Index to the Diaries', in 'Medley', 3/296, 7 February 1882.

135 W. Denton to Deakin from Hamilton, N.Z., 21 and 25 September 1882; on the Denton psychic experiment, 'Crude Index ...', 3/296, 9 September 1882.

136 'Spiritual Diary ...', 5/1453, 14 January 1882, p. 68.

137 At one seance in March 1881 Deakin was warned of 'revolution & civil war' over the Council deadlock, and it ends: 'I believe that the Reform Bill will as previously predicted be passed though much modified': 'Spiritual Diary ...', 5/1453, no. XXII, 26 March 1881. Professor La Nauze has candidly written, concerning Deakin's lifelong interest in and early involvement with the 'occult' and mysterious: 'It may be as well for a biographer to say frankly that he is not impressed by it, though he does not doubt that Deakin was. There is a good deal in Deakin's early "spiritual" adventures, and in his somewhat later flirtings with theosophy, to justify the opinion of some who knew him, as reported by Ernest Scott in 1923, that in these early days "his mind was birdlimed for any stray notion to settle and stick upon"': La Nauze, *Alfred Deakin*, vol. 1, p. 65. Scott's seems a harsh judgment from an undoubted admirer, especially given his intimate links by marriage to Theosophy; J. Roe, *Beyond Belief* ..., p. 80.

138 Literary Memoranda, typescript, 3/302, 8 October 1882.

139 'Spiritual Diary ...', 5/1453, 14 January 1882, p. 68.

140 Ibid.

141 See, for instance, 'Medley', 3/296, 'Clue' no. 766, 18 November 1900; 'Clue' no. 790, 24 August 1902, for Deakin's ideas about Jesus.

142 Literary Memoranda, typescript, 3/302, 14 January 1882.

143 Ibid., 22 January 1882.

144 Ibid.

145 There are six books of consecutive 'Clues', comprising 953 mostly numbered and
     dated entries of varying lengths, and spanning 25 years. Five are volumes of 'Clues',
     and one volume is the 'Medley': (a) volume 1, 'Clues', 3/283, nos. 1–260, January
     1882 to 21 July 1896; (b) volume 2, 'Clues', 3/288, nos. 261–341, 18 July 1888 to
     18 May 1889; (c) volume 3, 'Clues', 3/287, nos. 342–537, 27 July 1889 to 12 June
     1892; (d) volume 4, 'Clues', 3/286, nos. 538–709, 18 June 1892 to 21 July 1896;
     (e) 'Medley', 3/296, containing 'Clues' nos. 710–856, 23 August 1896 to November
     1910; (f) volume 5, 'Clues', 3/282, nos. 1–97, 30 July 1907 to 13 June 1909.

146 'Clues', vol. 1, 3/283, no. 237, 27 May 1888.

147 'Il y a mon Dieu, j'ai une âme, il ne me faut rien de plus pour être sage': 'Clues',
     vol. 1, 3/283, January 1882.

2

The Mission Revealed

The Youth, who daily farther from the east
Must travel, still is Nature's Priest,
And by the vision splendid
Is on his way attended;
At length the Man perceives it die away,
And fade into the light of common day.

William Wordsworth
'Ode: Intimations of Immortality'

From private writings considered in isolation, one might gain the impression that Alfred Deakin's commitment to politics in his early career was not wholehearted. Probably even then he was being less than sincere with himself; and among the fascinating patterns observed in his life is a seeking, an expectation and a gradual fulfilment of a sense of Divine sanction for that career, a process whereby he came to believe he was after all best placed to assist a Greater Purpose. This is less a comment on the career of the most successful and best-liked politician of his generation, than on a mind that always sought higher ground; perhaps too it gives a hint as to the role of private writing in that life. As his political career unfolded, this theme of hesitancy or unworthiness for the task at hand, expressed at times as vague and lingering aspirations to the literary life, resurfaced periodically in his private meditations. Now, after only three years in public life, inspired by Seeley's *Natural Religion*, he was thinking that he might 'go "teach & organise the outlying world" of so-called heathendom'.[1]

The increasingly religious tenor of Deakin's journals reflects the powerful influence of Swedenborg, while a strong sense of being a 'man apart' is conveyed in his meditations upon the 'prophetic information' that had so far attended his life and career. With the election in March 1883 of the Berry–Service coalition; another prophecy recorded in 1880 came to pass, that he would 'hold the reins of power within three years'. Each leader brought three members into the Cabinet, and Berry chose Deakin as Minister for Public Works and Water Supply.[2] While we cannot know whether an expectation thus engendered may have affected the result, it is true that Berry had been impressed by Deakin from the first; indeed in 1880, when Deakin had been in Parliament only two weeks, Berry had offered him the portfolio of Attorney-General! It was sensibly refused. He administered these offices in a way that compelled the silence of opponents who had decried him as a 'mystic'. With increasing responsibilities and a ministerial salary, Deakin felt he could now retire from journalism, whose narrowness and smug certainties he was finding increasingly grating. After five years he was free of 'its confidence, dogmatism, & the superficial exteriority of its judgments & remedies for all the ills that flesh is heir to'. He also wished to be more politically independent of the *Age*. On July 6 he wrote his last 'Verandah' column.[3]

Four days before he became a Minister of the Crown, Deakin inscribed a journal headed 'Two Paths', which reveals a consciousness of having come of age politically, mixed with a curious, almost apologetic tone:

> Every youth is ... an adventurer ... a major selection must be made between the two great paths ... he must be for or against the social order, within or without society, remain a son of the church & strive to purify it, or stand outside & seek to destroy it ... The social order is ... in places rotten, in places sound—Those who accept its badges, its restrictions, its labours, reap its rewards, & are entrusted in some measure with its powers ... those who refuse to wear its livery gain in freedom & lose in influence.[4]

These thoughts of bifurcation first appear six weeks before, probably when he first heard of the offer, regarding 'two strains': 'unhappy he who commingles the two strains & who born among the philistines in an unhistoric land ... feels a stranger in the land.'[5] The youth who had refused confirmation would continue to refuse the 'livery' of the social order in knighthoods, honorary degrees and Privy Councillorships; yet he did not now count himself among the 'outer', for he adds: 'It is given to very few to walk with one foot in each path & take steps alternatively with the friends of order & the friends of reform.'[6] If it is an absurd image, it reflects a growing tension of aims, and Deakin seems presently to have missed a step with the latter.

At a meeting in the Town Hall in May 1883 chaired by the radical Justice Higinbotham, the reforming community of Melbourne came together, with C. H. Pearson calling for the opening of museums and galleries on Sunday afternoons. The Sabbatarians, mostly conservative Presbyterian and Methodist clergy, opposed not only the opening of public institutions, but also the showing of the painting 'Chloe', Sunday trams except to go to church, and Sunday papers. As Pearson trenchantly remarked, in opposing these but not other Sunday events, well might they 'avenge themselves on sin when it has no balance in the bank'.[7] Curiously, Deakin took no part in the Sabbatarian controversy, although Pearson and Higinbotham, two men he greatly admired, were conspicuously present and, along with hundreds of others, so were his father-in-law Hugh Junor Browne and most of the V.A.S. committee, and Thomas Walker and the Secularists. Perhaps as a new minister his presence was deemed inappropriate, but it sits incongruously with his professed radicalism. The Sabbatarians won, and public institutions remained closed on Sundays in Victoria for the next twenty years.

Much of Deakin's leisure was consumed in reading, thinking and commenting on the ideas of others. He was searching more earnestly for a reasonable 'system' of religion that would harmonise with his own insights and experiences. Of the more than one hundred books Deakin listed as having read in 1883, Matthew Arnold figures prominently, including *Culture and Anarchy* and *God and the Bible*, which he commends for the distinction of the 'secret & method of Jesus' and the unity of natural and revealed religion; but like Seeley 'what unhappy conclusions his ignorance of Spiritism in its common sense, & of spiritualism in its larger sense, plunges him.'[8] In his critique of *Esoteric Buddhism* by the English Theosophist A. P. Sinnett, Deakin ventured a kind of smorgasbord system. With Arnold's interpretation of Christ and the Bible:

> ... taking thus together Jesus & Buddha, as now interpreted, with Plato & Swedenborg, & with Martineau & Emerson as modern commentaries, I begin to see a religious system of belief & action, of faith & philosophy, which I can not only accept, but act upon, as indeed I am acting upon & could even preach if necessary.[9]

As events after Federation would show, Deakin's desire to 'preach' was never far below the surface.

On 1 August 1883 Justice Higinbotham again outraged conservative opinion with his famous lecture on 'Science and Religion', delivered at Scots Hall. It was chaired by the Reverend Dr Charles Strong, and its criticisms *inter alia* of the Christian clergy and the Westminster Confession, would hasten Strong's break with his Kirk and his expulsion from the Presbyterian pulpit, and would lead to the founding of the Australian Church.[10] Although he did not attend, Deakin must have read the lecture because a journal written ten days later on the 'Divinity of Christ' explores similar themes. Of what did Christ's divinity consist? It was not his body, confessedly human, nor his miracles, for he was only one of a host of wonder workers, nor even his mind. Though he was 'pure, royally unselfish, intuitively wise, simple & yet profound', and though his was patently 'an intense devotion, an exalted faith, & a resplendent course of conduct', other men had approached if not equalled him in these virtues. His divinity is unprovable, but if Christ is divine, Deakin concludes, 'then is humanity divine too in diverse degrees'.[11] Here then is a lasting image, a Gnostic conception of Jesus as the zenith of human development, that rejects the Trinitarian man-god for the moral and spiritual Master of Wisdom whom humankind in the mass might seek to emulate. In his critique of the biography of *Sister Dora* the previous year, Deakin regarded it as unproven that Jesus was the only son of God 'in the Trinitarian sense or in any sense denied to Buddha'; he then proceeded to dilate on the 'utter insufficiency of the old theory of proportion between Christ's suffering & the redemption he was supposed to have purchased by it'. Elsewhere Deakin reflected that, if Christ had been a god with infinite foreknowledge, 'his greatest sacrifice would not have been to be nailed in a body to a cross for a few hours, but to be misrepresented by millions for so many centuries'.[12]

The year 1884 was possibly the most important to date for Deakin's inner life. It seems to have been the locus for a conscious decision to 'find out God', when he inaugurated the practice of recording prayers in a special book. In this year also he penned the first of his formal 'Gospels', the 'Gospel According to Wordsworth', where he sought the springs of inspiration of the Lakeland poet and mystic, the essence of whose gospel of Nature he believed to be contained in the lines:

> *O there is life that breathes not,*
> *Pains there are that touch each other to the quick in modes*
> *Which the gross world no sense hath to perceive*
> *No soul to dream of.*

Intrigued always by the original message, its essence, and the personal power which originates reform, rather than the glosses of lesser men, these pre-Federation 'exegetical' studies were conceived as part of a dual pathway to God: prayer and meditation, together with insights derived from the study of the lives and the revelation of great men. Put in its most general terms, and based on an evolutionist world-view, Deakin's was an implicit Victorian belief in the availability of absolute knowledge, which presupposed the positive relationship of knowledge to virtue.

On 1 July 1884 William Terry came to see Deakin, and they strolled and talked.[13] Deakin was falling away from the 'Cause'; he had not attended a committee meeting nor lectured at the association for over two years. Terry gently persuaded the now important Minister of the Crown to address the Lyceum where he had once been Conductor, which Deakin did on his birthday, 3 August. Spiritualism, he reflected in a current journal, although now not 'a whole' was still a potent force in his life.[14] Early in the same year, seeking to give 'an impartial view' Deakin had listed as its strengths: '(1) history (2) human mind (3) fact'; its weaknesses lay in: '(1) no clear results as to future state (2) silly people & silly phenomena (3) identity very difficult, superstitions attached'.[15] When the English Spiritualist writer Gerald Massey came to town Deakin attended his lectures, and had him to dinner several times; on one occasion they dined at David Syme's together with C. H. Pearson.[16]

Deakin's twenty-eighth birthday, 3 August 1884, was a Sunday; it marks an event of especial significance to his inner life, the inauguration of the practice of written prayer. This special and very busy day displays a range of activities, and illustrates a gamut of feelings from frivolous gaiety to deep orison, reminding us again of the existence in this complex man of a deep, almost pietistic religion alongside a broad humanity and a real sense of fun. The day began, as he explained in a frothy letter to his young niece Alice Browne, when he was awakened by his infant daughter Ivy. He had wished to go back to sleep, but was 'thwarted by Pattie' who pulled him out of bed. He was then given his present, a silk handkerchief, about which he now asked Alice's opinion. Drawing a series of stick figures showing the kerchief in the various styles he had already tried, as a turban, a necktie, in the breastpocket, as a sash, he asked: 'Please let me know which of these you think best.'[17] That afternoon, largely as a favour to his erstwhile mentor Terry; he addressed the Spiritualist Lyceum on what was to be the final occasion. Later, in an hour of deep reflection Deakin inaugurated the 'Boke of Praer & Prase', the mock Gothic title perhaps betokening a return to 'old style' religion. He wrote solemnly by way of preface:

> Almost always I realise the existence of God. Always I believe in Him with my intellect & turn to Him with my heart. But I am anxious for a closer & more permanent relationship. Almost always, I believe in the spiritual efficacy of prayer, & often I am inclined to pray. Sometimes the power to put my cry in words will come. Sometimes it will not come. I shall write those prayers I can express so as to open the channel wider, & enable me to recall past prayers when I cannot uplift fresh appeals. Let me know my wants if I can know nothing else.[18]

The archaic title and sonorous prose were matched by a sense of dramatic timing. Almost certainly the inauguration of this enterprise on this auspicious day was intimately connected to an inner spiritual decision to try to reach God directly, without intermediary, in which the symbolism of seven featured prominently. We have witnessed this numerical symbolism already in the 1880 'changing spheres' seance. To occultists the age of twenty-eight is the beginning of the 'fifth cycle' in the 'seven ages' of man, each of seven years' duration.[19] Deakin believed in the power of prayer, and he retained the habit of writing his prayers out until 1913, recording more than 400 in these twenty-nine years. For historians these meditations are a particularly rich source of insights into Deakin's changing ideas about what he called the 'invisible', and his perceptions of his own self, of his Duty and destiny. It was through these pages that his ranging intellect and compulsion to 'find out God' were given their most intimate expression, in a richer vision of reality which accommodated the phenomena, while appropriating the vocabulary and many conceptions from Spiritualism and Theosophy.

It has been said with only slight exaggeration that Alfred Deakin 'devoured whole libraries'.[20] The gustatory metaphor is entirely appropriate, as in the following 'Clue' where his love of books approaches the sensuous:

> What a delight, too, to pause before well-filled bookshelves in an hour of absolute leisure, & without any sense of duty to direct the lingering choice—there rises to one's palate the fine flavours of the masterpieces over whose titles the eye glances in a rapture of timid suspense—a great name or two perhaps in them, below a new title, having been stored up long for some fitting hour of sacrifice & prayer. There are keener pleasures in life—a few—& in Nature—a few—but few altogether rarer, purer, or more exquisite than this.[21]

'Without any sense of duty'; these oft repeated words leap out from the page. Already the heavy demands of ministerial office meant stolen hours of leisure. In addition to 'Clues' and special journals devoted variously to prayer, to literary criticism and to the recording of other 'hints & humours', Deakin maintained several alphabetical and thematic indexes, intended for his own quick reference. He had a penchant for snappy titles, like the journal 'Praises Phrases & Crazes' which recorded extracts from his wide reading. Hence under 'E' we find: 'earthliness, eating, education, error, evil, East & West', etc.; and under the subheading 'Eclecticism' he quotes F. D. Maurice: 'There is nothing so emasculating as the atmosphere of ...'; similarly under 'Parliament' he records Amiel's observation that: 'The more wise men you heap together, the less wisdom you obtain.' Given the volume of reading processed in this way, it must have been a very time-consuming practice, taking up a good deal of Deakin's diminishing leisure.[22]

The 1884 Parliamentary session was one of hard work. Now as Solicitor-General and Minister for Public Works the 28-year-old minister enjoyed considerable status, and his commanding oratory and backing by the powerful David Syme, made Deakin the object of jealousy and invective in some quarters. Moreover the coalition was not popular with some Liberals like Dr John Quick, who questioned the propriety of an alliance with the Conservatives. In this session Deakin caught some of the enmity and jealousy from former allies of Berry, as he had from Longmore in 1881 when introducing his Protection of Animals Bill.

Another former ally dropped by Berry was Major W. Collard-Smith, member for Ballarat West. He was not fond of Syme, nor of the upstart Solicitor-General, speaking in not very veiled terms of the 'newspaper offices of which all governments appear to be formed'. In a previous speech Deakin had described a meeting to form a Railway League at Camperdown which, along with shire councillors, Major Smith and another local M.LA., he attended to promote the connection of the country west of Ballarat. Turkey and champagne were provided, and when the hour to leave came: 'the Major was not to be found. When there was no more turkey and no more champagne, the Major would not go a step further.' On another occasion, he continued, the Major was discovered: ' "Under a spreading chestnut tree" with a shako over his eyes and a bottle by his side.' Deakin was reminded of Damon and Pithias when he reflected on the former friendship between Smith and Graham Berry, 'at whose heels at one time the honorable member trailed his sword and his trumpet'. This led to a misunderstanding as to whether Deakin in a *lapsus lingua* had said 'strumpet'. Gaunson also got into the act, responding to Deakin's jibe that he was 'the publican's puppet [who] must move as the wires are pulled', matching the alliteration by calling Deakin 'the poodle dog of a newspaper proprietor'. It was not a very dignified performance all around, but it shows the depth of animosity over the coalition in some quarters, and that, although he hated the tactic of personal slander, Deakin could display a mordant wit when he chose; he preferred not to play the game.[23]

It was in this session that Deakin first announced his support for the idea of Federation. In this he was influenced by the rapidly growing Australian Natives Association which was becoming his political power base, and by his leader James Service, whose recent initiative of a conference of all Colonies to discuss the formation of a Federal Council had met with a lukewarm response, especially in New South Wales. In debate Deakin criticised the previous speaker Dr Quick for his vacillation. While 'staunch, bold, and fearless in his support of the theoretical idea of Federation', Quick had concluded this was not the time to deal with the question, and he objected to the Federal Council as a 'one horse' option.[24] Deakin did not agree. Referring to current fears over German and French designs which had prompted Queensland's attempted annexation of Papua the previous year, he reminded members of the relative powerlessness of any Colony to gain a hearing with a foreign power, or indeed with the imperial government.[25] The time was not right, but the positive commitment to the idea by an Australian 'native' of Deakin's stature was of some importance, and his statements in Parliament foreshadowed his vigorous stance at the Imperial Conference three years later.

James Service was a demanding taskmaster who insisted that all items on a Cabinet agenda be dealt with before adjourning. Like Berry he was impressed with Deakin's thoroughness and imagination, especially his work concerning legislation on factories and shops and on irrigation. In 1884 Deakin was appointed chairman of a Royal Commission into irrigation. The vision of lush greenery on a desolate northern Victoria appealed to his poetic sensibilities, for in La Nauze's felicitous image 'no one could more vividly conjure up visions of two blades of grass growing where none had grown before';[26] but he was also prepared to do the hard background work. At the end of the year Cabinet sent him to the United States to research the American experience. The resulting thorough and well-informed volume *Irrigation in Western America*, written by a lawyer with training in neither hydrology nor engineering, was for many years a standard text on the subject in the United States.[27]

Deakin left for America on Christmas Eve 1884, returning on 9 May 1885. His wife and daughter travelled as far as San Francisco, and he continued across the west with a final dash to the east coast.[28] Deakin learned a great deal about Americans and about irrigation; in a letter to F. T. Derham he complained, 'I have talked water drunk water & dreamed water ever since I arrived', and he assured his theatre-going friend that 'neither theatres nor the performances have equalled ours'. He was also critical of Americans' mode of living, all those 'heated rooms & cars, rich food, mixed dishes & any quantity of them', though he noted that alcohol there 'is not used to such an excess as with us'.[29] He was at first denied entry to Salt Lake City because he was taken for a U.S. marshal![30] While in California Deakin met the Chaffey brothers, who would largely be responsible for the implementation of schemes of irrigation for northern Victoria as they had for Ontario. He called on Leland Stanford, railway magnate and founder of the Stanford University, whose brother Thomas Stanford he knew from the Spiritualist Association, and who probably approached his brother's wealth through his exclusive Australian rights to the Singer sewing machine and his property deals.[31] Deakin also kept 'American Notes', some of which were transposed and expanded in journals after his return.

Beyond family and Parliamentary duties there was Deakin's duty to realise the Ideal. From the first, written prayers sounded a theme whose significance increases in later years, a growing sense of being called to a Divine Mission. In the everyday world there were 'rumours, disquietudes, temptations, & failing of heart'; these meditations gave him 'hope, confidence, strength, & the trumpet tongues of Thy messengers'.[32] Always adopting the formal archaic tone when addressing his God, he prayed, 'give me Light that I may learn to serve Thee, & enable me to serve Thee that I may win more Light.'[33] The idea of mediation by a spirit world, prominent in early prayers, would in time almost disappear. Sometimes these petitions assumed ponderous forms, as in a long and complicated prayer in October 1884, where Deakin asks for 'the presence of those pure spirits who enjoy a fuller portion of Thy Love & radiance', so that without dimming that 'most supernal light which pierces me direct from Thee' they might surround 'the innermost temple of my being with acceptable sacrifices of elevated thought & loyal inspiration'.[34]

Pleas for certitude—'Give me O God the faith in Thee ... & I can await in patience the uplifting of all other veils'—and for eventual revelation are frequent, for an opening of his inner sight such as Swedenborg had claimed. 'Thy will be done in what it shall please Thee to give me in the way of spiritual gifts', he asked with meekness in one prayer, while in another he constructed in imagination a Swedenborgian scenario as to how that revelation might occur: 'Give me to breathe as often as may be the purer air of the higher spheres of Nature, & enable me to translate into the terms of life act & idea the inward inspiration which I may there derive.'[35] An even more dramatic plea, along with kabbalistic imagery, appears in a December 1884 prayer beseeching direct ascent: 'give me often times that freedom of the limbs of the immortal man which may fit them for higher exercises in higher spheres.' Assurance as to his Duty, he ventured elsewhere, must come 'within me in some confident intuition of transmutation of reason into inspiration'.[36]

Deakin's mode of prayer followed a similar pattern. He would first praise God and give thanks for his mercies; then would follow confessions of self-perceived deficiencies of character, and invariably petitions to the Almighty for 'gifts' and for certitude. The baring of his soul in confession and contrition is in sharp contrast to the image of the 'affable' politician and man of letters, and had no obvious causes in the circumstances of Deakin's life. Probably there exists in all humans reared in relative affluence a sense of not being deserving; and a consciousness of guilt and imperfection is common to the religious, and especially the Christian, believer. Yet Deakin's frequent expression of these feelings seems especially poignant, and unique in being occasioned by a consciousness of the overall ease of his secular path and the happiness of his 'outer' life. Certainly at this distance it is unwise to speculate about motivations and the deeper recesses of the individual psyche, but it cannot be denied that this very ease, given his growing notion of the role of 'sacrifice' in spiritual development, convinced Deakin that cosmic justice would in time extract the just measure in payment for his precocious success in the world. This was a dynamic and half-conscious structure in his belief system, perhaps best understood as the other side of his very real ambition. The related notions of spiritual worth, usefulness and sacrifice were now inextricably connected with his moral Idealism.

An October 1884 prayer asks: 'give me Thy guidance that I may fearlessly pierce into the depths of my own being.' The development of latent faculties, he believed, required first the removal of 'masks', especially from one's self. And, closing with an allusion to the prophetic series of four years previous, he asked that 'to & through me some further vision of Thy Grace' might be imparted.[37] Already in Deakin's prayers there was a subtle change in rhetoric in a written discipline now only a few months old. He desired more evidence of prophecy, but now not only 'to' but 'through me'. The next day he wrote: 'I trust & in trusting pray that I may further Thine eternal purpose, & be chosen as one of the instruments in working out Thy Will.'[38] Again in November Deakin prayed directly, 'to make me Thy servant & the servant of my race, & to grant me greatness & thoroughness of service, though at every step of service I must sacrifice myself.'[39] Duty, mission, service, self-sacrifice, all the elements that would permeate his activity for the rest of his life, were present in these petitions before Deakin had reached his thirtieth year. He asked for the Light to 'lighten' his load, like Christian in *Pilgrim's Progress*, and to 'light' his path, which he now suspected, however reluctantly, to be politics.

It appears that this consummate success in public life precipitated what can only be described as the first crisis in Deakin's adult inner life. How far private writings reflect the overall concerns of a life, especially a life as complex and varied as Alfred Deakin's, remains problematic. Yet something of those deepening tensions can be seen in the 'Two Paths' tract, which he wrote before taking up ministerial office, and in the sombre tone developing in the prayers. All that is known about Deakin apart from his writings describes anything but a religious fanatic or a wowser. Hence the duration of a morose and indecisive mood following his return from the United States in May 1885, which achieved an uneasy resolution at the end of the year with his election as Liberal leader, indicates a crisis both real and prolonged, that colleagues could not have suspected from the always courteous and 'affable' exterior.

The first indication of this new mood appears in the rough diary for his birthday 3 August, which observed somewhat hypercritically: 'Birthday 29 & nothing done', and inscribed below:

> *Not yet awhile my soul*
> *Not yet awhile shalt thou be free.*[40]

On this always significant day, looking backward and then forward upon his life as a whole, Deakin introduced an introspective, almost a brooding, tone. But this protracted mood was present already in the 'American Notes' written some five months before, probably on one of those interminable train journeys across the American midwest when he was separated for the first time from his wife and child. There, in particularly evocative phrases, he traced the path he had thus far been obliged to tread. In essence the earliest of several retrospectives on his life, these lengthy 'American Notes' present a rather self-serving picture of a gradually evolving awareness. They refer first to his early days, to the 'hour of rambling in which I felt no tie & scoffed & flouted all doctrines surrounding me'. Gradually it became clear to him that 'the creed of negations was nothing but negations', and here he seemed to be alluding to the Spencerian ideas of his university days. Soon, the need for 'seriousness & reverence' began to assert themselves, and 'Wordsworth & Swedenborg became my teachers; slowly, though insensibly, the darkness lifted.'[41] It was with a certain smugness that he added: 'I fancy that in mine own person I can trace the irresistible power of destiny', and he wondered 'what lies still capsulate in my nature'.[42]

Deakin was occupied writing his report on irrigation for some time after his return. When he opened his book of prayers on 23 August 1885 for the first time in eighteen months, the retrospective mood had taken real hold of him. This is indicated first by the parenthetical heading: '(After a long silence the floodgates open)', which was probably added later. The lengthy prayer inscribed on this day even as his political ascendancy was sure, which elaborates some of the 'American Notes', merits careful examination:

> O God it is with the most absolute gratitude & humility that I acknowledge myself a creature of Thy Grace. Not of myself, O God, & not in myself has come my blessing. Weakly & slightly was I framed in youth, & any chill blast would have nipped & blighted me. Not of Thy glorious ones was I O God gifted by Thee ... A vague & vain childhood— a boyhood with only a dim love of knowledge, a youth of feeble purposes & vain enthusiasms. I was singled out for the conspicuous manifestations of Thy Grace. Such gifts as Thou didst give were taken & abused. The bloom of manhood half-robbed by my own unripe & wretched self indulgence—was made by me a means of selfish satisfaction at the expense of others ... Still unchastening, still forgiving, still endowing, I rise only to sink again deeper & more darkly than before. Out of the pit didst Thou pluck me. Out of the mire didst Thou raise me & set me at once upon the altar of a pure spirit. Even the way I must walk was smoothed ... Thy vision of what was better gave me fellowship even with some of the godly. I became through Thy merciful training stronger & clearer & more energetic, & yet how frail. Thou didst advance me O my God over my elders ...[43]

In this periodic ritual of self-searching, the summing up of his life to date and projecting into the future, two themes common to Deakin's prayers are illustrated in particularly vivid images that bespeak high emotion: a deep self-examination, unmercifully honest, mixed with the discernment of a salutary pattern of guidance.

Deakin was weighing up the antinomies of Grace received against the insufficiency and wretchedness of his efforts, as though in vivid counterpoint to the triumphs attending an already brilliant public career. At its root, this feeling was due in part to his still hesitant commitment to politics, and vague literary aspirations. The Factories and Irrigation Bills marked him as an innovator; his oratorical performances in Parliament were masterly, and clearly he was the rising star in the Liberal ranks, and knew that he was destined for the leadership.

Despite his feebleness, which we note was both moral and physical, he had been 'singled out for the conspicuous manifestations of Thy Grace', by which

Deakin means those 'signs': the trip to Fiji, his marriage, his ascent to ministerial office. These however were 'taken & abused'. After an oblique reference to Pattie, bringing events for the moment to the present, he confessed, 'I rise only to sink again deeper & more darkly than before.' He then returns to the period of 'negations', enumerating his many blessings and referring to Spiritism with his 'fellowship with the godly', when Providence slowly became manifest in political life: 'Thou didst advance me O my God over my elders.' Greatness to come based on past blessings is implied in the dramatic and patently emotive closing passage:

> I tremble before Thy mercies O my God, & foreshadow Thy trial of me while still the sky is clear & the air serene. I can as yet discern no cloud. Yet have I turned my face towards repentance, yet have I summed up the count of the past, yet have I looked in the face of Retribution, & cried 'what hast Thou in store for me?' Behold I meet it with meekness, I bend myself to the rod, I will strip the leaves from the branches & make rods myself if only Thou O God will guide me & smile upon me.[44]

One wonders what the repentance is for. It were unprofitable and reductive to infer meanings from such images in an evocative passage written at a furious pace in a stream of consciousness, as suggested by the sharper angles and wider spaces in the penmanship. But if melodramatic, it was not an unhappy petition. The Old Testament cadences, the archaic language and the poetic imagery add a sacramental dimension, and even the litany of failings implies the unearned fruits of Grace in a life destined, at the cost of eventual sacrifice of self, to yield an even lusher harvest. In a bizarre way, Alfred Deakin was his own best prophet.

Another journal entitled 'Belief' inscribed on the same date, 23 August, sheds additional light on his present mood: 'If I could be always convinced of my personal relation to the Soul of the Universe ... have this made permanent, & then know myself enough to know my path & duty—nothing would be hard then.' What he needed was 'the deep assurance that I am not befooling myself'. He averred that he had 'surfeited' of material success, and shifting suddenly back to the archaic prayer mode, he was now anxious for 'Light and evidence of Thy Will'. In conclusion, and for the second time on the same day, Deakin linked together the three important predictions of his life. Having been 'thrice blessed ... in Thy revelations by opportunity hitherto ... to Thee & Them I trust for further guidance.'[45]

A diary note just one week later proclaims: 'Realising happiness';[46] and his next prayer in mid-September offers stark contrast to the dolorous tones of 23 August: 'I am overcome with Grace & thankfulness for the Light Thou hast given me. Let me walk by it O God. Let me realise it in deed & creed. Let me multiply it in precept & example.' He now desired 'a closer communion with the qualities which are Thine & the manifestations of which underlie & compose the world we see'.[47] Something in the course of events, perhaps the progress of the Federal Council Bill, had spoken to him of Providence.

There were further swells and troughs, as in a restive prayer which records 'stirrings within me as of change, dim gleams of promise in my eyes, & unsatisfied yearnings in my soul'. He knew not what they forebode, and again he insisted that he craved no 'loftier position'. Its closing passage outlines Deakin's present dilemma succinctly:

> For the world & for my worldly self, I might well be at peace. But I cannot yet realise that I am placed where my nature & my efforts might best serve Thee, & until so assured

of the attainment of my end in Thy sight, I cannot devote myself entirely, even to that which lies so close at hand.[48]

This is a long way from the Christian idea of service, which makes no conditions and demands no certitude beyond Faith. Deakin did not see then, though he certainly did in later life, the paradox of such a position, the egotism of a proclaimed subjugation to the Divine will which imposes qualifications of certitude.

The medium in 1880 had told him 'you are the boy', and so far she had been right. His meteoric rise in public life was unprecedented, yet, as I have argued, this very facility underscored a sense of inadequacy and foreshadowed a Divine sacrifice. A current prayer, largely abandoning the formal language, echoes the concerns over his private and public strivings, which came together in an insightful passage that reveals a more introspective, and a sadder, frame of mind:

> Me afflicted at last with sense of wasted life—unearned ease, undeserved blessings & unmerited response. Me shallow & poor & frail in spirit, in mind & in flesh. Me selfish & barren, even to bitterness & blackness of soul. Me the mere creature of other wills, though closed to Thine. Me the mere counter of the ideas of others, producing none. Me the figure upon the stage of life letting all power slip past me, without use or benefit. Me sunk in dreamy sloth & wayward idlenesses. Me humiliated—me shamed.[49]

This self-image of sloth and ineptitude in the handling of power seems a harsh judgment. Certainly political power was not slipping from his grasp, for even as he lamented his personal worth, Deakin was shepherding through the Assembly a magnificent piece of social legislation in the Workrooms Factories and Shops Bill. His interest went back at least to 1879, where at a public meeting, along with E. W. O'Sullivan and Bishop Moorhouse, he had spoken in support of factory reform.[50] To Liberals like Pearson and Deakin its most important provisions were those against 'sweating', the exploitation of piece workers by entrepreneurs, but the intransigence of the manufacturing interests and the opposition of the conservative press caused many of their intended measures to be blocked in the Council. The second part of the Bill dealing with shops was more successful, its chief victory being the regulation of trading hours. As always in debate, Deakin displayed a fine wit and ready humour; he observed after a melodramatic speech against early closing by the former butcher J. Patterson that:

> The honorable member seemed to argue the case without knowing very much about it ... First it was tyranny, then it was an interference with liberty, then it was gloom and darkness, and lastly it was something highly calculated to promote immorality. Ghastly visions of poor unfortunates treading benighted pavements floated across the mind's eye, and in the rear of the dismal procession was the very darkest personage of all history.[51]

Though he was prepared 'to follow the honorable member into the utmost recesses of the metaphysical arguments he hinted at', he wondered why his sympathies were not equally with the young men and women behind counters 'whose daily work was a round of monotonous drudgery, the effect of which was made worse by the want of exercise both of body and mind?'[52] In these comments we see something of what Liberalism meant to Deakin; other provisions reflect prevailing social attitudes he shared, like the requirement that furniture be stamped to indicate whether made by 'Chinese or European' labour, which the Council changed to a stamping as to origin. Overall it was a pioneer piece of legislation of which Deakin was justly proud in later years, despite its mutilation by the Legislative Council.

The crisis of vocation developing since the American tour appears to have been resolved in a peculiar and characteristic fashion, by a double divination reminiscent of his 'consultation' of Chaucer seven years before. It is another example of what his friend Watt called 'the oriental' cast of Deakin's mind.[53] On 17 October he finished Carlyle's *Past and Present*, first read in 1873. This precipitated what he called the 'Two trials of the Sibyls'. As he explained (to whom?) in a journal the next day, he was 'anxious about my work & considering that politics is my best field', and opening Chapman's *Homer* randomly, his finger had rested on these lines from Book XIII of the *Iliad* which he copied, underscoring two lines in the stanza:

> *Far-seeing God grants some the wisdom of the mind,*
> *Which no man can keep to himself,*
> *That tho but few can find,*
> *Doth profit many, that preserves*
> *The public weal and state,*
> *And that who hath, he best can prize.*[54]

This was the first part of the 'Trial'. He then turned to Carlyle. His critique of *Past and Present* the previous day had praised it as a great book despite incompleteness and obscurity, which seems an understatement. It is difficult to relate this work, essentially an attack on laissez-faire in economic and social policy, easily to any 'sign'. However, education, emigration, factory and sanitation laws— in short, the kinds of concerns Deakin's own work was addressing—are discussed at length. This seems to have given it a keener providential significance. Carlyle's 'superb' discussion of religion was of special importance; religion was not a 'Morrison's pill' taken from without, but a 'reawakening of thy own Self from within', whose essence was to keep that 'Inner Light ... alive & shining'.[55]

Though it may sound prosaic and even odd to the reader, it appears that Deakin counted as providential Carlyle's relation of religion to Protectionist-style politics, which spoke to him of his own life's aims. The influence of Carlyle, whose *Sartor Resartus* was the first book the twelve-year-old Alfred had bought with his own money, was still potent. Among his favourite quotations from Carlyle was 'Blessed is he who has found his work; let him ask no other blessedness'; appearing first at the front of the 'Boke of Praer & Prase', it bade him consider the overall value of his political work. Deakin was particularly drawn to his heroic and elitist view of history where reform is brought about by the 'strongest' men. As he summarised one passage: 'having got the best let them govern in reality & not by laissez-faire.'[56] He could willingly follow Carlyle's gospel, expressed as a parody on Socrates to 'Know thy work & do it', as a call to Duty, a providential 'sign' which he interpreted together with the lines from Homer:

Could anything be more significant or perfectly apropos than these two trials of the Sibyls—the one of the inner the other of the outer, the one of the past, the other of the future. None but myself can know how marvellously they have fitted my moods of late.[57]

In essence the divination revealed that: Wisdom of mind is a gift from God, *'which no man can keep to himself, [and] That tho but few can find'*; it is the Duty of those so gifted to share for the commonweal. Hence the two 'Trials' concerned both the 'inner' and the past, what he called the *'Sortes Homericae'* relating to his responsibilities to his Creator, and the 'outer' and the future, to apply his gifts to social and political reform, especially to Protectionism. The intimate relation between politics and religion is never articulated very far, but it was very much on Deakin's mind. A 'Clue' written a month later refers indirectly to the two 'Trials':

> There is plenty of room for the *super-natural* ... Nine tenths of the life of man is *artificial*. The social scheme is so complicated that what we term the *accidental* fills a very large space. Here is the sphere of the *providential*. A chance remark, a chance lifting of the eyes, a chance opening of a book ...[58]

It was out of such events he continued, in which 'our will is silent & our reflection asleep' and when we act 'as by impulse from the unseen', whence come 'the currents which change our lives'.[59]

Deakin's nomination as Liberal leader was of course the decisive factor in shaping his decision. By December 1885 he was once again 'strong in the certainty that thus I best work for Humanity'.[60] The 'Two Trials' had brought home the selfishness of leaving a field where he was achieving great success in ameliorating the lot of the masses. The Factories Act was now the law of the land, and Carlyle's heroic stoicism recalled Deakin once more to gird himself to the Ideal. When he was nominated as leader on the last day of the year Deakin again had second thoughts:

> Old year closes with my nomination as leader of the Liberal Party—Will the new year give it? Is it worth taking? Is this not leading me farther & farther from my true Goal? In God I trust.[61]

The indecision was momentary. On 19 January 1886 Deakin noted *'Caucus elected leader unanimously'*.[62] We might wonder why he quoted the American motto, and what he now regarded as his 'true Goal'. Athough he continued to doubt and at times even to despise politics, with this accolade Deakin's life was set on the political path surely and finally. Not yet thirty, he became Chief Secretary in addition to Minister of Water Supply, and assumed co-leadership in matters of policy with his coalition partner, the Conservative Premier Duncan Gillies. The other serious contender had been C. H. Pearson. How badly Deakin wanted the leadership is indicated by his acceptance of Gillies as 'good enough to be a Liberal now'. Pearson and other Liberals like Quick had great reservations. Pearson felt the Conservatives had not fought hard enough for the Factories Bill, and in committee he disagreed with Deakin on certain provisions. He was unhappy that the clause against sweating had been removed and the eight-hour principle 'lost sight of'. For Deakin however this was not mere opportunism, though it signals his ambition. To his mind the political reality of continuing a stable coalition was preferable to the series of unstable ministries in the early part of the decade; half a loaf was better than none. As political pragmatist he knew which measures could not pass the Council. Throughout his career some would accuse him of facile swings of opinion and allegiance, and of being primarily interested in staying in office. More ominously for the immediate future of the Victorian economy, and correctly as events would soon show, Pearson was unhappy about the rapid growth of government expenditure and of overseas borrowing.[63]

The year 1886 was extremely busy, with his new duties as Chief Secretary and the Irrigation Bill. Deakin had little time for reflection or prayer, beyond the occasional book review in the journal *Links*. Hence no prayers were recorded between the end of 1885 and the middle of 1887 when he returned from England. The Water Supply and Irrigation Bill introduced in June was justly praised as a thorough measure based on a large body of empirical data. The most radical provision was the investing of all riparian rights in the State, except for domestic and stock purposes. It provided regionally funded irrigation trusts and head works, as well as national works, canals and other infrastructure funded directly by the Victorian government.[64] Had it not been for the devastation of the 1890s depression, and factors like salination unknown at the time, it might have been an even greater success. Some members were clearly jealous. Gaunson huffed that to settle an issue that had taken other nations centuries on the basis of 'one young man who went on a short trip to America' was absurd. Patterson got his own back for being outflanked on the shops debate, observing that Deakin's speech had been 'full of poetry but not of water'.[65] Deakin's real interest in irrigation was in opening up the land and improving the quality of life. Yet for all its present benefits, he saw further:

> when this Colony forms part, as I hope it will, of a Federated Australia, that will be renowned I trust all around the world for the richness of its soil, the enterprise of its people, and the freedom of its government ... if there is a spot meriting the proud title 'Australia Felix', it is the Colony of Victoria.[66]

It was in this year that the infamous Half Caste Act was passed, for which Deakin as Chief Secretary was responsible. During debate, the Member for Mandurang questioned the ten thousand pounds allocation, for he observed that if the Aboriginal race was dying out, there ought to be a reduction instead of an increase in the sum. Deakin agreed with the honourable member, who had 'very properly described the Aborigines as a nearly extinct race, and therefore the expense attending their maintenance ought to become less and less'. But he advised a plan to 'get rid of maintenance of the half caste and quarter caste Aboriginals' which would enable a reduction in these expenses.[67]

Deakin's attitudes to the Aborigines are well illustrated in an 1890 'Clue', which suggests a work of monumental proportions to celebrate 'The Meeting of the Two Races'. One group in black marble comprising an Aboriginal father with spear, and a mother and child, would bring out 'their beauties of wiry vigour' as well as 'their defects of form'. The other group in white marble would depict a young white settler on horseback, wearing riding trousers, booted and spurred, and holding in one hand a revolver 'ready but not pointed', the other hand being 'extended as inviting peace', with his wife and child also behind him. They were to be depicted in their physical perfection, the settler wearing a 'close fitting singlet so as to discover his shape', while his wife, sheltering behind him from the spear, would be 'in sufficient undress to disclose all her perfections'. The banality of the composition underscores the extent to which Deakin accepted popular views of his day, in keeping with the common 'ethnographic' and Darwinian assumptions regarding the inevitable demise of the Aboriginal people which should be made as painless as possible. As an imperialist, he never questioned the rationale of domination. What is puzzling is that as a religious seeker, he never seems to have inquired, and he certainly never wrote anything about, Koorie spirituality.[68]

The annual summation, now a regular feature, at the end of the 1886 diary shows that Deakin had reached a state of equanimity, or at least a professed detachment, of his innermost Self from the vicissitudes of a public career. It commenced:

> (A Polycrates ring) A successful year publicly. Still rising higher & higher—Have a presentiment that my fall will be all the more sudden & from an even greater height. But the fall will be public as the rise has been. If I really rise or so far as I may rise in reality, that is in spirit & in faith, I cannot fall unless I fail myself.[69]

The detached tone rings a little hollow when we recall his anxiety twelve months earlier about the leadership. The note was a caveat to himself regarding his rapid rise in politics, a reminder to himself, to his 'true' Self, of his real aims. The parenthetical 'Polycrates' heading, probably added later, while it invites varying interpretations, depending on whether it refers to the tyrant of Samos or to the Christian bishop with the same name, confirms a relation in Deakin's mind between the political power he was beginning to taste in earnest, and this admonitory message to himself.[70] He had recently been reading a biography of Epictetus, a philosophy, as we shall see, that would have increasing significance in later years, and the ambience of stoic detachment is evident in this note. He was sanguine about his anticipated 'fall', but he predicted it would be from 'an even greater height', perhaps the premiership? He now warned himself against allowing apparent success to become 'necessary or even pleasant to me'. The important thing was to stay 'cued in on one's own duty'. This two-page caveat, now become a prayer, concludes with gratitude for his many blessings 'so far as it has pleased the Power manifest in events & appearances to crown me with every success of political & public nature'. It closes with a final consecratory paragraph redolent with emotional force:

> To the Inner Life, to the Inner Light, I turn myself at the close of this year full of gratitude for the grace of inward things ... It is in other works & other triumphs (if capable of gaining them) that I set my heart, to realise the Light, to see clearly by it, to walk by it, kneel to it & spread its radiance. Thus ... to serve & follow the Light 'which lightens every man that comes into the world'.[71]

It was a sincere plea for grace, for seership, for religious service. Deakin remained instead the most successful politician of his era. Perhaps this tells of continuing tensions, for he would continue to long in his depths for 'other works & other triumphs'. But it testifies also to the Idealist conception of personal progress as the motive force in his inner life. The ambiguity of the term 'lightens' provides an epigrammatic comment on his life henceforward. What he gained in the lighting of his life did not 'lighten' his load, for Deakin pushed himself harder in his work, while striving for an inner realisation and adhering to a lofty code of conduct that temptations of office and the fulsome environment of politics did little to assist. Conversely he believed the Light he gained considerably lightened his load, rendering insights into otherwise inexplicable events and processes, and preventing him from sinking into the morass of politics. This was a very real fear, as the 1890s prayers will show.

Less than a week later, while engrossed in the composition of his 'Gospel According to Shakespeare', Deakin received a sudden response to a 'prayer of many years': a response that would transform his inner life and determine his public career, and would ultimately have far-reaching implications for the political future of Australia. On 6 January 1887 he learned that he was to be sent to London as leader of the Victorian delegation to a consultative Colonial Conference just called by the imperial government.[72] Deakin was elated. Not only would the colonies now be afforded a chance to voice their many grievances directly; privately, this conference was interpreted as the fulfilment of that third prophecy made some seven years previously 'through' a Spiritualist medium that 'before long, I should be officially sent to London to appear for Victoria before a tribunal ... which she described as the highest in the land.'[73] The inner significance of this event was profound, lifelong, and absolute. To him it would stand always as 'irrefragable evidence that the world as we know it is but glimpsed at one or two angles & remains for us absolutely uninterpretable'.[74] More than a quarter-century later he recalled that he had been unable to shake the medium's confidence in her declaration at the time that this tribunal was to mark 'a national new departure'; Deakin added: 'so it proved to be.'[75]

With the sudden announcement of the conference, Deakin had received an answer to his petitions as to how his energies should now be channelled. Moreover as a Providential 'sign', it signified the direction his career should now take. Deakin's immediate call for the achievement of the old dream of Australian Federation upon his return from England was intimately connected with this 'sign', as was his indefatigable advocacy of the 'Federal Ideal' over the next decade, which drew its motive power from his faith thus bolstered by the fulfilment of the Grand Prophecy.

By 1887 Deakin had come of age, both as statesman as he proved in London, and as believer in a Divine Providence. Through his energetic performances at the conference, not only the Colonial Office but the English press and public were made more aware of Australia, of Victoria and, incidentally, of Alfred Deakin. The 'pilgrim' had progressed at an astonishing rate in the 'outer' world, but the continuing paradox in his life is illustrated by the 'Polycrates' caveat, and by his aspiration for 'other triumphs'. We can only guess what these might have been. Power was outwardly sweet and inwardly repugnant, and indeed in later years it seems to have become all too 'necessary'. Following this stupendous confirmation of the power of prophecy, Deakin's life would never be the same, in either the 'inner' or the 'outer' spheres. Previously, he had craved knowledge as to which path to follow, though not necessarily in politics. After 1887 he would occasionally lose heart, but seldom again did he doubt his calling, or the operation of the Divine will in human affairs. Personal spiritual development and public career converged in the Christian Ideal of service—to God, race and kind. To be sure, this Ideal developed over a long period; but with the Grand Prophecy of 1887, the capstone was set on the edifice of his faith.

Notes

1 Literary Memoranda, typescript, 3/302, 8 Oct 1882.

2 La Nauze, *Alfred Deakin*, vol. 1, p. 80.

3 Red Spine Book, 3/281, 6 May 1911; 'Crude Index ...', in 'Medley', 3/296, 6 July 1883.

4 Literary Memoranda, typescript, 3/302, 4 March 1883.

5 Ibid., 21 January 1883.

6 Ibid., 4 March 1883.

7 Tregenza, *Professor ...*, p. 178; Serle, *The Rush to Be Rich*, p. 157.

8 Literary Memoranda, typescript, 3/302, 21 January 1883.

9 Ibid., 7 October 1883.

10 George Higinbotham, 'Religion and Science', lecture delivered at Scots Hall Melbourne, 1 August 1883; C. Badger, *The Reverend Charles Strong and the Australian Church*, Melbourne, 1971, pp. 55–66.

11 Literary Memoranda, typescript, 3/302, 11 August 1883.

12 Ibid., 7 May 1882; 12 April 1884.

13 Diary, 1 July 1884.

14 Literary Memoranda, typescript, 3/302, 6 October 1883.

15 'Clues', typescript, 3/301, no. 57, undated, c. October 1884.

16 Diary, 30 August and 7 September 1884. Gerald Massey was a self-improver, a rationalist and Chartist later introduced to Spiritualism. From the 1860s he wrote arcane books on the keys to psychic mysteries in ancient Egypt. Deakin read his *Book of Beginnings*, 1881, and *The Natural Genesis*, 1883: Oppenheim, *The Other World ...*, p. 41.

17 Deakin to Alice Browne, 3 August 1884.

18 'Boke of Praer & Prase', MS 5/1457, typescript 5/818 ff., 3 August 1884. The typescript, with reference numbers for each page, has been used almost exclusively in this study.

19 Regarding nineteenth-century occultism and the seven ages of man, H. P. Blavatsky's *The Secret Doctrine*, like her other works, consists of two heavy tomes, 676 pages of vol. 1 'Cosmogenesis', followed by vol. 2 'Anthropogenesis' in 798 pages. 'Sevens' like 'Threes' figure prominently. Hence 'Seven Races' and 'Seven Eternities' etc.; on the Seven Root Races, related to the Seven Stages in the individual life, see vol. l, p. 650 and *passim: The Secret Doctrine, The Synthesis of Science, Religion, and Philosophy*, Pasadena, 1970.

20 Murdoch, *Alfred Deakin ...*, p. 19; La Nauze, *Alfred Deakin*, vol. 1, p. 26.

21 'Clues', vol. 1, 3/283, 27 July 1884.

22 'Praises Phrases & Crazes', 3/11, 1884, p. 20; p. 65.

23 'W. Collard Smith', *A.D.B.*, vol. 6, 1851–90; *V.P.D.*, vol. 45, pp. 92–3, 12 and 17 June 1884.

24 'John Quick', *A.D.B.*, vol. 11, 1891–1939.

25 *V.P.D.*, vol. 45, 12 June 1884, p. 85.

26 La Nauze, *Alfred Deakin*, vol. 1, p. 84.

27 Murdoch, *Alfred Deakin* ..., p. 90. Deakin wrote *Irrigation in Western America*, 1885; *Irrigation in Italy and Egypt*, 1887; and *Irrigated India*, 1893.

28 H. Brogan, *The Penguin History of the United States*, Ringwood, 1990, p. 70.

29 Deakin to F. T. Derham, 10 February 1885.

30 *V.P.D.*, vol. 51, 6 July 1886, p. 575.

31 L. E. Fredman, 'Thomas Welton Stanford: An American in Exile', *Victorian Historical Magazine*, vol. 33, no. 1, August 1962.

32 'Boke ...', 5/820, prayer IV, 17 August 1884.

33 Ibid., 5/823, prayer IX, 14 September 1884.

34 Ibid., 5/824, prayer XIII, 19 October 1884.

35 Ibid., 5/823, prayer X, 20 September 1884; 5/820, prayer IV, 17 August 1884; 5/824, prayer XIII, 19 October 1884.

36 Literary Memoranda, typescript, 3/302, 23 August 1885.

37 'Boke ...', 5/824, prayer XIII, 19 October 1884.

38 Ibid., 5/825, prayer XIV, 20 October 1884.

39 Ibid., 5/828, prayer XVIII, 23 November 1884.

40 Diary, 3 August 1885.

41 'American Notes', 10/102, 21 March 1885.

42 Ibid., April 1885.

43 'Boke ...', 5/829, prayer XXI, 23 August 1885.

44 Ibid.

45 Literary Memoranda, typescript, 3/302, 23 August 1885.

46 Diary, 31 August 1885.

47 'Boke ...', 5/830, prayer XXII, 13 September 1885.

48 Ibid., 5/834, prayer XXIV, 27 September 1885.

49 Ibid., 5/837, prayer XXVII, 11 October 1885.

50 Mansfield, *Australian Democrat* ..., p. 34.

51 *V.P.D.*, vol. 50, 10 November 1885, p. 1755.

52 Ibid., p. 1758.

53 W. H. Watt, Obituary Testimonial, 23/74, 22 October 1919.

54 'Clues', vol. 1, 3/283, no. 75, 18 October 1885.

55 'Links', 3/5, 17 October 1885.

56 Ibid.; 'Notebook IV', 3/91, 17 December 1873; 'Boke ...', 5/1457, preface, 3 August 1884. In a 1903 interview Deakin said *Sartor Resartus* was the foundation stone of his library, the first work that had turned his thoughts to more serious channels: *Punch*, 1 October 1903.

57 'Clues', vol. 1, 3/283, no. 75, 18 October 1885.

58 Ibid., no. 79, 30 December 1885.

59 Ibid.

60 'Boke ...', 5/840, prayer XXXIV, 6 December 1885.

61 Diary, 31 December 1885.

62 Diary, 19 January 1886.

63 Tregenza, *Professor* ..., p. 201.

64 *V.P.D.*, vol. 51, 24 June 1886, p. 433.

65 *V.P.D.*, vol. 52, 14 September 1886, p. 1447.

66 *V.P.D.*, vol. 51, 24 June 1886, p. 447.

67 *V.P.D.*, vol. 52, 7 October 1886, p. 1810; B. Attwood, *The Making of the Aborigines*, Sydney, 1989, p. 96.

68 'Clues', vol. 3, 3/287, no. 374, 26 January 1890.

69 Diary, 31 December 1886.

70 The Polycrates he was referring to is suggested by a journal notation made 25 years later, where he gave a hint of the meaning it held for him. Polycrates, tyrant of Samos, in dread of his constant good fortune, sought to propitiate the gods by sacrificing his proudest possession. He threw his crown in the sea, whereupon it returned in the maw of a fish as a warning 'that his offering was not accepted, & that days of grace were over': Red Spine Book, 3/281, 7 May 1911.

71 Diary, 31 December 1886.

72 La Nauze, *Alfred Deakin*, vol. 1, p. 89; the official designation was 'Colonial', but the colonists insisted on 'Imperial Conference'.

73 Autobiographical Notes, typescript, 3/300, June 1910.

74 Counsel Fees, 3/290, 12 November 1913.

75 Ibid.

3

The Grand Prophecy

For one fair Vision ever fled
Down the waste waters day and night,
And still we follow'd where she led,
In hope to gain upon her flight.

A. Tennyson,
'The Voyage'

A certain *outrecuidance*;[1] that was the aristocratic Prime Minister's private view of the presumption and audacity of 'Greater Britain', especially those very vocal Victorians. At the behest of his Colonial Secretary, Lord Salisbury had put aside other matters of state to address the Colonial Conference at its opening on 4 April 1887. He spoke again on 26 April in his capacity as Foreign Secretary, when the vexatious question of French designs in the New Hebrides (now Vanuatu) was under discussion. On this second occasion he came unprepared and gave an impromptu talk, full of *politesse* and generalities, on the grave business of running an Empire and the need for unity, emphasising that where imperial and 'local' interests clashed, the 'general good of the Empire' should prevail.

As he sat down to hear the responses of the grateful colonials, Salisbury was even less prepared for what followed. The first speaker, from New South Wales, thanked the Prime Minister with 'bated breath and whispering humbleness', as Deakin characterised it in the *Federal Story*, for explaining the situation, and spoke in glowing terms of Empire. Even the 'cool and dignified analysis' which followed from Griffith of Queensland implied an acceptance of the status quo.[2] Now came the turn of the Victorians, first James Service and then Graham Berry, who spoke with 'great warmth' on a theme that his successor as Chief Secretary would elaborate further, the security of British interests in the Pacific.

With none of the formal and faintly obsequious tone adopted by colleagues from other colonies, though perhaps without the fire of that 'demagogue' Berry, the tall and youthful Alfred Deakin rose to deliver, with engaging bonhomie, a devastating critique of Salisbury's speech. In a 'downright but not offensive' manner, he struck a theme that was to remain constant during his many clashes with the Colonial Office: that with proper consultation, there ought to be no inherent conflict between imperial and colonial interests.[3] The recent annexation of Samoa and part of New Guinea by Germany and the designs of the French in the New Hebrides made this a most contentious issue for the Australian colonists. After the Queensland government's abortive attempt to annex Papua for the Crown in 1883, the Victorians had nearly followed suit in the New Hebrides. The Marquis looked on, at times staring, as his talk was gracefully analysed, dissected, and rebutted point by point, beginning with the imperial government's assumptions as to the 'general good of the Empire'.

Lord Salisbury had admitted that France had not kept faith with the present treaty, because of a chaos of changing ministries. If this were the case, Deakin observed drily, with the recent humiliation in New Guinea now to be repeated by the loss of the New Hebrides, the colonists might wish 'that the evenness of political life in England which sacrificed their interests might be displaced by a chaos which should preserve them'. They had been told that to attempt to negotiate a great power like France out of its place in a joint protectorate was presumption, yet 'a greater power', the British Empire, was asked to consent to be so negotiated without protest. It would be 'startling' to those delegates presently assembled to consider how to 'maintain and extend' the Empire, to learn that the British Empire was 'less high-spirited, less powerful, and less jealous of its honour' than the French Republic. Victorians would never consent to the cession of the islands on any terms, Deakin warned darkly in closing, and the 'Australian born' would forever resent the humiliation of surrender, which would 'immensely weaken their confidence in an Empire to which hitherto they had been proud to belong'.[4] These were strong words, delivered with dramatic effect by the young and articulate representative of the Australian 'natives'.

Deakin was given to dramatic entrances. His resignation tendered after his maiden speech to the Victorian Parliament eight years before had caused a sensation. Now a wider issue was to generate an even greater sensation in Australia, when a 'son of the soil' stood up to the aristocratic leader of the great power situated at the centre of their mutual world, and while remaining a committed imperialist, proclaimed the right to consultation and the coordination of British policy with its dependencies. A refreshing frankness and eloquent tongue were beginning to earn for Deakin a reputation as the voice of emergent colonial nationalism, not only in Victoria and Australia, but also in Great Britain.[5]

On the voyage over Deakin had taken thirty-four French authors—and given his castigation of the Republic there is a faint irony in the fact—and their English translations, following Pearson's advice to use the leisure to perfect his French. Rousseau's *Confessions* and works by St Beuve and De Maistre, as well as Balzac and lighter Dumas romances were among them. By the end of the trip he could skim light French novels in a 'rough and tumble way' sufficient not to find them tedious.[6]

Deakin's letters from London to his sister Katie reveal him at his most witty and incisive, applying his journalist's powers of observation and a keen sense of humour. In April he wrote that having 'summed up and dismissed the whole of it', he could now pass judgment on English aristocratic society. With a democratic temper, but also with the fascination of the provincial, he informed her that titles do not grow out of a person, 'they are stuck on from the outside ... and are always artificial and often ridiculous'. He was 'delighted to find society at its best has so little that is tempting', for the dukes and earls and their ladies were all given up to 'small talk, giddiness or emptiness or clever courtness [sic] or mere sensible educated good manners at best'. It was with some smugness he later informed her that 'Lorimer [Victorian Minister of Defence] has accepted the knighthood I refused'.[7]

Yet for all these stern judgments, the social side of his first trip 'Home' was invaluable. Deakin made important contacts with publishers and some lasting friendships, as with that tragic figure Charles Dilke, who became an admirer of the Australian politician. Ever the intrepid tourist, he visited the great haunts of English history, had tea with his mother's relatives in Wales, and met many of the Immortals he had only read like Matthew Arnold, George Meredith and John Seeley, author of *Ecce Homo*, with whom he dined at Cambridge and in whom he was disappointed. He was surprised that at Westminster Abbey 'the sacred ground within did not affect me as much as I anticipated.' And he was much disappointed in the palace at Versailles, 'an enormous barrack after all' which, he added, was 'not a bit prettier or more imposing than our Government House'.[8] He wondered also how his own performances would be viewed in Victoria. The benefits of the conference would be largely intangible, he speculated in one letter to Katie, closing aphoristically with: 'we do what we are intended to do & what we intend even & much more what we desire plays but a small part in the piece.'[9]

One of the salutary effects of the voyage was to show him the quality of the men who held power in Great Britain—most were found wanting. Lord Rosebery he judged as 'affected & selfish', although John Morley was 'a man of force & capacity'.[10] Incredibly, he describes Gladstone as 'eagle-like' but probably 'wayward if not weak in the central will which knits a man's life & purposes into one long chain'.[11] He describes the formal occasions: 'lines of carriages in waiting—titles on every lip', and London itself, where he found 'not many pretty faces ... but plenty of healthy ones & heavy figures the rule. Young men short, young women bunchy, old women stout.' Some of his letters contain actual gossip. He confided to his sister that Matthew Arnold 'goes to church and takes the sacrament'; and with an evident sense of shock, that George Eliot 'married in the most conventional manner'.[12] If it strikes a provincial tone, none of it is malicious; but one cannot help feeling that Deakin was not a little disillusioned by the humanness of his heroes, and even gullible, as with his reference to Ruskin and Carlyle's alleged love affairs with various women.

At Queen Victoria's Golden Jubilee Ball, Deakin was resplendent in his official uniform with feathered hat and sword. Entering into the spirit of revelry, the young colonial entertained a number of people, joking and enjoying himself thoroughly.[13] The delegates were feted continuously, in part of their own choosing to publicise their cause, but also one suspects because they were refreshing to the jaded social world of London. The official banquet given by the Duke of Cambridge included 'Purée à la Victoria', and 'Tindal à la Colonial', but the côtellete was 'à l'Imperial', and perhaps more importantly, the poulard braisée was 'à la financière', a not so subtle reminder that the 'main course' was the province of the 'Home' government.[14]

Deakin clearly took pleasure in a sort of inverted colonial snobbery. Even as co-leader of an alliance with the Conservatives, he regarded himself still a non-conformist and a radical. He was well aware of the proper graces, and familiar with the stereotype of deferential colonials who dropped their aspirates. His critique of Salisbury's speech, like his refusal of a knighthood, can be viewed as aspects of his performance as the 'mouthpiece of Victoria' (as one newspaper article put it).[15] Deakin did use to good effect the fact that he was to the English aristocrats a somewhat exotic (though surprisingly cultured) specimen, to make his points to the British press, government and people. It was a pattern of frenetic activity to be repeated on his two further visits to London over the next twenty years, when he would again clash with the Colonial Office and the imperial government on behalf of Australia, employing the print media effectively to publicise his cause.

Professor La Nauze has cautioned against attaching too much importance to this conference, 'Colonial' to the 'Home' government, 'Imperial' to the Australians. Its actual accomplishments were modest: a de facto annexation of Papua; no concessions to France on the New Hebrides; and a financial contribution to be borne by the colonies for an Australian-based naval defence squadron. While he is probably right about the political consequences, La Nauze does not sufficiently assess the significance of this event to the imperial-minded colonists, for whom the conference served as a powerful symbol of a greater autonomy. No-one symbolised these values better than Alfred Deakin, particularly among the Victorian 'natives', and his political fortunes were to benefit therefrom, especially in the next decade with the personal following he gathered among the 'young men with ideas' of the Australian Natives Association.

Inextricably linked with these events in Deakin's mind was their spiritual dimension. There are several indications of a profound sense of secular Mission whose dramatic, if veiled, expression has been observed already in his animated performance at the conference as a 'tribune' of the people. The most compelling evidence for the private significance of these events is found in sketchy reflections inscribed at the back of his travelling diary while in London and on the voyage home. These private notes illustrate what I take to be Deakin's current mood of quiet elation, which in turn sheds light upon his extraordinary performances in London and his political activity thereafter. They disclose a process of deliberation, and Deakin's current attitudes to the recent astounding prophetic fulfilment, along with a recasting of his entire past experience with prophecy. In the first, under the heading for 4 July he wrote:

Sudden changes of scene & life & fashion in a dream—faithful to principle of conduct in all & undisturbed—most go mad—you have learned the lesson. 24.5.87 [16]

The use of the second person suggests another, and higher, authority for this judgment. And as with the 'American Notes' two years before, being a significant insight to its author this note was later expanded, in light of his current reading, in the journal 'Clues', to which we shall return. The next two entries, inscribed at various times though not under the date indicated, relate directly to events occurring in England. These notes were entered at the back of this diary, and he commenced a new rough diary upon his return home. Under the date 6 July 1887 Deakin recorded:

Spsm
Hodgson asked obligation
Ten years elapsed
Mediums like Doctors consult one another
Religious side mysticism
Quakerism
A dream—an ideal or a truth— [17]

To some extent this shorthand can be unravelled. On 24 and 27 March Deakin had long discussions with his friend from university days Dr Richard Hodgson, who had come up to Cambridge to study with the moral philosopher Henry Sidgwick. He was already achieving fame as a professional psychical researcher with his recent exposé of Madame Blavatsky, and when Deakin visited him in 1887, Hodgson was about to leave for the United States as inaugural secretary of the American branch of the Society for Psychical Research.[18] Although it had many detractors, psychical research also had important supporters, and not only among the Spiritists. There was not then the impassable gulf between the study of normal and pathological, and the study of supernormal, behaviours. The principal mover in getting Hodgson to Boston was William James, who required his expertise to 'experiment' upon the medium Mrs Leonora Piper and others, in search of his 'one white crow' who would give evidence of the untapped powers of the human mind. It was Deakin who had been responsible for introducing Hodgson to this 'occult' world by taking him to his first seance while they were at university, thereby, it could be argued, having an indirect influence on the path which research on the unconscious would take over the next twenty years.[19]

'Spsm' refers to 'Spiritism'. It had been ten years since the first political prophecies, and Hodgson the cautious professional sceptic asked what obligation Deakin felt to this sort of prescience. Probably in a discussion on duty and revelation, as the second part implies, Hodgson advised that a religious interpretation beyond or even despite the thin 'scientific' evidence might be more fruitful, for which a pattern might be found in the experiences of Quakers, and among the great mystics. He pointed out that corroborative or seemingly continuing readings given 'through' one medium and then another, which had greatly impressed Deakin, might simply be the result of collusion. It must be remembered that Deakin was speaking to no philistine, but to a sceptical professional who long withheld judgment on questions like 'survival' after death.[20] We note the need for a male confidant, where Deakin divulges events to Hodgson of the most intimate significance which he had not yet discussed with either Pattie or his sister Katie. Whether they broached the topic of the Grand Prophecy we cannot know, but it would seem consistent with the notations that ensue. Had it been a 'dream', an 'ideal' or a 'truth' with which he had so suddenly been presented?

The next entry under 8 July, probably arose from his second tête-à-tête with Hodgson, and it relates also to Deakin's spiritistic experiences:

> *Spsm—personal exps. as keys (1) Table L M*
> *(2) Adelaide clergy (3) Blakeville*
> *age 16 to 21*
> *'Light of common day' Spirit with spirit can meet*
> *How pure in heart how sound in head.*
> *Kant's experience & spiritism.*[21]

This note also divides into two parts, the first summing up and weighing 'evidences' deriving from his own experiences, the second confirming these experiences by placing them in a larger spiritual context. As Deakin saw it, the keys were three. First were the inexplicable movements of the table in his first circle back in 1873. 'L M' refers to Letty Martin, A. P. Martin's sister, the most unlikely and sceptical candidate, who turned out to be the 'medium' of the table-tilting group. The second refers to one of only two 'readings' ever given by Deakin during his short career as 'medium' in Dr Motherwell's circle. On this occasion he had to his own real surprise 'felt' the presence of two deceased persons, and he found himself claiming them as relations of a visitor to the circle. This visitor, an Adelaide clergyman, remained noncommittal, and Deakin felt a little foolish. Then some weeks later he received a copy of an article written by this clergyman which praised the accuracy of these 'evidential' descriptions of his father and brother. For Deakin the continuing source of wonder was less its accuracy than the bizarre nature of the experience itself. Third was the presaging of an instance of political treachery at Blakeville by one of the three mediums in 1880.

The second part of the notation seems in a manner to confirm these personal experiences by reference to a poetic tradition, and to philosophy. The quotation, taken from Wordsworth's 'Ode', permits the inference that between his sixteenth and twenty-first years, Alfred had in diverse ways been shown the 'vision splendid' that continued to sustain his religious faith.[22] The next line, from Tennyson's 'In Memoriam', proclaims the soundness and purity of those who would hold 'an hour's communion with the dead', and the final reference to Kant probably arose out of his current reading of Swedenborg. In his 'Gospel' written two years later, Deakin recounts a story concerning the two contemporaries who had known each other only by reputation. Kant, hardly an admirer of Swedenborg, had sent an agent to investigate the Swedish mystic, who later confirmed his alleged dramatic displays of clairvoyance.[23]

Taken together these various notes represent an extended reflection, probably of several weeks' duration, which shows Deakin's strong disposition to focus upon mysterious experiences. Had it been, as Hodgson cautioned, an artless collusion? The prophecies had come between the ages of sixteen and twenty-one, and they came no more. Were they somehow a preparatory ground, a providential stimulus to his faith, at the beginning of his career? The second part, though not to be pressed too far, offers some sort of response to these puzzles. Wordsworth's 'Ode' celebrates the intimations of the Divine origin of the soul as it comes into earth experience 'trailing clouds of glory', retaining a remembrance, 'not in entire forgetfulness' of its Divine estate. It is perhaps also a lament for the end of those days of vision for, as in Wordsworth's 'Ode', the Man sees it fade and die 'in the light of common day'. Tennyson's lines were written over a period of seventeen years after the early death of his friend A. H. Hallam, and they seem to confirm that 'Spirit' (capitalised) can meet with 'spirit'.

The briefest and most accessible of these jottings is the final entry, made probably on the return voyage, under the heading 12 July, which firmly places Deakin's musings in a political context:

> *Athens after Delos*
> *Rome after 2nd Punic*
> *natives—opinion—*
> *awaken them—*[24]

In this succinct notation with its classical allusions, we arrive at last at compelling indications of the Mission which Deakin now saw clearly before him. The reference to Athens and Rome, coupled with what comes after, suggests an element of self-congratulation on his recent oratorical performance, though this is muted by his anticipated role as an Australian Demosthenes. Of the numerous parallels that could be postulated, the most relevant seems that of peaceful conquest or unification. Just as Athens after conquering Delos was the most important financial centre in the Athenian Amphyction, and Rome became an even greater power in a similar period of peace and prosperity after the second Punic war, so Melbourne and Victoria, the extrapolated logic suggests, might become in these prosperous times the centre of an Australian amphyction, a federation of the colonies.[25] Several factors encourage this view, among them Deakin's meetings while in London with the constitutional expert James Bryce, author of *The American Commonwealth* published the next year, which became the virtual Bible of the Federation Conventions of the 1890s.[26] With the depression still three years away, his confidence in the leading role for 'Marvellous Melbourne', as G. A. Sala had recently called it, in such an amphyction was the embodiment of a faith in progress he shared with many others. If this interpretation is correct, this brief notation confirms Deakin's commitment to a Mission. He felt deeply and sincerely that he was now called upon to stir opinions regarding the old and mostly forlorn dream of Federation in the hearts of the 'natives', that is, to 'awaken them'.

Deakin's first trip to London was a watershed. With his faith in a Divine Providence dramatically confirmed, with talents, capacities and enthusiasm at their apogee, and his hold on political power growing more firm and sure, public life was still 'a joyous experiment & field for adventurous explorations'.[27] The images of Alfred Deakin are protean: the 'silver tongued' orator, the master of parliamentary manoeuvres, the 'affable' politician who treated all persons from ministers to messenger boys with equal respect, the leader whose personal integrity was never questioned, even by those who condemned what they regarded as his political opportunism. There was also a private, sombre and introspective, more deeply religious side to his nature. Can we relate in any coherent way the 'silent student', the budding mystic of the journals and prayers, to Professor La Nauze's political adept? The very disparity of these images tells us something about the complexities, even the paradoxes, in the character of this remarkable man. Paradox is to varying degrees a feature of all human life, and justification, rationalisation and the building of a personal mythology are present in all writing, no matter how private. Yet, perhaps because of the remorseless introspection, and the articulateness, of their author, there does emerge from the historical artefacts a picture of Alfred Deakin which conveys something of the 'texture' of self, confirmed by others' accounts, helping to shed light on his inner world at a time when he felt the mantle of Divine instrument descend upon him.

Among those who had known him, Deakin was 'flashing, a sword through dullness'. They remembered that he had made them laugh, had roused them to excitement, yet they could not recall what it was about him that had affected them thus. He was 'a most friendly soul', and many remembered particularly 'his outstretched hand when he came at you across a roomful of people'. They also spoke of his sense of fun, and his immense courtesy, that had in it 'a hint of stateliness'.[28]

In photographs of the federal conventions Deakin seems dwarfed by giants like Kingston, Forrest and Lyne, but he was a tall and strikingly handsome man of over six feet, with a 'scintillating personality' and a powerful physical presence. With a medium complexion, a fine, rather long oval-shaped head and dark bushy hair, and a beard worn long in his 'radical' days and later trimmed in the Van Dyke style, he had a slightly foreign look.[29] A strong attachment to race is illustrated in his reaction to a journalist writing for an American publication that in looks he was 'tall, straight, and dark like the rugged impression of Phillip [sic] II of Spain'. When immediately Deakin wrote to complain, he was assured that she had 'meant only your features'; nevertheless his face reminded her 'of a portrait of Phillip II which used to hang in New England schoolrooms ... in my girlhood days'. One suspects he was offended less by the alleged physical resemblance than what he must have taken as a questioning of his Anglo-Saxon origins.[30]

What is most remembered about Alfred Deakin, besides his courtesy and a direct and engaging manner, were his eyes, deeply set, almost hypnotic, and of a luminous brown colour, and his voice, a light baritone with 'a wonderful ring in it' that has been compared to Menzies'.[31] His accent, like Barton's, was said to be indistinguishable from that of cultured Britons. He would delight his daughters when reading them stories aloud, as his own father had done, by taking on the voices of the various characters. Deakin shared with his sister advanced ideas on the education of women, and his daughters were raised according to progressive ideas, encouraged to think for themselves and to develop useful talents—seldom punished except when they told an untruth, and never praised for duty well done.[32] Though they never lacked for anything, they were dressed economically, with none of the curls and frills then in fashion, wearing their hair tied back plainly.[33]

Deakin always carried himself very erect, overcoming an early tendency to stoop, and he kept himself fit through deep breathing and exercises.[34] His tastes in all things but books were modest. One enduring image has Deakin enjoying a simple lunch of steak and eggs at a favourite haunt near Parliament House, a book propped beside his plate, discussing politics with any chance comer who happened along.[35] He was not a club man, preferring to entertain his few close friends at home. He ate sparingly and drank little, in part due to a delicate digestion; as a young man he did smoke the occasional cigar. He had remained a vegetarian until 1879. In the Deakin home there were constant discussions on hygiene and the constituents and values of various foods.[36]

Like his parents, Deakin was a lover of home. He presented Pattie with a new poem on each anniversary and on her birthday, and would write individually to his infant daughters when he was away. His family life was ordinary, if very close, but there were tensions between wife and sister vying for his attention, which surfaced from time to time. Like Henry Parkes, Deakin was surrounded by adoring women who gave support and meaningfulness to his life. F. W. Eggleston has provided some incisive comments on the women in Deakin's life, especially on Catherine whom he knew in her advancing years:

> It was Deakin's fate to be surrounded by women who worshipped him, but did not agree with one another. He was very largely brought up by a sister who never married. She had helped to educate him and to inspire him with literary tastes, and she had assisted him in his early political struggles. She did not think that anyone else could do for Alfred what she could...[37]

He added that 'she was a grand old lady and her jealousy of his wife was only in the natural order of things, but it was resented very much.' He remembered Pattie Deakin as a magnificent-looking woman, not beautiful but 'tall and stately, a commanding figure', who was devoted to her husband and his interests. Pattie is largely silent through the pages of Deakin's private writings, appearing, like parents, sister and children as a sort of icon, praised as among his many blessings, but never acquiring a definite shape. It is not clear how much of his inner life she knew about, for Deakin kept his journals locked up, and he insisted that no others ever saw them. And it would seem that, early on, Katie rather than Pattie shared his intellectual tastes. Among the reasons for keeping journals was 'the closing of the safety valve of speech', and elsewhere he noted: 'These journals indicate a lack of conversational companionship on the intellectual side, a lack of courage if not of opportunity to speak one's mind.'[38]

Eggleston's account gives an interesting insight into Deakin's 'cocoon' of protection, which was also a source of animosity. Pattie had 'formed the idea that Alfred was unworldly, as indeed he was; and that she must exercise an influence on his relations with others'. He was 'an emotional politician, surrounded by a possessive sister, a possessive wife and possessive daughters, [who] must have been, I think, sorely tried at times'. Eggleston concludes that 'It would have been well for the Deakin women if they had been relieved of the burden of Deakin's greatness.'[39]

Deakin was regarded as a true gentleman, and even his political opponents liked and trusted him. What impresses one most is Deakin's humanity and sincerity. To our cynical modern age, these may seem unhelpful qualities for success in politics, but even in a more genteel era Deakin stood out among his peers. All who knew him attested to his absolute personal integrity. His first London trip brought him notoriety equally for his refusal of a knighthood, and for returning half of his official expense allowance, some £500, to the Treasury. Yet his friends were few, and his closest confidants, once his relationship with his sister Katie inevitably changed with maturity, became his journals. David Syme in early days was both friend and father figure. Some, like Ernest Joske and the peripatetic Dutchman Alkemade, remained his friends long after their days together at the V.A.S. Later in his career, Deakin became close to Charles Strong, and to Edmund Barton and Richard O'Connor, who alone among his political colleagues were considered close friends; with their 'retirement' to the High Court Bench, and the crushing responsibilities as head of government, Deakin grew more aloof. The most intimate friendship of Deakin's life was probably with Herbert Brookes, who became son-in-law and confidant, and later fellow political worker in the federal era. Popular with all men yet known by very few, and befriending even fewer, 'affable' Alfred presents many paradoxes.

Deakin's oratory has become part of the Australian legend, a 'burning, bristling and commanding eloquence' capable at times of swaying a Parliament against its will.[40] Like Dr Bromby, he spoke rapidly, varying his delivery with significant pauses, then rising dramatically to staccato rhythms. Ernest Scott has left a vivid account of his oratorical style. In a policy speech extending over two hours, Deakin used:

> every variety of gesture, from a simply lifted forefinger to a windmill whirl of arms ... Body spoke as well as tongue, and every sentence was animated by its appropriate action ... passages delivered with the throb of passion in every syllable ... shot out of the mouth like lightning flashes ... accented by the emphatic beat of fist upon open palm; passages spoken in an eager stride across the platform ... rhythmic with movement and glowing with fervour ... [then] the orator slowed down his speed, folded his arms across his chest, stood quietly by the table, and drew to a quiet and earnest conclusion.[41]

King O'Malley in later life said that after Sir Josiah Symons, Deakin was the finest speaker Australia had ever produced; but he added, he was more than that, 'he was one of the kindest men who ever walked the earth.'[42] It was this kindness, directness and unprepossessing manner, revealed in various ways, that gives more than a hint to the practical side of Deakin's religion, in a rigorous personal code of conduct. His daughter Ivy's statement that 'he would invariably discover the best in people' has the ring of truth and is supported by anecdotal evidence.[43] For many years and without fanfare he took Sunday dinner to a Miss Cowben, an old white-worker; when he was in town, also bringing jam and fruit and carrying letters.[44] It was the characteristic act of a generous soul, like the not inconsiderable help he gave to struggling Australian artists such as Sydney Jephcott and William Gay, and the practical assistance he rendered to others like his bohemian friend Alkemade. These actions—and examples could be multiplied—indicate a tenderness and sympathy that even the rough and tumble of politics could not extinguish.

There was also a spartan quality about the man. He 'awed and horrified' his colleagues when, in London as Prime Minister of the Commonwealth, he preferred a 'cheap lodging house and a nine-penny chop' while his colleagues 'lorded it at the Hotel Cecil'.[45] His pleasures were simple: reading, writing, walking the dogs, gardening, and good conversation. An 1890 'Clue' describes in considerable detail his 'ideal day':

> My ideal day to which the actual occasionally approaches blends the physical & the mental: begins early with a game of tennis, gardening or wood chopping, something that inflates the chest & sends the perspiration streaming from the pores—a quick leap under a cold shower & vigorous rub down brings one into a breakfast of wheaten bread, butter 'Tasting of flora & the country green', & pure milk, for luxury flavored with real mocha. Then a stretch in a deep armchair, a ship chair with some of the great or the delicious authors, poetry, philosophy, or critical or humorous essay. The notebook is hard by & is taken up to prolong the trance till lunch time. This meal is light, embracing fruit, salad or sweets, rarely meat & no liquid. After this the book or the chat & then the walk in the later afternoon with conversation & good tempered dispute. If I were rich this should be a canter into the hills or along the sea shore. Back to a good dinner, either French or light, a little good wine, a romp with the children whose chatter brightens every meal & then good music, a song & a little closing comment on the day which fades into silence of swift coming sleep with my wife's last kisses warm upon my lips.[46]

Notice, besides the patriarchal tone and bourgeois aspiration, the primacy of books. Deakin's principal delight was his 'harvest of reading' during the annual holiday at the beach, when he could read steadily and without distraction, covering an astounding range from biography and history, poetry and philosophy, to science and geography. Deakin's tastes varied from the French masters to light novels like those of Hilaire Belloc, but they tended, especially later, to religion. A selection from 1887 when he was overseas for half the year, shows the catholicity of his tastes: biography, especially religious biography, with *Marcus Aurelius* by Long, Potter's *Aeschylus*, and Huxley's *Life of Hume*; religious works like *Study of Religion* by the Unitarian James Martineau and Newman's *Grammar of Assent*, philosophic treatises like Kant's *Theory of Ethics* and Sidgwick's commentary on it; a lesser emphasis on political works like Rousseau's *Confessions*, Dilke on *Greater Britain* and De Tocqueville's reflections on *Democracy in America*; in French a constant favourite was St Beuve, that year it was *Portraits Litéraires*; and for the new task he saw ahead of him Bryce's *The American Commonwealth*.[47]

A reviewer of Deakin's first biography, George Cockrill, writing for the *Age*, felt the disjunction between the portrait rendered by Walter Murdoch, who relied greatly on Deakin's private corpus of writing, and the man he had known well.

His criticisms underscore La Nauze's warning that 'religious musings could, perhaps, reflect a whole man; in fact they rarely do.'[48] Cockrill had known an Alfred Deakin 'less introspective and much more human' than Murdoch's portrayal suggests. Murdoch had also known Deakin, but only slightly and under more formal circumstances. Cockrill recalled Deakin as 'more boyish in his good humour and love of fun, more vital and companiable [sic]' than the sombre individual presented in Murdoch's sketch.[49]

The most marked characteristic observed from youth was an augmenting dichotomy between Deakin's 'inner' and 'outer' worlds, characterised in early years by a jealous guarding of the creative side of his nature. Gradually with the call to Mission, this became an 'aloofness' evidenced already by his habit of private written prayer. It appears that, as politics became tougher, there was firstly the solace of the home environment, closed to all but a few, to which Deakin retreated; beyond that was the rejuvenation of his self-communings, in books and poetry, in speculation, and in prayers invoked 'through the pen'. Rising early, especially in the federal era, when he suffered from chronic insomnia, he would inscribe his journals early in the morning and late at night.

This core of solitariness became more deeply established with age. By 1904 he could confess with stark honesty in a birthday reflection: 'I act alone, live alone & think alone.'[50] 'Nervously active in temperament, cheerful, inquiring, speculative, unprejudiced' was how the American Idealist philosopher Josiah Royce described Deakin after their week together in the Blue Mountains in 1888. He was 'an admirer of America and of good scenery, a lover of life, of metaphysics' and, Royce added with perspicacity, 'of power'.[51] This acute observation seems to sit oddly with his consistent refusal of honours, in Deakin's day an important badge of power, but here too there is both paradox and a certain coherence: while fond of power and fiercely imperial in his views, Deakin rejected the symbols of title and class; he cared little for money, preferring an abstemious life to banquets and processions, and his tastes were reflective and scholarly while he occupied, and would long continue to occupy, the most powerful position in any Parliament. In his private religion Deakin eschewed creeds for direct inspiration, avoiding slavishness to systems of thought and pursuing an eclectic, almost encyclopaedist search for truth which, like his political Liberalism, placed a high premium on individual authority. With important exceptions like John Morley he was not enamoured of those who ruled Britain, yet he was attached to the Kiplingesque idea of the Anglo-Saxon race and hence to Empire; and while an admirer of Hinduism, Islam and other religions of the East, he was also an architect of the 'White Australia' policy and of legislation against the Chinese.

Deakin's steadfast refusal of accolades—over the years he refused other knighthoods, a Privy Councillorship, and a doctorate of civil law from Oxford, the first Oxonians had seen rejected (he did in 1915 accept an honorary doctorate of laws from the University of California)—suggests an Australian nationalism and a democratic temper. Like Higinbotham he believed that honours should originate from the community served, and were inherently undemocratic in placing some men above their fellows. But Deakin's consistency in such refusals came also from a personal discipline of humility. A central theme in private reflections was a self-disgust at his 'egoism', a disgust related to the pseudo-Buddhist Theosophical belief that the path of self-realisation lay in 'extinguishing the ego'. Allied to these ideas was another and contrasting theme: the ease of his 'rise and rise', while still a very young man, in the world.

There are, especially in prayers, frequent reminders to himself of the undeserved ease of his political rise and happiness of his personal life. We have seen, with the advent of the Grand Prophecy, an apprehension of a 'sacrifice' to be extracted. The idea that payment was in some way necessitated by the very ease of his ascent had complex strands, and was probably also influenced by Theosophy's popularised notion of 'Karma', understood as spiritual cause and effect. These elements, their relative status in Deakin's overall view of reality, and their importance in his ethos of active faith formed the dynamic elements of his personal 'web of significance': the ease, the resultant guilt and the expectation of retributive justice at some later time.[52]

Deakin seemed in 1887 to have everything: a remarkable mentality, great personal charm, the zeal of the reformer, an oratory of singular style and penetrating power. Added to these native gifts were other blessings, of loving parents and sister, a beautiful and devoted wife, healthy children; the educational opportunities and the persons and circumstances that always seemed to make his path relatively effortless: a profession chosen (on a whim?) at the suggestion of Theodore Fink, a journalistic, and then a political career initiated by Syme, and ministerial office at twenty-six that had brought overseas travel. Now only thirty, Deakin was leader of his party and co-leader of a government presiding over a period of unprecedented progress, and the champion of an epoch-making (for the Australians) conference predicted several years before by the spirits. Providence had smiled on him, but at the cost he believed, of an eventual sacrifice of self. These were powerful factors in shaping Deakin's world view. How far his protestations of ease in private meditations were the rhetoric of supplication and humility, and how far they reflect his actual feelings, must remain problematic; yet they do seem to go some way toward explaining his increasing 'aloofness'.

Lest we caricature this vital human being as an unwilling victim of his fate, we must balance the ethereal images and the spiritual resolve with the dissenting opinion of another contemporary from Murdoch's biography. The anonymous reviewer (probably Richard Hain, a shadowy aide of Deakin's federal career) complained of the erroneous impression conveyed by Murdoch that Deakin found himself in politics in spite of himself, that he loved his ease and literature more than public work, to which he was 'willingly chained [as] to a wheel from which he longed to set himself free'. This impression, the reviewer insisted, 'is exactly what Deakin was not'. Always fighting for a cause, Deakin enjoyed the 'clash of aims in politics as few men do'. The opinion is an important corrective, a reminder of the dangers of biography that relies too much on the private writing, and hence on the projected ideal image, of its subject.[53] Like Cockrill, this reviewer insisted on Deakin's zest for living, his competitive nature and enthusiasm; these were qualities that the sombre and introspective side of the man, expressed through his journals and prayer books, could not convey.

Professor La Nauze perhaps put the matter best in his introduction to *Federated Australia*: 'His distinction of intellect and bearing was patent; his political character was a matter of debate, and to some extent still is.'[54] To some he was an Australian patriot who achieved much in a period when 'parties' were fluid and unstable. To others he was seen, especially in his late federal career, as a 'smooth negotiator' primarily concerned with remaining in office. These are dramatic contradictions, or seem so. Some reviewers had complained that La Nauze's biography had not 'told them precisely what I think about him'. He regarded this a compliment, for 'I do not know precisely what to think ... about a man as complex as Deakin'.[55]

I conclude this attempt at a portrait by concurring in La Nauze's perplexity; contradictions and paradox are inherent in all human life, but in a person like Alfred Deakin, they stand starkly in their definition and contrast.

To return to the Grand Prophecy, and the diary note composed in England and initially headed 4 July: it was entered later as 'Clue' 155 under the date of the original inspiration, 24 May 1887, and expanded upon:

> 155. A sudden change of scene, locality, country, circumstance, language, rank—(See Miscellanies—J. H. Newman, p. 128) Remains faithful to principles of conduct. 'Most go mad'—You have learned the lesson of life. Call 'the next street'.[56]

The added reference to Newman is illuminating, as it relates these inner concerns to events in his outer life, and particularly to a conspicuous decision Deakin made while in London—declining a knighthood. Newman's essay entitled 'The Greatness and Littleness of Human Life' is a sermon constructed around the idea of the Limitless Horizons of life despite its limitations. Speaking to Christians Newman wrote that though life be a long and painful discipline which abounds in 'littlenesses', and however unprofitable when viewed in itself, we should remember:

> that we are immortal spirits, independent of time and space; and that this life is but a sort of outward stage, on which we act for a time, and which is only sufficient and only intended to answer the purpose of trying whether we will serve God or no ... and in which it is our duty to act as if all we saw had a truth and reality, because all that meets us influences us and our destiny ...[57]

This passage, with its exhortation to duty and destiny, despite life's dream-like quality, struck a deep and resonant chord in Deakin. Newman's writings concerning a Divine government of the world, and of inspiration residing in an 'Illative sense', exerted some later influence on Deakin's ideas. While this significance can only be adumbrated, given the elation at his new found 'sign' and resounding success in defending the rights of his 'country', both diary and journal undeniably express satisfaction that by rejecting the 'livery' of the social order in refusing a knighthood, he had somehow overcome the temptation of ambition. This was the essence of the 'Polycrates' warning of six months previous, just days before Deakin learned of the conference, a caveat that he could not 'fall' unless he 'failed' himself. Perhaps in his own eyes these events had been a personal test, and he was now morally fit to call on the 'next street' of life experience, the realisation of the 'Federal Ideal'.

On his return to Victoria, Deakin was received as something of a celebrity. As Professor La Nauze observed there was in all the pomp a 'comic solemnity about what amounted to self-congratulation'; but the event was important politically for Victoria and personally for Deakin.[58] The *Age* was clearly behind him. He had returned from his 'Ithaca' after witnessing many wonders and going through as many temptations as Ulysses. Continuing the parallel, the article notes that he had refused the 'bribe of Immortality', that is a knighthood, perceptively adding that he had obtained as much distinction for coming home without one.[59] Practically the entire Cabinet met the special train at Ballarat that had carried him from Adelaide, where his ship had docked. After giving a speech at Spencer Street station, Deakin drove home. His diary expressed his overall feelings: 'Thank God—Very tired Early to bed.'[60]

Deakin lost no time in declaring for Federation. But first he shared this great Truth with his wife. His diary for 21 June contains a cryptic entry: 'Illuminations—P—', recording a sharing of his revelation with Pattie, and rejoicing together in its outcome after his ecstatic reception home.[61] The A.N.A. banquet given in his honour on 12 July was his first large forum. One reporter observed 'an impression of fatigue'. As the *Argus* reported, Deakin told the enthusiastic audience that until very recently relations with the responsible ministers had come only 'through an intervening veil of irresponsible officials (Hear Hear)'; so that the ministers of Great Britain were perceiving the colonists 'through an official glass darkly (Hear hear)'. In this speech Deakin the politician was careful to enunciate his position clearly. It appeared to him that the proposals for 'separation', that is a republic, meant 'all loss and no gain', but neither was he for an Imperial Federation of sovereign States under the British Crown. Their next object he declared was for a Federation of Australasia, after which 'we might be prepared to consider another kind of federation'.[62]

The following day, 13 July, Deakin attended a seance, his first for some six years, with Mrs Stirling, one of the trilogy of prophetic mediums from seven years before. In his diary he noted:[63] 'Gillies better in 4 months—change beginning—show in 3 months—clear in 6 culminate in 9—Min not last long—Great change in world outside in 2 years—Health—struggle soon—'. It is beyond my competency to comment on the ontological status of these predictions, but they indisputably had a marked effect on Deakin. The young Chief Secretary might well have regarded it a successful reading, although she was wrong about the ministry, which lasted another three years, as did Gillies' leadership. There was indeed a great change that began within two years, caused by a mixture of intemperate investment in railways and unbridled land speculation, and tolerated if not encouraged by his government. It was to signal the end of the 'boom' and the beginnings of the depression; he might also have interpreted the maritime strike of 1890 after the fact as the 'struggle' alluded to.

Whatever interpretation Deakin placed on his reading with Mrs Stirling, the first Imperial Conference became the impetus to nationhood, with himself its prime mover in Victoria. It was a herald to him—with it his political destiny had been sealed and sanctified. He had seen 'Thy Will be done' in action, in working to realise that vague hope of Federation. It is only this conviction of prophetic fulfilment which makes comprehensible both his actions at the conference and his political activities thereafter. Armed with what he believed to be prescience as to its outcome, we can well understand his unexpected force of conviction, his jubilation, even his *outrecuidance*. Deakin's actions over the next few years, most notably his refusal of political office and his return to the Bar, which he truly disliked, so as to work for Federation, speak louder than the speculations of historians. The clearest testament to Deakin's newly discovered, yet long anticipated, Mission appears in a prayer penned at the end of that eventful year. On 26 November 1887, for the first time in almost a year, he prayed:

Merciful God I thank Thee—
I thank Thee for Thine inexhaustible bounty of experience; for what I might deem a peculiar & personal grace if not ever conscious that I am but the instrument among millions of instruments to perform the part for which I was conceived & reared & trained so far as my faculties would allow—O God I thank Thee nevertheless for the tide of blessing; for the means of knowledge & for the power which has brought me through

many trials without permitting me to fail. For a long work accomplished beyond my daily work I thank Thee—For grace to wife & child & safety of all loved & joy in all their love I thank Thee O my God—I thank & thank & praise Thee.[64]

It is the prayer of a man who has found his Purpose; but it is also a reiteration in varied form of the ideas and sentiments expressed in the 'American Notes' and the 'floodgates' prayer two years before. As in those records of previous encounters with his feelings, aspiration and ambitions, yet more succinctly, it courses over the same perceived path of development and celebrates the arrival at a preordained and useful destination despite, as always, momentary falterings and personal limitations. In some ways Deakin prayed throughout his life a single prayer.

Notes

1 La Nauze, *Alfred Deakin*, vol. 1, p. 99; *outrecuidance* is defined as: 'presumption; overweening conceit; audacity.'

2 A. Deakin, *The Federal Story*, J. A. La Nauze (ed.), Melbourne, 1963, pp. 21–2.

3 *Age*, 17 June 1887.

4 Undated note, 9/444, circa 1887.

5 La Nauze, *Alfred Deakin*, vol. 1, p. 96.

6 Deakin to F. T. Derham, 26 February 1887.

7 Deakin to Catherine Deakin, 14 April 1887.

8 Ibid., 31 March 1887.

9 Ibid., 30 April 1887.

10 Deakin to F. T. Derham, 31 March 1887.

11 Deakin to Catherine Deakin, 21 April 1887.

12 Ibid., 30 April 1887.

13 Pattie Deakin, Reminiscences, 19/281, undated.

14 Menu, Banquet of the Duke of Cambridge, 20 April 1887.

15 *Age*, 11 June 1887.

16 Diary, 4 July 1887.

17 Diary, 6 July 1887.

18 In one letter Royce tells Deakin: 'I shall soon send you a long psychical research article for which [Hodgson] has furnished the facts and I have spun out the fictitious theories': Josiah Royce to Deakin, 20 February 1889; A. T. Baird, *Richard Hodgson*, London, 1949.

19 Richard Hodgson to Deakin, 26 March 1899; see G. Murphy and R.O. Ballou (eds), *William James on Psychical Research*, Clifton, 1973; for major developments in social thought from the 1890s, see H. S. Hughes, *Consciousness and Society*, New York, 1977.

20 For different perspectives on the 'Mahatma letters' controversy, see A. Gauld, *The Founders of Psychical Research*, New York, 1968, pp. 202–3; and A. Conan Doyle, *History of Spiritualism*, 2 vols, Melbourne, 1926, vol. 1, p. 64.

21 Diary, 8 July 1887.

22 'The Youth, who daily farther from the east
    Must travel, still is Nature's Priest,
    And by the vision splendid
    Is on his way attended;
  At length the Man perceives it die away,
  And fade into the light of common day.'
  W. Wordsworth, 'Ode: Intimations of Immortality'.

23 'How pure at heart and sound in head,
    With what divine affections bold
    Should be the man whose thought would hold
  An hour's communion with the dead.'
  A. Tennyson, 'In Memoriam', section XCIV. See chapter 4; one instance, that to the agent's knowledge proved perfectly true, occurred while Swedenborg was dining with friends some 300 miles from Stockholm where he lived. He suddenly announced that a fire was raging there, and later he added with some relief that it had been quenched only four doors from his own house, which on investigation was confirmed. George Trobridge, *Swedenborg Life and Teaching*, New York, 1976, pp. 198–9.

24 Diary, 12 July 1887.

25 *Oxford Classical Dictionary*, pp. 321–2; D. Dudley, *Roman Society*, Ringwood, 1970, p. 83.

26 J. A. La Nauze, *The Making of the Australian Constitution*, Melbourne, 1974, p. 18.

27 Red Spine Book, 3/281, 6 May 1911.

28 Kylie Tennant, preface to the play *Tether A Dragon*, Sydney, 1952, p. 15.

29 A. T. Woodward, *The Link*, Melbourne, 1 April 1929; see also J. A. La Nauze, 'Who Are the Fathers?', *Historical Studies*, vol. 13, no. 51, October 1968.

30 The article is dated 6 March 1890; 11/5; the letter from Zadel Gustafson to Deakin in reply to his is dated 16 April 1890.

31 Interviews with Atlee Hunt, undated, and with Elsie Bannister, 29 March 1961, La Nauze papers, series 5248, N.L.A.

32 Reminiscences of Pattie Deakin, 19/285, undated.

33 Interview with Ivy and Stella Deakin, circa 1952, La Nauze papers, series 5248, N.L.A.

34 Ivy Brookes, text of speech given in 1951, 19/327.

35 *Catholic Press*, 16 January 1913.

36 Reminiscences of Pattie Deakin, 19/279, undated.

37 A. W. Martin, *Henry Parkes*, p. 15; F. W. Eggleston, historical notes; my thanks to Dr Warren Osmond for providing me with this material.

38 'Clues', vol. 1, 3/283, no. 260, 15 July 1888; vol. 4, 3/286, no. 598, 17 December 1892; see also Clue no. 537, where he asserts that their existence was 'unguessed by anyone else': Vol. 3, 3/287, 12 June 1892.

39 F. W. Eggleston, historical notes.

40 W. H. Watt, Obituary Testimonial, 23/74, 22 October 1919. One instance was the second reading of the Judiciary Bill in the Federal Parliament, when Deakin captivated an unruly House for over three hours by close discussion of fine legal and constitutional points relating to the establishment of the High Court: Diary, 9 June 1903.

41 E. Scott for the Melbourne *Herald*, 1906 Policy Speech Ballarat, cited in A. Davies, *Politics as Work*, Melbourne, 1973, p. 50.

42 King O'Malley, A.B.C. broadcast 'Guest of Honour', 28 January 1951, transcript in La Nauze papers, series 5248, N.L.A.

43 Ivy Brookes, text of speech given in 1951, 19/325.

44 Reminiscences of Pattie Deakin, 19/283, undated.

45 *Catholic Press*, 16 January 1913.

46 'Clues', vol. 3, 3/287, no. 429, undated, c. August 1890.

47 1887 Diary, back.

48 La Nauze, *Alfred Deakin*, vol. 1, p. 79.

49 George Cockrill, 'Biography under Difficulties', *Age*, 18 August 1923.

50 Autobiographical Notes, typescript, 3/300, 3 August 1904.

51 Josiah Royce, 'Impressions of Australia', *Scribner's Magazine*, January 1891; quoted in La Nauze, *Alfred Deakin*, vol. 1, p. 124.

52 Clifford Geertz has provided a useful adaptation of an image drawn from Max Weber, an heuristic conception which views the analysis of culture in terms of recovering culturally defined meanings, aiming to 'explicate' as far as possible the constellation of meanings and their relations in 'natives' understandings': 'Thick Description: Toward an Interpretive Theory of Culture', in *The Interpretation of Cultures*, New York, 1973, p. 5.

53 *Adelaide Advertiser*, 13 August 1923; for a discussion of biography and its attendant dangers, see A. Martin, 'Henry Parkes: In Search of the "Actual Man Underneath"', *Historical Studies*, vol. 16, no. 63, October 1974.

54 J. A. La Nauze, *Federated Australia, Selections from Letters to the* Morning Post, Melbourne, 1968, p. 3.

55 Ibid.; for criticism of Deakin's political career, see Frank Anstey, *Thirty Years of Deakin*, Melbourne, 1913.

56 'Clues', vol. 1, 3/283, no. 155, dated 24 May 1887.

57 J. H. Newman, *Miscellanies*, London, 1890, p. 128.

58 La Nauze, *Alfred Deakin*, vol. 1, p. 105.

59 *Age*, 17 June 1887.

60 Diary, 17 June 1887.

61 Diary, 21 June 1887.

62 *The Australian*, 12 July 1887; *Argus*, 12 July 1887.

63 Diary, 13 July 1887.

64 'Boke of Praer & Prase', 5/841, prayer XXXIX, 26 November 1887.

4

God and Federation

He who sings to the gods a song of hope will see his wish come true.

Aeschylus

It was characteristic of the two most powerful advocates of Australian Federation that one, at the beginning of his career and fired by a conviction of Divine guidance, should seek in Talmudic fashion for evidences of the Law in the lives and thoughts of divines, while the other, wishing to crown a long career and secure his place in history, should voice his call publicly. Thus in October 1889 as Alfred Deakin the future 'apostle' of the movement was engrossed in a commentary on Emanuel Swedenborg, the leonine and secular-minded Premier of New South Wales, Sir Henry Parkes, was calling for a federation of the colonies from 'the rooftop of Australia' at Tenterfield.[1] The announcement was a complete surprise to Deakin, although they had held private discussions on the subject at the beginning of that year. While he was under no illusion about Parkes' motives, this unexpected support was regarded by Deakin as the 'sign' in the course of events sedulously searched for since that glorious prophetic fulfilment two years before. He now knew that the movement was to come to fruition.[2]

Things moved quickly from the time of Parkes' pronouncement. An Australasian Federation Conference was held in Melbourne five months later in February 1890 to which delegates, including those from New Zealand and Fiji, were sent by their legislatures. Deakin spoke twice during the one-week conference. The sweltering heat visited on delegates did not help matters, and almost immobilised old Henry Parkes. On the opening day, 10 February, 'Big Tom' Playford of South Australia, in a prickly and aggressive speech exacerbated perhaps by the oppressive weather, had attacked *inter alia* Victorian Protection and self interest, New South Wales, and Henry Parkes. Deakin, who took the podium next, was the soul of conciliation. Sensing that such insensitivity could stir up that 'something more than rivalry' between colonies which James Service had warned of early in the decade and wreck their nascent enterprise, he reminded delegates that lines between colonies were imaginary, that 'we are one people in blood, race, religion and aspiration'.[3] Then coming quickly to the heart of the matter, he avowed that self-interest was 'most assuredly' an impetus toward Federation not only in Victoria, but also in the other colonies. Threats making union imperative, like the 'recidivistes' France was sending to the New Hebrides, and the influx of 'inferior races' into the north, were matched by its many advantages: control of ports; a federal judiciary; post; and a common currency. Thus whether guided by the 'forces of sentiment' or by self-interest, Deakin implored delegates to shape their course so that all might reach the 'haven of Federation'.[4] In the closing to his second speech on the last day, referring to the duty of the forthcoming convention to frame a Federal Constitution which he called a work of 'transcendent respon-sibility',[5] Deakin paraphrased Washington's appeal to the delegates at the American convention, and urged colleagues to work to choose nothing but the best proposal, and then to leave the issue 'in higher hands'.[6]

In these two brief but masterful performances, the youngest delegate to the conference had courteously rebutted Playford to allay the suspicions of the 'smaller' colonies, had outlined the threats and advantages, and elevated the tenor of the assembly by invoking the very model of democracy, which he deftly linked to the Divine Providence. It was upon the generation now coming, he declared, that fell the great task of framing the Constitution, yet he 'could not despair of the result, nor question the ultimate triumph of those who are now entering upon the hour of their labour and their trial.'[7] Speaking thus in general terms, Deakin was pondering his own commitment.

The next speaker, the conservative Freetrader McMillan of New South Wales, remarked that if anything could have swayed delegates, 'it would have been the charming eloquence of our friend, in whom the church has certainly lost an extraordinary light'.[8] In general, a positive ambience attended the conference. The remaining speeches voiced general approval of the idea of Federation while remaining divided over issues to become even more fissiparous in future debate, especially the relative powers of the 'smaller' and 'larger' States in an Upper House, the resolution of deadlocks, and the money powers of the Senate. Plans were made for a full convention to be appointed by the colonial legislatures, to which delegates now left to report.

We have glimpsed Deakin on the public platform, in debating style, at this first national gathering of federalists, soothing and smoothing in his affable manner and calling delegates to match their highest ideal of a federated Australia. Deakin preferred to work behind the scenes, as shown in the *Federal Story*, his account of the Federation movement written at the end of the decade, where he focuses on the roles of others; regarding himself he wrote with seemly modesty:

> Of Deakin it is unnecessary to say anything except that on seeing the impression created by his fellow-Victorians he devoted himself from the first to the task of smoothing away resentments and overcoming difficulties, preferring to support amendments rather than move them as so many coveted to do, and in every way subordinating his votes and speeches and silences as he believed would most contribute to the attainment of Union.[9]

Here then was his method and mandate. The religious images are significant: he 'devoted' himself to a background role while others 'coveted' the sponsoring of amendments. His votes, speeches, even his 'silences'—and we may wonder what is meant here, for it has an almost mystical air—were subordinated to a 'Higher' end. Deakin's silences may have been partly due to his status at thirty-four as the youngest delegate, and his relative inexperience in the law. With a strong faith in spiritual guidance, and both a natural disposition and conscious exercise of humility, he endeavoured to move through the chaos of competition and factional interests to bring about harmony. He would try to effect compromise, applying his familiar 'affable' political style, to inspire others to give of their best. At least that is how Deakin perceived his own role. He added: 'Many others were actuated by precisely the same motives, but none followed it in precisely the same manner of self-suppression in public coupled with continuous activity in private among the members.'[10]

Committee debates were not recorded, but one issue resolved at this first gathering gives an idea of Deakin's style, and attests to his penchant for investing names and dates with special significance. After being suggested by Parkes, the title 'Commonwealth' had been rejected in the Constitutional Committee of which Deakin was a member because of its flavour of republicanism and separation. As he recounts the event in the *Federal Story*, after 'a night's reflection' Deakin became 'enamoured' of the name, and he reopened the debate the next day, attacking other names as 'barbarous, clumsy and uneuphonious' and taking an 'energetic personal canvass' on its behalf.[11] A master of persuasion who in each case knew his man, Deakin appealed first to the 'streak of republicanism' in the elderly Adye Douglas. Inglis Clark, Griffith and Barton supported it out of friendship to Parkes, and Sir George Grey because it was the 'most radical' name proposed. It was finally carried by one vote in the fourteen-man committee. We might wonder at the significance of the name or the nature of the intervening night's reflection—might it have been an unrecorded prayer responded to by a 'sign'? While never a republican, as a Liberal and a democrat Deakin had a strong sense of the primacy of the People's House, as in his forcible and eloquent address in its defence in the Victorian Parliament the following year. He spoke of the days of Hampden and Pym, when important issues were decided like the 'assertion of Constitutional liberty ... the supremacy of Parliament ... the right of the nation to concede no taxation excepting through ... Parliament ... to be tried by their own courts ... and [for their] representatives to speak in Parliament without danger of arrest by the Myrmidons of a despotic king.'[12] Apart from its inner significance, the name 'Commonwealth' sat well with Deakin's political Liberalism.

The die was cast. Over the next ten years he would work for the realisation of the 'Federal Ideal' in numerous ways—organising, publicising, arguing, testifying. He suffered momentary lapses, not as to the overall design, but from lack of confidence in his own capacities and moral fitness for the task, or out of frustration with the many obstacles. It is significant that the *Federal Story* commences with the events of 1887.

The profound spiritual significance of a federated Australia to this politician reformer can never be adequately conveyed, but its impact and stresses can be gauged somewhat in the most intimate record extant of Deakin's inner life, the prayers he recorded as he prayed. That vital interrelation between the 'inner' man and his activities in the 'outer' world, refracted to varying degrees in all of Deakin's private writings, is clearest in these poignant petitions, especially during the troubled 1890s. In these writings, always sincere, sometimes touching, frequently eloquent, we see a deeply religious man conversing with his God, struggling to do His will.

There was also the struggle against himself, his wayward faith, weaknesses of character and temptations that thwarted his determination to 'hold the plowshare steadily'. He prayed frequently, sometimes daily, to know the Divine will in these secular matters, both to be a more effective instrument, and to satisfy his deep hunger to understand some of the 'inexhaustible mysteries of life'. The prayers, then, are useful barometers to the troughs and swells in Deakin's faith.

Previously he had prayed for the capacity to serve, to be granted 'greatness & thoroughness of service', although not necessarily in politics, so that he might be 'chosen as one of the instruments in working out Thy Will'.[13] After the Grand Prophecy a new theme appears, a new confidence and refinement of aim. His prayers were now for power to achieve that service, beseeching God to 'let me have no ambition for power but for usefulness'. The first unequivocal declaration for that Mission of national endeavour appears in an August 1888 prayer:

> O God grant me that judgment & foresight which will enable me to serve my country— guide me & strengthen me, so that I may follow & persuade others to follow the path which shall lead to the elevation of national life & thought & permanence of well earned prosperity—give me light & truth & influence for the highest & the highest only.[14]

We know that permanence of prosperity was not vouchsafed to Victoria. But this plea for divinely inspired secular service, penned more than a year before Parkes made his famous pronouncement, is pragmatic; it asks that a singular trait of character, Deakin's influence as conciliator, might be used toward a higher purpose. Prayer LII inscribed the following month asks: 'Let me know my special task if I have one, my special power if I have one, or let me grasp at the general duty which belongs to me as a man in my true place, calling & capacity.'[15]

Along with the 'occasional visitation of fire & strength' came doubts about his Mission, especially during the dark years of economic collapse of 1892–3. Above all else he wished that his utmost effort might be 'wrung' from him.[16] In more confident moments he felt he could read 'Thy will in the course of events' and asked to 'obey the demands of my time & country ... so that I fill the need which would otherwise be unfilled'.[17] Yet as before in times of tension, journals throughout 1889 spoke of being torn between 'two voices', whether to serve the 'laws & functions of the state' or 'another quieter & holier way.'[18] This conflict, framed in Idealist terms, was succinctly expressed in a later prayer: 'that I am guided is plain—That I err & fail is plainer. That I must submit & accept my lot & yet that I must spurn it & aspire is incontestable.'[19] To this existential dilemma of vocation, which continued well into Deakin's federal career, were added strong doubts as to his health and capacities. In a typical prayer he bemoaned a life that had seen 'youth fled & manhood beginning to flee with naught accomplished such as I aspire to.' He prayed that he might spend his 'short life & feeble forces' to the best account—'Let me feel again the pressure of Thy hand upon me & see the pointing of Thy finger', he asked in 1890, '& know even in failure that I am about Thy chosen work.'[20] Yet his next prayer, written a month later after the successful debate in the Victorian Parliament on the forthcoming convention, shows little trace of this sombre pleading: 'Gracious God who hast been pleased to make me Thine instrument in what appears to be success in a good cause, I thank Thee that Thou hast given to me a small contributory part in forward movements.'[21]

On 3 August 1890, his thirty-fourth birthday, Deakin visited his childhood homes in George and Gore Streets, Fitzroy. The prayer written on this special day, always an occasion for deep reflection, illustrates the augmenting theme of 'feebleness', and reveals a stark realisation of advancing age: 'Youth has passed & manhood unfolded to its full, but I find myself still feeble, still doubting, still uncertain of my life & part, still a scholar learning little & all unfit to rise or rule.'[22] As usual he declared his unfitness to lay claim to 'worldly ease & blessings.' This perception of an unearned political rise, like that of 'feebleness' is a significant view of self that gradually recedes in the federal era. Fortunate and blessed in every respect with adoring parents and sister, with wife and family, with success in business and ministerial politics, how could he claim no right to them? He would wish, in the life remaining:

> to retain the hope, the enthusiasm, the trust of youth with such ripeness as my nature permits of at its maturity ... I would also crave to do something for my country & my kind, if ever so fractional, & pray to be shattered & crucified, rather than aid anything contrary to Thy will & Their elevation. Let me serve somewhere & somehow Thy purposes & for myself I seek no more.[23]

He turned then to inscribe 'Clue' 423, noting that 'in prayer there is at times an outbursting of passion & a returning glow which seems a response.'[24] Recorded on the anniversary of his birth after a sentimental journey, these thoughts bear considerable conviction but, it should be noted, they also reveal an underlying egoism in an aspiration that seeks power, and in the unspoken assumption that he would take a leading role in future events.

A subtle shift is observed during the six years since Deakin began the regular habit of inscribing these prayers. Earlier doubts as to a Divine government became doubts as to his part in a Greater Plan, and finally as to whether this Plan, now intimately including him, was best aided through these public exertions. We note the sacrificial image of 'crucifixion' and the continuing tension between higher and lower in his nature, a disjunction between a consummate success in the material sphere and an aspiration to transcend it intellectually, morally and spiritually.

Extravagant speculation in urban land values, and the resulting depression, together with public displeasure over railway appropriations and the government's handling of the maritime strike conspired to bring down the Deakin–Gillies government in October 1890. On 10 August Deakin noted wrily: 'Socialists decapitated my effigy.' That night he prayed for 'Thy Truth [to] elevate & stimulate my faltering steps in the path of duty'.[25] Frank Anstey and others have contended that Deakin and the Cabinet were trying to suppress the workers' right to strike, but current prayers seem to belie this view, at least so far as they record his own highest intentions. On 30 August, the day of the riots, he sought wisdom to 'act with power & promptitude to suppress violence' but he asked also that 'the enfranchisement of the many should receive no check', and that the 'bonds of labour be loosened for the free growth of humanity.'[26] The swearing in of 2000 special constables equipped with batons resembled Wellington's measures against the Chartists in 1848, when Pearson had been among those enrolled by the 'forces of order' while a student at King's College, which suggests that he was instrumental to the government's tactics in combating the 'gasconade and violence' of those who were 'endeavouring to incite the passions of the unionists.'[27]

Nevertheless as responsible minister Deakin was held accountable for the infamous Cabinet decision to send in the Mounted Rifles. Several years later in

Parliament, the Labor member for Footscray and leading trade unionist, with the improbable name John Hancock, accused the coalition government of 'bringing out the gatlings to shoot a pickpocket', but sought to excuse him personally. Deakin responded quickly and emotionally, taking full responsibility for the Cabinet decision.[28] His petition to his God at the height of the riots, if it was not empty rationalisation, confirms that he had agonised over the matter, but in keeping with the public trust, he had seen his paramount duty as keeping the peace, not as Hancock suggested, against the workers, but against the 'reckless and lawless' elements who would have turned the anarchic situation to their own advantage.[29]

Following a vote of no-confidence on 30 October, the coalition was removed from office. Deakin turned to the law for the first time in earnest, unlike his desultory practice in the late 1870s, working hard to repay the 'calls' after losing both his own and his father's savings in the waning days of the 'boom'. From 1892 he remained a private member. On the same day that the ministry fell, David Syme offered to send him to Egypt to write some articles on irrigation. It would be a welcome respite from the unpleasant events surrounding the strike, enabling him to recover his diminished health. They agreed on India.[30] Characteristically Deakin put the three months away to productive use. *Irrigated India* was a sequel to *Irrigation in Western America*, an exhaustive survey of India's massive projects under the Raj. He also found time for a series of articles for the *Age*, later collected as *Temple and Tomb in India*. This was a personal and at times eloquent guided journey through the spiritual centres of India, especially its history and religious architecture, as with his alliterative impression of the Taj Mahal:

> White as poppies are, when their pale petals fleck the ryot's fenceless fields, like flocks of fairy butterflies; white as the lotus is, floating upon the sacred pools of the south, as the camellia is, but free from its formality; white within and without, as the incomparable lily is ... the wealth and witchery of this marvellous mausoleum are artistically transformed to forms and hues, suggesting purity and chastity alone ... A shrine rather than a tomb, in which the stone of despair is rolled from the sepulchre, and its gloom irradiated as with the glory of a shining presence, this peerless pearl of visionary loveliness, fascinating the mind, and ravishing the memory, also seeks, finds and subdues the heart ...[31]

Within a fortnight of his return Deakin was off with his family to Sydney for the National Australasian Convention. Almost immediately conflicts surfaced between Liberals and Conservatives, Freetraders and Protectionists, 'small' and 'large' colonies, generating considerable acrimony in some quarters. The Victorians' bitter experiences with the 'obstructables' in the Legislative Council caused them to regard deadlocks, the co-ordinate powers of the two chambers, and the money powers of the Senate as important issues; and the weight of debate on these matters testifies to their influence in both conventions. Deakin's only speech at Sydney did not mince words. Losing momentarily the mantle of conciliator he declared that, like other radical Liberals, he wanted responsible government 'answerable only to one Chamber, and that Chamber responsible to the whole people'.[32] The convention produced a skeleton Constitution through the efforts of that remarkable jurist, Sir Samuel Griffith, which served as the basis of debate at both conventions, though the second was ostensibly begun from scratch. With the appearance of a Constitution, as Dr Quick put it, 'the era of vague generalities ended, and the era of close criticism began.'[33]

In May 1891, with the hectic convention over, Deakin returned to his prayer book after 'long silence, great changes, distant voyages, & new experiences, both of myself & the world' for his first entry in over six months. He offered thanks for being 'carried at least passably through great affairs'. Despite the apparent fortunes of the Federation movement, this prayer has a strangely depressive quality whose cause is left undefined: 'I turn O God once more to Thine altar stairs & with a sad faith, half doubting & half-ashamed, [I] bow down my brow to where my knees have been before.'[34] It is a dramatic, if not a ridiculous, image. Perhaps his recent conversations with the touring Theosophical leader, the American Colonel H. J. Olcott whom he heard lecture on Buddhism, had given him a poignant perspective on his own egoism, of which in later years he was all too aware. He was also beginning with many others to realise the full effects of the economic depression. In any case, speaking of his 'humiliation' he now stood before God 'colder harder denser coarser & feebler' than ever before, blessed yet 'fallen, thankless, indifferent, more selfish in confession'.[35]

By the end of November disaster had struck. The crisis in Victoria was exacerbated by the inept handling of the Munro government, and building societies were beginning to close their doors. It was a time of extreme confusion, and efforts toward Federation were stalled for several years. Deakin did not escape the public odium. Images of 'purity' and expiation are prominent in writings of the period, and they bespeak his puzzlement and his sense of shared responsibility for the disaster. '[O]nce more the waters have gone over me. I am drowned in dissidences, all faith eludes my grasp ...'.[36]

As chairman of directors of the City of Melbourne Building Society, an established company that had suffered a fate similar to more questionable ventures, Deakin was to chair a stockholders' meeting on 3 December 1891. On the previous night he prayed for 'wisdom & ... courage to temper the blow ... & guidance to enable me to assist to rescue them in the best way ... so that our country may reap only good & useful lessons from its privations'.[37] The next day a crowd of four of five hundred disappointed people were gathered, less interested in 'good & useful lessons' than in getting their money back. A magazine article tells how Deakin stood at the door silent and possessed, as those who would 'gladly have shaken his hand a week ago, and felt honoured with the touch' now walked past with heads averted. But as he rose to speak, an incredible transformation occurred; his oratory worked its magic, and his speech was a masterpiece of exposition: 'in a twinkle every man in the room was in possession of every fact relating to the society, and then the appeal to their manhood'.[38]

A 'Clue' written a few days later took the cosmic perspective, arguing a vaguely social Darwinist line that 'Nature's purposes run through us, use us, & achieve themselves independently of our selfish existence.'[39] A repatriated English journalist explained that what English financiers could not comprehend was the 'colossal incompetency, the utter lack of the commonest caution and the outright barefaced dishonesty' in that great game of 'Grab' as played in Australia, and in Victoria in particular. He asked Deakin if he would now 'play the Herculean part of cleaning the Augean stable of dishonesty and incapability with a stream of your eloquence?'[40]

With the Queensland shearers practising drill and erecting barricades against the pastoralists, and the rancour of the defeated maritime workers still alive, some considered these hard times as precursors to revolution, as suggested by two seances

Deakin attended when tensions were at their height. On 9 August he heard through Mrs Cohen:

> Great changes within 12 months, probably less, political & a revival of industry. depression pass away—hold hand federation if carried as it is other colonies will combine for free trade & adopting free trade lead to terrible blow to Melbourne & to a local uprising like a revolution ...[41]

Did Deakin merely record, or did he really believe, that other colonies would gang up on Victoria to force free trade, and that this might lead to an armed uprising? The alleged communicator, Dr Motherwell, advised a month later: 'self from Dr Rest on oars—Quite satisfied mantle for dangers—action change of Govt few months shall be called suddenly'.[42]

He should 'rest on oars', that is, relax his efforts for Federation, now that his 'capacity for public usefulness' was diminished, as were 'my possibilities of literary work ... by this failure which appears to push me back into private life & professional drudgery'.[43] The repayment of his father's money and the support of his family were further considerations. On the first day of January 1892 Deakin took up *Stephens Digest* before going back into chambers. A letter from Charles Pearson rendered sound advice in the hope that 'you will stay at the bar long enough to make a moderate competence, before you take a leading position again.' There was nothing to risk, he insisted, for 'you can command the highest place in Parliament whenever you wish for it.'[44] It is another impressive index to the substance of Deakin's faith that even at this nadir in personal and federal fortunes, he was improving his knowledge of the law and scrupulously repaying his many debts, until the right moment for action toward Federation would be revealed by the Providence guiding events:

> About once more to change my walk of life I do so despairing of usefulness in my public life, waiting for further developments of events which are subject to Thy will, & also in the faith that this divergence may fit me in the general opinion & in some degree in actuality, for a return to larger responsibilities under more auspicious conditions.[45]

To Charles Dilke in England he communicated his intention to write a book about 'The Coming Commonwealth'.[46] His private writing at this time includes a significant outburst of speculation on death in verse and prose, and strangely dissociated narratives, some of which we shall consider later. The principal themes in Deakin's prayers were failure at a personal level, and a consciousness of having reached a halfway point in life with little accomplished. Common enough throughout his writings, these sentiments acquired a greater intensity in these dark days. But there was hope too, and an abiding faith in the Cause.

A prayer dated 13 February 1892 begs for the 'virtue of sincerity & the voice of truth' so as to 'speak the word & do the deed best for this country & its people'. Theosophical ideas, and probably the influence of his recent tour of India, informed Deakin's wish to 'extinguish the ego', to subordinate his private and public aims so that he might repeat the message 'without admixture & without regard to the welcome it may procure for me'.[47] More significant is the recurring image of himself as 'channel'. He had recently discovered in Xenophon's *Memorabilia* a very different Socrates from that presented in Plato's *Dialogues*, as a mystic who had claimed guidance throughout his life from a *daimon,* or voice of admonition. One journal proclaims excitedly: 'Socrates accused of evoking spirits ... *this is new.*'[48] And three months later in a parody on Demosthenes entitled 'Truth! Truth! Truth!', Deakin identifies even more closely with Socrates when he asked to 'enter the places of public speech', and devoting himself 'absolutely to the endeavour':

> to say therein the best of which I am capable as if there stood before me at all times some sign of Thy presence & resounding in my ear a voice of admonition & exhortation to Truth ...[49]

The phenomenon of a 'voice', as we shall see, would assume profound significance in the private religion of the older Alfred Deakin.

The period from early 1893 to the 'bank holiday' in May was an especially gloomy time to live in Victoria. The Dibbs government in New South Wales, with Opposition support from George Reid, avoided disaster by passing a Bank Issue Bill.[50] As Deakin informed Pearson in England, the news was not good; there was a threatened foreclosure by the Bank of New South Wales of the Union Finance Co., in which he had 800 shares, and he was 'drained dry by similar calls in other institutions'.[51] In September 1892 and again two months later Deakin was 'Pressed to take leadership' by the powerful David Syme.[52] He resisted, wishing to maintain the independence to speak out on issues, as he explained in letters to Parkes and Royce, and to devote himself exclusively to 'the great cause of the nation.'[53]

The Federation issue was enjoying a revival by the beginning of 1893, even if Victoria's finances were not. Through the militancy of the A.N.A., a conference was organised in August at Corowa, where the novel 'Quick formula' put life back in the movement.[54] The motives for such a revival were mixed. The depression and bank failures had subdued Victoria, and made intercolonial free trade behind a national tariff wall a more attractive prospect for Victorian manufacturers. A common defence was another important factor, since the 'yellow Hordes' as well as the French and Germans were still perceived as threats.[55] During these lean years in federal fortunes, while practising at the Bar Deakin continued his advocacy of the 'one true faith' of federalism via direct involvement in organisation, in the Victorian Parliament, through speeches, interviews and articles like one, arising from his new passion of cycling, entitled 'What Federation means to every cyclist, tourist and colonist', along with a prodigious personal correspondence.[56]

In Victoria, the links between the A.N.A. and the Federation Leagues were very close. Dr John Quick was president of both in Bendigo, one of the bastions of federal sentiment. When a central Federation League was formed by Edmund Barton in Sydney, the Prahran branch of the A.N.A., of which Deakin was a member, proposed a Victorian League, formed on 4 June 1894, to link up with Barton's efforts. Deakin was indefatigable in the campaign leading up to its formation. During 1893 he presided over the A.N.A. Metropolitan Federation Conference, and helped to plan an educational campaign. He also addressed numerous country and suburban branches. He courted the establishment, addressing the Chamber of Manufactures and Trades Hall, the Council of Melbourne University, the Sons of Temperance, the Railways Union, Derham's Victorian Employers Union, and the Law Clerks Association, also rallying Parkes, Berry, Shiels and other luminaries to preach the virtues of Federation. He believed Federation would succeed only by the 'labours of the everactive band in whose hands fortune will place the trowel that will strike the foundation'. A reporter has left the image of Deakin's hectic life in these days 'rushing from court to a Federal Executive meeting, then away with bag and rug, then to court next morning'.[57]

The exit from Spiritualism in the early 1880s had been induced partly by its inane contradictions and a poverty of theoretical basis. In Swedenborg, and again in Theosophy, Deakin sought a synthesis. If Spiritualism was too vague, and Swedenborg too confidently dogmatic and Christian, the lofty aims and sweeping generalities of Theosophy seemed to blend the best of all these, incorporating the 'spiritistic outbreak' within a more or less coherent theoretical system. At the suggestion of the remarkable Dr Annie Besant (now president of the society following Blavatsky's death) during her visit in 1894, Deakin became a member of the society for a trial period, even forming the 'Ibis' branch that met in his home, of which he was secretary.[58] He resigned after one year, and on the same day he joined the Australian Church. During the 1890s Deakin regularly attended the Australian Church more or less weekly, sometimes with his daughters or his sister, but seldom with Pattie. He contributed articles as 'Student' to the organ of the church, the *Australian Herald*, on topics like 'In the Beginning' and 'The gospel of Buddha', which defends the doctrines of karma and reincarnation. Prayers around this time reflect these influences in paradoxical statements like: 'Nothing for myself but all for others, for myself only when not a self & when devoted to others.'[59]

In these middle years of his relatively short active life—Deakin died at sixty-three, but the last decade was a lengthy period of sad decline—a compulsion for private literary expression remained, and its modes even increased, but in different directions than in his young manhood, when he had aspired to creative endeavours. Prayers and gospels satisfied the emotional and intellectual aspects of his faith; 'Clues' continued to fulfil a more 'literary' role, varying from tidbits gleaned from reading and observations on life, to story sketches and reflections on the activity of writing. Just as he compartmentalised his life between private, family, and public, so too he compartmentalised his writing into 'zones', at least until the period of his decline.

Deakin's prayers seem somewhat akin to the automatic writing of former years, the hand rapidly forming the words even as the thoughts came into the consciousness, only now the 'dictation' came from a higher source, whether within or outside the self is never made clear, though it mattered not, for he believed this influx to emanate ultimately from Deity. In this way aspiration and inspiration were linked in a two-way process. Powerful and evocative metaphors attest to the emotional stress in some passages. On 12 May 1895, for instance, he asks that he might take 'the quivering flesh & force it though it be against iron with the sense of going forward & fulfilling what lies within my power—Utility ... conquest ... victory & defeat are not without but within'.[60] The mood in prayers varied from such heights of devotional feeling to depths of contrition and self-blame, but it always invoked the Ideal.

Deakin's literary indexes and journals, principally 'Clues' (also the 'Medley') continued the more exteriorised reflection, such as commentaries on his reading. Commenting in 1893 on Milton's *Paradise Lost*, Deakin focused on its hopeless incongruities: though there had never been war in Heaven, after the Fall all the angels are 'armed, drilled, organised & practiced in strife'; there are no female angels, no employment except in 'military exercises, song dance & banquet', and he points out the want of interest in a combat in which only one side can be wounded or injured, and of a Heaven where God the Father 'speaks in sarcasms'; he concludes that 'the style saves it all.'[61]

Other 'Clues' include occasional story lines, like one from November 1885 where he renders a deft outline, suggesting a personal experience in these days of continuing struggles between squatters and selectors. 'An Australian Sketch', probably arising from his irrigation experience, treats of a Royal Commission: 'its political secretary, its anti-physical, spectacled, narrow theoretical town chairman, land question, the members, the table, men, partisans ... bush towns-people, famous homestead, narrowness of other kind, things of chips & sawdust, & painful literalness'. One wishes he had filled in the sketch further.[62]

Private reflections in 'Clues' and other journals frequently throw light on public events. Looking back on the dark years of the depression when conditions began to improve, Deakin included himself in his trenchant observation that the 'Day of Humiliation & Prayer' then proclaimed by the churches had really meant 'humiliation at failing to make money & prayer to be able to make it in the future', when it ought to have been 'humiliation at the descent into self-consciousless greed & prayer for higher ideals & purer living.'[63]

On 24 May 1895 Deakin experienced a spiritual breakthrough. Prayer CCXIII introduces a new tone of optimism, even ebullience, absent during the dark years of economic malaise, mixed with a strange sense of resignation concerning spiritual gifts:

> At last! O God! At last! I turn to Thee with no pitiful prayer for self, but with a deep & perfect thankfulness pouring out of my whole being for the answer that Thou has vouchsafed to my fitful & broken prayers ... The Light has shone around me all my life but my darkened gaze was unable to discern it until now. I have at last bathed myself in its flood & seen enough & more than enough to render me humble, submissive & content. I have at last realised that I am neither entitled nor qualified to perceive more, that I have no need of more, that far more has been discovered to me than I can put into practice...[64]

Whatever Deakin came to understand on this day was connected to the paradoxical notion that his former blindness was due to his narrow absorption with 'seeing' in the Swedenborgian sense. He understood now that 'the clear duty lying before me is to spread the light I have, to absorb it into my own narrow character & shallow ability, so that I may make myself as a gutter pool does a mirror, for its reflection to any observant eye.' The metaphor of the gutter pool suggests that he now felt empowered, though soiled, weak and imperfect as he knew himself to be, to serve, to reflect Truth according to the limits of his capacity. Probably his formal connection with Theosophy bade him consider his former egotism, and in the rising tide of renewed interest in Federation he discerned at long last signs of a coming triumph. He now prayed for:

> the power to pray unceasingly, the energy to work unweariedly & wisely, the devotion that will annihilate self, the courage that will ignore obstacles, the insight that will despise a career, the patience fearing no rebuff or failure, the resolution unshaken & unsubdued; the judgment that will guide all effort; the affection that will permit itself no resentments reproach or regret—God Almighty help me to fulfill my pledges my vows to Thee now Thou hast overwhelmed me with mercies innumerable grace unspeakable & with a signal blessing of Thy Light.[65]

Some powerful experience, we cannot know what, took hold of Deakin on this day. Was it one of those 'visitations, lofty ideas, high purposes, generous moods & noble aspirations' that at times 'descend upon or glow before me, bringing with them glimmerings of deep blessedness & pure peace'?[66] The date may be a clue: the 'sudden changes' insight jotted at the back of his diary, transcribed and then expanded when he returned from England in 1887 also bore the date 24 May, although this could be mere coincidence, as indeed might be his joining of the Australian Church exactly one year later. Taken in context this prayer proclaims a reconsecration to 'my pledges my vows', to the Ideal.

From 1895 Federation was more assured, after the 'excellent agreement' achieved at the meeting of the Federal Council and the Premiers held in tandem in Hobart.[67] The 1896 Bathurst 'Peoples' Convention' generated further momentum, as did the Enabling Act legislation and the positive action of the newly elected Reid government in New South Wales, in placing Federation at the top of its agenda, which superficially at least challenges Deakin's opinion of George Reid as an enemy of Federation. Following a great deal of lobbying and intrigue, which included further conferences between the Victorian Premier George Turner and Reid, a convention was organised to meet in Adelaide in March 1897. The popular election of delegates showed a more democratic intent than in 1891. The *Age* put forward ten candidates in Victoria, all of them elected, with Deakin polling third. Upon receiving the results, Deakin turned to his book of prayers, expressing first his thankfulness, then his aspiration for the convention:

> Infinite Spirit of Unity Order & Harmony, be present with us in our gathering of representatives, fitting us our words & work & aims utterly & absolutely to Thy divine will for the best results to Thy people here & elsewhere, to all Thy peoples everywhere & to the coming of Thy Kingdom ...[68]

Then he prayed for himself:

> For myself O God obliterate me thoroughly, shut my self & my interests from my sight or consciousness, in my surrender to Thy will as Thine instrument, for any office however mean or poor in the opinion of others or in my own, so that I subserve Thy Beneficence, Thy Justice & Thy Love.

Two days later Deakin again asked for 'sufficient clearness of vision or sufficient antagonism of failure' to carry through these endeavours that would 'affect potent causes operating for far-distant times'. At the convention's first venue in Adelaide, following the election of Charles Kingston as president and other formalities, they went to a Government House garden party, where they were entertained by an 'Indian juggler'.[69]

At these second conventions during 1897-8, Deakin's desire to keep a low profile was motivated partly by an awareness of the general unpopularity of the Victorians over issues like stock taxes, railway rates, and Protection generally. Convinced of his mandate and aware of his own strong points—'affability', natural good humour, popularity with all men, unquestioned integrity—he left greater constitutional experts to plan and debate while once again with self-effacing, though not obsequious, humility he took a subordinate but crucial role.

Though he minimised its religious guiding motive, Professor La Nauze remarked that 'even in the public record his devotion to his self-imposed role is evident.'[70] What is remarkable about Deakin's work over these seven years is the consistency of the role he had marked out for himself as far back as August 1888 in that first petition for the 'elevation of national life'.[71] That role, so far as we may glimpse it, was manifest most clearly in Deakin's efforts to create an harmonious atmosphere where the best work could be produced by delegates called to their highest Ideal. It was in 1897 an older and wiser, but no less devoted 'apostle' who again set to work to be the midwife of Federation.

Deakin was aware that it is difficult to steer events, for it takes a good grasp of the individual to influence him effectively, especially if he came determined to defend certain political principles, regional interests or prejudices. This is not to say that on some issues, particularly those dealing with 'moral' questions, he was in any way reluctant to press his views on the convention floor. As a Temperance man, Deakin was for the retention of control of alcohol and opium by the States; he supported the proposal even though it endangered the principle that commerce between States should remain 'absolutely free'. Nor as a radical Victorian was he inhibited in expressing strong views on issues like the 'deadlock' provisions and money powers of the Senate.[72] He favoured Canadian-style responsible government, but without a nominee Senate and States lacking 'virility and individuality'; and he did not want a U.S.-style administration, with its extra-parliamentary executive.

The delegates had voted to start afresh in considering the Constitution, but in fact they largely adopted Griffith's 1891 draft. We first see Deakin lobbying delicately but energetically for his 'compromise of 1891' when, following a South Australian measure, he had proposed that the Senate should have power only to accept or reject, but also to make 'suggestions' on amendments to money bills. George Reid opposed the idea, believing that any Senate power of 'suggestion' would lend it equal status with the Lower House. Deakin was convinced of the need for a balanced Constitution, with an Upper House 'of weight', but he also wanted a limitation of the Senate's veto; as there are to be two Houses, one must predominate, just as 'when two men ride a horse, one must ride behind.'[73] Before the vote on 14 April 1897, while on a visit to Broken Hill, Deakin, along with Wise, Abbott and O'Connor, was lobbying the Tasmanians Lewis and Brown, whose votes for the compromise were crucial; they agreed, and the measure was later passed on a division by just two votes. His diary playfully referred to this as 'Proprietary time'.[74]

Deakin brought even more conspicuous lobbying to bear on other issues like federal legislative power over old-age and invalid pensions. Initially proposed by Howe, this measure was finally won a few weeks later on a second division. As Professor La Nauze observed, the Victorians who changed their votes in the interim—Higgins, Turner, Fraser, Zeal and Trenwith—very likely did so with the assistance of Deakin, 'the most persuasive of men', who urged them to take account of strong Victorian trade-union support of the federal power.[75] Regarding fiscal matters, Reid quipped that asking New South Wales to join without resolving the issue was 'like a reformed drunkard setting up house with five unreformed brethren, leaving the question of beverages to be decided later by majority vote.'[76] Another measure 'Deakin's clause' provided for the maintenance of duties on intercolonial imports for Western Australia on a 20 per cent per year diminishing scale.[77] His energetic lobbying for this provision, although it too went against his own political principles, helped to secure Western Australia for the union and circumvented another round of tariff squabbles that could have rent the fragile cohesion so painfully built up in the previous sessions. With masterful powers of conciliation, and a sound political sense, Deakin knew when to retreat and how much to concede.

Curiously enough, given his private sensibilities, Deakin had little to do publicly with the 'religious' issues at the conventions, the 'recognition' of God in the preamble and Section 116 of the Constitution, which prohibits religious tests and official favour or prejudice toward any religion. He supported and probably helped promote the sentiment expressed in the preamble: 'humbly relying upon the blessing of Almighty God', although his preference for 'Divine Providence' was rejected, like his other proposal to 'unite in' a federal Commonwealth.[78] Considerable pressure was applied on the already harassed delegates from bodies like the National Scripture Education League on one side, and the Catholics, secularists and Seventh Day Adventists on the other. In the final days of the Melbourne convention Patrick McMahon Glynn, a South Australian barrister and a Catholic put forward by the 'recognitionists' to give the cause an interdenominational aura, moved the 'recognition' amendment to the preamble.[79] Glynn had conferred with unspecified others, one of whom almost certainly was Deakin, whose only public contribution to this debate was a humorous jibe against the Victorian Legislative Council. A related issue was that of prayers in Parliament, and when in reply to a question it was reported that openings of the Legislative Council included reading the Lord's Prayer, Deakin quipped that 'nearly all the members know it now.'[80]

With a hiatus to permit the Premiers to sail to England to attend Queen Victoria's Golden Jubilee, the convention met in close conference for over five months in the twelve-month period from its opening session in Adelaide in March 1897. It was an exhausting process, with delegates assembling thereafter in Sydney, then in Melbourne for another sweltering summer session as in 1890. The Melbourne session was the most arduous. Working sometimes until 4 a.m. delegates would commence again at 10.30 a.m. the next day. Deakin's diary notes frequent exhaustion and acute diarrhoea. In a letter he complained of 'no time for any literary work—no time to think—sometimes not enough to live.'[81] Delegates were trying to iron out the last items of contention, and already bearing the pressure of competing parochial interests in their colonies. It is small wonder that the *Federal Story*, commenced around this time, speaks of 'conditions of great nervous exhaustion and irritability' attending the delegates.[82]

But with Federation apparently so close, in these waning years of the 1890s decade there arose several unexpected hurdles, whose crossing would further tax Deakin's conciliatory powers, and his energies: firstly in forcing the dramatic turnaround of the *Age*; then the first failed referendum, and the successful efforts of the Federalists on a second try in 1899, followed by the 'defence' of the Constitution in London; and finally the 'Hopetoun blunder' which almost saw William Lyne, an enemy of Federation, become the first Prime Minister of the Commonwealth.

On 15 March 1898, while the Federation Convention was in the crucial last week in its final session in Melbourne, Deakin was called away by a previous engagement to address the annual conference of the Australian Natives Association at Bendigo. On this Ides of March, given his strong belief in significant dates, in portents and prophecy, he might well have mused on the inauspicious date and pondered its implications for their present labours. On the train to Bendigo, Deakin would have occasion for gloomy reflection on the numerous present obstacles to Federation, and some confusion about events he believed to be in essence divinely mandated.

Having survived a savage depression, colonial antagonisms and public apathy, the Federation movement, its fortunes always 'trembling in the balance', was again in danger from several quarters. As they were nearing the end of an exhausting process of deliberation and debate, there was still no consensus among delegates on the Australian Constitution Bill soon to be put to public referendum in each colony, and these last weeks were alive with bargaining over fundamental issues, even about the desirability of a federal compact. Rallied against the Bill were practically the whole of New South Wales, and in Victoria Higgins and the 'radical and labour wing'. Even more ominous was opposition from David Syme, fearing a diminished role for his newspaper, and through his pervasive influence, from the Turner ministry, which included three ministerial delegates to the Convention.

If, already into his Federation narrative and feeling the general atmosphere of gloom, Deakin did regard the date as an inauspicious omen, it seems to have spurred him on to redouble his efforts. His celebrated 'Bendigo speech' delivered late that evening with considerable fire and eloquence, in what many contemporaries regarded as being among his highest flights of oratory, urged the A.N.A. stalwarts:

> Let us nail our standard to the mast. Let us stand shoulder to shoulder in defence of the enlightened liberalism of the constitution. Let us recognise that we live in an unstable era, and that, if we fail in the hour of crisis, we may never be able to recall our lost national opportunities.[83]

Deakin's diary records that he 'Declared for Bill' and that there was 'Immense enthusiasm'.[84] Privately, the 'providential' interlocution of the A.N.A. conference reinforced his conviction that this and myriad other events on the rocky path to Federation formed part of a Greater Purpose, and perhaps for this reason his narrative attaches too much importance to it. Yet it is clear that the exhortations of Deakin and J. L. Purves, another A.N.A. enthusiast for Federation, in defiance of Syme and his lieutenants, did have important political consequences; they gave the lead, and a new impetus to the flagging faith of the 'natives' at this important juncture in the protracted Federation campaign.

Deakin's 'Bendigo speech' has rightly been judged a watershed in Federation history.[85] But there was a personal side to the episode. He closed with a tribute to a local poet, William Gay, who had died only three months previously. Although they never met, for the last three years or so of his short and penurious life, Gay had maintained a correspondence with Deakin, in which they discussed art, politics and philosophy. Deakin had Gay's poetry reviewed in newspapers and journals, and even used his political influence on Gay's behalf toward the end to make his way easier. Now, in a characteristic gesture at once elegant and opportune, Deakin asked his audience to remember 'the stirring appeal of the young poet of genius ... whose grave is not yet green in your midst', quoting the sestet from William Gay's sonnet on Federation:

> *Our country's garment*
> *With hands unfilial we have basely rent,*
> *With petty variance our souls are spent,*
> *And ancient kinship under foot is trod:*
> *O let us rise,—united,—penitent,—*
> *And be one people,—mighty, serving God!*[86]

Had it been merely a device for rounding off an appeal to work for the 'Cause', Gay's poem would still have substance, and relevance to the occasion, although in a silent emendation Deakin changed the first line from 'Her seamless garment, at great Mammon's nod'. Rather than being merely the 'contrived "happy touch" of the skilful politician',[87] Deakin's gesture was in the nature of a personal tribute to the poet.

Apart from the private dimension of its closing, the Bendigo speech crystallised A.N.A. support, the rank and file passing a unanimous resolution for the Bill. Against formidable opposition as Deakin tells it, a handful of young 'natives'—among them Deakin's friends Hume Cook, Theodore Fink and W. H. Watt—finding that Deakin along with Dr Quick was 'prepared to support the Bill at all hazards and against all adversaries', threatened Alexander Peacock, Education Minister and member of the A.N.A. Executive, with a breach.[88] He fell into line, and through him so did the Cabinet. The defiant and impassioned pleas at Bendigo by Deakin and Purves to members to 'seize the opportunity to leap to the front and make the measure theirs'[89] brought Syme, sensing public opinion, to a nominal support of the Bill on 31 May 1898, the eve of the poll.[90] More important still, although the Bill was lost in the first referendum in June, the solid Victorian support ultimately helped carry the day for the Federalists, after further haggling and concessions to New South Wales, in a second referendum the following year.

Deakin wrote that 'other influences' were brought to bear on Trenwith, the only Labor delegate to the convention, so that at the end of that important week, on the last day of the Melbourne convention, he also declared for the Bill. His endorsement was crucial in swaying the trade unions and helping to counter claims that the Constitution was a 'conservative' document. The prompting probably came from Deakin. Regarding these events, Professor La Nauze commented that there is at least a case for believing: 'that in taking action to secure their public endorsement of the bill, if not their wholehearted enthusiasm, Deakin's part in the victory was not less significant than his direct appeals to the public.'[91]

For Deakin it served as another signpost of the essential Providence guiding the movement. Still fascinated with the place of 'chance' in human affairs, in the *Federal Story* Deakin speculated that if a few 'ardent Federalists' had wavered, or if 'the handful of young members of the A.N.A. had not intervened just when and where they did',[92] the 'merely selfish energy' would have died down since an enthusiasm for union, manifest in all to some extent, was the dominating factor 'only among the young, the imaginative, and those whose patriotism was Australian or Imperial'.[93] In this praise of the patriotic sons of the soil, echoes of Herbert Spencer and of current myths of the 'Coming Man' are interlaced with Swedenborg's supreme Ideal of Unselfishness. It is clear that Deakin orchestrated these lobbying efforts, but less clear whether in this narrative he was implying a Divine influence at work, or simply commenting on the superb moral character of 'natives' like himself. Having 'accepted' God and separated responsibilities in the Constitution, delegates dispersed to report to their Parliaments and to stump for the Bill at the forthcoming referendum.

Deakin knew men. The marvellous pen portraits in the *Federal Story* attest to his uncanny judgment of their motives, qualities and vices, and his ability to express these in a strong and distinctive style. Privately he mused:

> Men as I find them are not as I expected to find them—Not as in my youth I pictured them—Not as philosophers describe nor yet as cynics portray ... My public life has

shown me little but littleness—Sometimes great talents, rarely fine characters, more rarely still in combination talents of a high order & character able to bear them—Selfishness rules all in much & most in all ...'[94]

Of 'Charlie' Kingston he observed that 'strong passions had crippled his self-development'.[95] William Lyne was 'a crude, sleek, suspicious, blundering, short-sighted backblocks politician'.[96] He called Dr Cockburn of South Australia 'a visionary by nature', and surprisingly he added that he was 'full of heterodox ideas in politics, religion and medicine'.[97] His portrait of the president of the convention, Edmund Barton, reveals a continuing belief in 'physiognomy', and some moralising. His face was a 'true index to the man'; his 'Apollo-like brow and brilliant capacities' offering contrast to his 'fish-like' mouth and 'large jowls', which indicated indulgence, so that his nobler qualities were 'chained to earth by his lazy love of good living.'[98] His masterly portrait of Henry Parkes, 'than whom no actor ever more carefully posed for effect', captures the vanity and pomposity of the man, together with the statesmanlike abilities that made him an effective leader:

> His studied attitudes expressed either distinguished humility or imperious command ... He had always in his mind's eye his own portrait as that of a great man, and constantly adjusted himself to it. A far-away expression of the eyes, intended to convey his remoteness from the earthly sphere, and often associated with melancholy treble cadences of voice in which he implied a vast and inexpressible weariness, constituted his favourite and at last his almost invariable exterior. Movements, gestures, inflexions, attitudes harmonised, not simply because they were intentionally adopted but because there was in him the substance of the man he dressed himself to appear ... He had both by nature and by art the manner of a sage and a statesman.[99]

Deakin saved his most trenchant observations for George Reid. No more opposite character could be found to Deakin, and in his opinions of Reid there was a blind spot: he detested him as a black devil who refused to share Deakin's vision of the federal dream. His catalogue of Reid's faults reads like the Seven Deadly Sins: a rank opportunist, a calculating and unprincipled pariah, a 'clever clerk' whose private life was characterised by 'indolence and geniality', and whose most distinguished accomplishment was as a 'squire of dames'.[100] Deakin sketches an almost predatory character, whose support for Federation was motivated solely by his efforts to undermine Parkes. It is an uncharacteristically jaundiced view. Reid's motives were far from pristine, but he did have claims to his boast to have 'picked Federation out of the gutter', which grated on Deakin considerably.[101] As Professor La Nauze observed, it is hard to reconcile Deakin's picture with the record of Reid's speeches on finance and deadlocks, which show 'both weight and cogency'. Deakin's attitude seems to have been based on a personal revulsion at the corpulence and common aspects of the man; he applied standards of 'manners and fastidiousness rather than of practical effectiveness'.[102] In one speech Deakin admitted that all Liberals were not Protectionists, though they clearly ought to be, and Reid retorted: 'on the principle of standing on your head.' to which Deakin then responded: 'Well if it came to standing on his head, I can understand the reluctance of the honorable member to engage in an exercise of that description.'[103] He blamed Reid's 'Yes/No' speech, in which he damned the Bill but said that he personally would vote 'Yes', for a failure to reach the amended minimum vote of 80,000 in New South Wales. The depth of Deakin's animus is transparent in an *Age* leader he wrote after the defeat of this first referendum on 3 June 1898. It seethes with sarcasm and controlled rage:

> His antagonism to the Bill grew in exact proportion as its prospects improved, until at last, acting from the highest motives, he contrived to bring about the failure of the movement which he claimed to have inaugurated by defeating a Bill he had pledged himself to support.[104]

It is significant, as La Nauze points out, that Deakin says nothing of Barton's own public commitment to some of the same amendments as Reid was seeking. Looked at more dispassionately, Reid's actions, even his early initiatives such as appointing Barton to the Legislative Council to take charge of the Bill, and his consultation with Turner leading to the second conventions, reveal a canny politician rather than a rogue.[105] A prayer inscribed on the day following the first poll alludes to the unsavoury developments he held Reid and his friends accountable for, and expresses his current perplexity: 'Father of Nations receive our psalm of thanksgiving. Enable us to pursue the cause of unity in spite of the obstacles which at present appear to beset our path elsewhere.'[106]

It is relevant to ask, toward what purpose, this Divinely mandated nation building? For some Federation meant simply devising 'a treaty between States'; others regarded it as a 'shabby deal between competing interests'.[107] For men like Deakin, and perhaps Glynn, O'Connor, Quick and others, religiously minded and well versed in the art of compromise and the expediencies of politics, these delegates were doing far more. The Constitution would embody their highest social and political ideals, drawing on the constitutional experience of the mother country and of Switzerland, the United States, Canada and Norway, while modifying the Westminster system to Australian conditions. Moreover for Deakin at least it was a Divine work, sketching the parameters of authority to guide untold generations, a document which could be altered with the 'progress' of society and its institutions, and which represented the highest fruits of reason, which is given by God—'By Thy Light shall we see light' was a favourite Biblical passage—and it would be a work, moreover, created in peace and espousing the best Liberal political principles that negotiations among men could secure.

Was the guiding ideal of Federation for Deakin the millenarian hope of the poet Bernard O'Dowd, or Marcus Clarke's 'Coming Man', or the prospect of a democracy in the Southern Seas to lift the race to its highest expression? Such ideas counted with Deakin, as did the imperialist ethos symbolised by the facile yet powerful metaphor of the 'oak tree' whose branches were the outposts of the New Britannia celebrated in Seeley's very popular *Expansion of England*. A more potent influence yet, especially on his immigration views, was another book written in the less buoyant 1890s by Deakin's mentor Charles Pearson, warning of coming perils to the race and the eventual hegemony through overpopulation of the inhabitants of the 'tropical belt'. *National Life and Character* was widely praised; it represents the current concern with 'National Efficiency', the very opposite to Seeley's smug optimism, while retaining that fundamental faith in the destiny of the Anglo-Saxon race. Deakin, like many in his generation, was greatly influenced by these two works.[108]

Ideas about politics and religion, about the individual and society converge here. Deakin's obedience to a Divine government, and his faith in the evolution of the human species harmonised with his political Liberalism, regarded as in Métin's

'Étatism' as the most effective means of creating the ideal political environment, and some measure of social justice, that would minimise class privileges so that the individual within society might reach his full potential enfranchisement, political, moral and spiritual. As Deakin saw it, they went together. At the Sydney convention, we see how far Deakin had come from his early advocacy of the 'plebiscitium', in criticising what he called B. R. Wise's 'rigid radicalism' calling for a direct referendum:

> A constitution embodies the principle of the rule of the majority not as its working principle or method, but as its final and ultimate test of the work done ... I hold that two Chambers and an Executive, such as we are aiming at, form no less an important part of constitutional government than the ultimate decision of the majority, and are in fact, the essential means by which we arrive at a decision as to what the will of the majority really is.[109]

His strong sense of their responsibilities as 'trustees for posterity'[110] through their present labours, is conveyed in an eloquent speech to the Victorian Parliament after the 1891 convention. In the current atmosphere of great optimism, Deakin had reminded members of the 'higher than human help' they were accustomed to invoke in their proceedings. It was with a feeling of:

> something like awe that we listen—and, while we listen, seem almost to hear the approaching march of the millions yet to be on this continent, the conditions of whose political life and the course of whose national development is perhaps about to be determined.[111]

Within three months of the successful second referendum in July 1899, Deakin's inner life once again underwent a dramatic transformation with a 'voice' heard in October 1899 while he was absorbed in prayer. We shall consider later Deakin's extraordinarily detailed account of this audition, which seems to have served as another 'sign', where the opaque inner life briefly assumes an astounding clarity. Here we note its rejuvenating power in the months ahead, since far from being assured, the fortunes of Federation would continue to 'tremble in the balance', and Deakin would need to marshal all his resources on two further occasions to help save the imperilled union, first from the Colonial Office in London, then from an eleventh-hour coup at home. We note further that as with Deakin's previous journey to the centre of Empire as 'tribune' of the people, an important phase in Australia's destiny in which he would play a central role was heralded by an esoteric private experience which signified a transcendental influence.

In January 1900 Deakin departed for London as Victorian representative to shepherd the Commonwealth Constitution Bill, which now required imperial sanction, through the Imperial Parliament. The three 'natives', Deakin, Barton and Kingston, were determined that the Constitution should pass unaltered from the form in which the Australian electorate had approved it. One point of absolute intransigence by that erstwhile radical Joseph Chamberlain of the Colonial Office, was in regard to Clause 74 on the rights of appeal to the Privy Council. The delegates stonewalled for months, conceding nothing, and they exploited all available avenues of publicity through the press, and through some forty-seven dinners. Finally the capitulation of the Premiers at home forced a compromise, and they managed to limit the right of appeal so that certification was required from the Australian High Court on the agreement of both parties, along with the right of the Commonwealth Parliament to legislate further on future conditions for such appeals. To most people at home this appeared a lawyer's concern, but the delegates knew that without these powers the autonomy of the Constitution would be undermined, since its ultimate interpretation would reside with a distant tribunal, however close the 'crimson thread of kinship'. It would mean, as Deakin had explained in 1891, that Australia 'was unable to produce judges of sufficient learning and ability to pronounce a final judgment' on the Constitution. There were enormous pressures on the delegates; the jubilation they felt when they forced the Bill through with these minimal concessions has been captured by the joyous image of Barton, Kingston and Deakin, with the door in the stately Westminster office closed behind them, reverting to the uninhibited behaviour of childhood, as they held hands and danced in a ring around the centre of the room.[112]

In London Deakin refused a Privy Councillorship, but was persuaded to accept the position of King's Counsel, since refusal would have seemed a strange action for the first Attorney-General of the Commonwealth. Before the ship voyage home Deakin was laid up in Paris for two weeks, suffering from nervous exhaustion and painful carbuncles. One eye was intermittently inflamed for at least two months.[113] For the remaining period of the interregnum until the new century and the birth of the Commonwealth, Deakin was occupied thinking about and planning its future organisation. He frequently prodded Barton to turn his attention to urgent matters like the various contenders for ministerial office, and the representation in Cabinet of the various States. Thus the composition of the Cabinet and the first crucial portfolios and officeholders were largely decided by Deakin and confirmed by a kitchen cabinet of two. Deakin's acute sense of the loyalties and jealousies, of the balance of provincial and national forces are evident in his memorandum to Barton on 26–27 September 1900 on the subject; his proposals were accepted virtually unchanged. He suggested that the head of the federal government 'ought to be termed the "Prime Minister"—a good old English title which will have the advantage of distinguishing him from the State 'premiers' as they are now invariably entitled'.[114]

He was strangely coy about his own inclusion, ostensibly to leave Barton absolute freedom to choose his own Cabinet, but this did not prevent him from commenting on others. In August Deakin remarked that Kingston expressed himself as still uncertain about whether to stand, but this 'I think points to his being a probable starter.'[115] Along with these foundational labours Deakin the journalist and historian, in a kind of house-clearing during a period of relative calm, completed his narrative of the remarkable events he had just lived through, recording that 'combination of circumstances persons and their interrelations' that had now brought them to imminent nationhood. Dashed off in a single draft, the *Federal Story* stands as a masterpiece of political journalism. Unable to remain idle long, he turned then to the beginnings of his career with *Crisis in Victorian Politics 1879–1881*, intended to link up with his Federation narrative. The tidying up of old affairs in preparation for a greater challenge in the national sphere was abandoned in December with the first rumblings of yet another sudden crisis, potentially most damaging for the imminent Commonwealth, which was resolved largely due to the fixity of Deakin's loyalty to Barton, and to his famed diplomatic art.

Arriving two weeks before the celebrations, the Governor-General, Lord Hopetoun, with breathtaking disregard for (or ignorance of) the politics of the moment and perhaps on Reid's advice, 'sent for' William Lyne, assuming that as Premier of the original colony he would automatically become the first Prime Minister of the Commonwealth.[116] He could not have made a poorer choice. Deakin, once over his astonishment and disgust, resolutely refused to join his ministry; his intransigence, together with his intense lobbying, set the tone for others. Lyne for his part was also lobbying energetically. He spoke with Turner, Symon, Holder and others, and even complained to Syme about Barton's 'negligences, unpunctualities, etc.'[117] Familiar behind-the-scenes tactics were fully mobilised to prevent Lyne from forming a strong ministry. That these would in time be added to the litany of providential events made for no less anxiety in the last fortnight of the colonial order. Deakin's motives went further than personal revulsion at the prospect of working under Lyne, whom he had described as a sleek 'backblocks'-style politician of mediocre talents, and an anti-Federalist to boot. His real fears as he wrote to Kingston were that a Lyne ministry could not last long, leaving the way clear for the Freetrader Reid to come in, which would be a calamity for the Protectionists.[118]

In the 'Slough of Despond' in which the Federalists found themselves on the very eve of union, Deakin took charge. Over several days before Christmas he wrote to all his colleagues, imploring them to stand firm. With what he believed to be a Divine mandate, his Duty was clear—he should do his 'best' to ensure that Australia's national life might begin under the best political conditions, with Protectionists and true Federalists at the helm. That this scenario might include himself seems beside the point. Deakin's own expectations, recorded in private notes, were predictably modest: 'later retirement altogether upon very modest earnings outside Federal public service or State unless duties very small to seek for leisure peace & study'.[119] He shared these beliefs with no-one except possibly Herbert Brookes, and as his prayers declare and his actions confirm, Deakin was willing to forgo personal ambition. Writing to Barton when the situation looked gloomiest he expressed what they both knew, that there could be only one answer: 'the Commonwealth first & one's self anywhere or nowhere so as to render the best service in the hour of need'.[120] His words must have caused them both anguish. Reluctantly, he advised Barton to join Lyne. The next day he wrote again, reminding Barton that 'Australia will suffer if you refuse to crucify yourself.'[121] A flurry of telegrams and letters, and shuttling by Deakin between Sydney and Melbourne over the next few days, brought a successful resolution for the Federalists on Christmas Eve.

As with the referendum battle two years before, Deakin again forced the *Age's* hand by applying pressure on the elderly Syme, prepared to sacrifice anything and anyone to ensure the survival of Protectionism, who had endorsed Lyne despite his anti-federalism. Deakin persuaded Syme at last that Barton was essential to the ministry, although part of the price was Lyne's inclusion in the Cabinet. If it was another indication of David Syme's role as power broker in the pre-Commonwealth era, to Deakin it was clear evidence that Providence had placed him on important occasions like these to influence his friend and early mentor. With this final difficulty overcome and the birth of the Commonwealth just hours away, Deakin closed his last diary for the old century with the thought that it had been 'perhaps the most eventful year of all politically'.[122] And indeed during this busy year he had been twice called upon to save the imperilled union. The numerous crises that characterised the long march to Federation further strengthened Deakin's faith in Providence, and they make comprehensible his gnomic declaration in the closing page of his commentary on Federation:

if ever anything ought to be styled providential it is the extraordinary combination of circumstances, persons and their most intricate interrelations of which the Commonwealth is about to become the crown.[123]

The Crisis in Victorian Politics 1879–1881 also belongs in Deakin's parlance to his 'outer' expression, but unlike the *Federal Story*, which speaks in general terms, it discloses an immediate, if still opaque, declaration of faith. Interposed in one passage in a rare personal digression, Deakin gives a remarkable summary of his life and career, which traces succinctly the pathway he had been 'obliged to follow'. Deakin related first how journalism had 'gratified, amused, rewarded but disgusted' him; he then went back further:

> Better acquaintance with the theatre had destroyed my boyish ambition to become an actor though this had filled me for years. A more extended knowledge of the drama destroyed the companion idea, still longer cherished, that I could write as well as perform poetic plays on the Shakespearean model. The growth of judgement next satisfied me that the poetry so long loved and its production practiced in secret for many years, was so poor by comparison with that of even the minor singers to be worthy of preservation. Finally my hope of doing anything permanent in prose died gradually away. The platform to which I then turned with the idea of preparing and delivering essays upon literary, social and religious issues from an open unsectarian Sunday pulpit also proved to be above my reach ... So it was at length I became a politician ...[124]

Thus after trying his hand as actor, dramatist, poet, prose writer and would-be pulpit orator for the Unitarians, as Providence was directing his steps toward what he strongly implies was a predetermined goal, Deakin discovered his true calling in politics. The passage has a curious air of resignation, mingled with a certain pride. He insisted that he had 'hugely' enjoyed his life as a whole, although politics had 'only by degrees become congenial to me and has only been accepted reluctantly when door after door which I should have preferred to open proved beyond my power to unbar'. We note that his ideal of service had triumphed over his own 'egoistic' desire, like many young men of his era, to excel in some branch of literature. Deakin ends this digression in his political narrative with an image of that life, such as he could never have survived, but which would always remain a far-off rustic Wordsworthian ideal to the busy cosmopolitan politician:

> To have spent my days in retirement without public appearances, public speaking or public notice under a veil of anonymity and largely in communion with Nature, represents the dream cherished by me with but slight alteration from boyhood up to the hour of writing.[125]

Notes

1 B. R. Wise, *The Making of the Australian Commonwealth 1889-1900*, London, 1913, p. 4.

2 The talks were held on 4 and 7 January 1889: Diary. According to Deakin, Parkes' motives included a fear of the exclusion of N.S.W. from a recently enlarged Federal Council, as well as a desire to crown his political career as founder and hopefully first Premier of a unified Australia. Still, Parkes had been speaking about Federation as far back as 1867, and it was on his initiative that the Federal Council had been formed in 1883, although N.S.W. then declined to join. See J. Quick and R. R. Garran, *Annotated Constitution of the Australian Commonwealth*, Sydney, 1901, pp. 103–4.

3 *Official Record of the Proceedings and Debates of the Australasian Federation Conference*, Melbourne, 10 February 1890, p. 77.

4 Ibid., p. 78.

5 Ibid., p. 94.

6 Ibid., p. 250.

7 Ibid., p. 95.

8 Ibid., 13 February 1890, p. 272.

9 A. Deakin, *The Federal Story*, p. 72.

10 Ibid.

11 Ibid. p. 49.

12 *V.P.D.*, vol. 66, 21 July 1891, p. 496.

13 'Boke of Praer and Prase', 5/828, prayer XVIII, 23 November 1884; 5/825, prayer XIV, 20 October 1884.

14 Ibid., 5/845, prayer XLVII, 12 August 1888.

15 Ibid., 5/847, prayer LII, 23 September 1888.

16 Ibid., 5/848, prayer LIV, 21 October 1888.

17 Ibid., 5/850, prayer LIX, 14 April 1889.

18 Ibid., 5/851, prayer LXIV, 3 August 1889; another 'Clue' expresses the desire for 'the life of frequent solitude with Nature for which I have always longed': vol. 2, 3/288, 25 April 1889.

19 'Boke ...', 5/874, prayer CXXIV, 1 January 1892.

20 Ibid., 5/854, prayer LXX, 18 May 1890.

21 Ibid., 5/854, prayer LXXI, 15 June 1890.

22 Ibid., 5/857, prayer LXXVII, 3 August 1890.

23 Ibid.

24 'Clues', vol. 3, 3/287, no. 423, 3 August 1890.

25 Diary, 10 August 1890; 'Boke ...', 5/857, prayer LXXVIII, 10 August 1890.

26 'Boke ...', 5/859, prayer LXXXI, 30 August 1890. See Frank Anstey, *Thirty Years of Deakin*; and R. Gollan, *Radical and Working Class Politics*, Melbourne, 1970.

27　Tregenza, *Professor* ..., p. 224; *Age*, 29 and 30 August 1890; for an account of Melbourne during the boom and the depression, see G. Davison, *The Rise and Fall of Marvellous Melbourne*, Melbourne, 1970.

28　*V.P.D.*, vol. 87, 12 August 1897, p. 1302; 'John Hancock', A.D.B. vol. 9, 1891–1939.

29　*V.P.D.*, vol. 87, 12 August 1897, p. 1303.

30　Diary, 31 October and 4 November 1890.

31　A. Deakin, *Temple and Tomb in India*, Melbourne, 1893, p. 44.

32　*Official Record of the Proceedings and Debates of the National Australasian Convention*, Sydney, 1891, p. 369.

33　J. Quick and R. R. Garran, *Annotated Constitution* ..., p. 129; R. B. Joyce, *Samuel Walker Griffith*, St Lucia, 1984.

34　'Boke ...', 5/863, prayer XCIII, 24 May 1891.

35　Ibid.

36　Ibid., 5/871, prayer CXVI, 2 November 1891; see A. W. Martin, 'Economic Influences in the "New Federation Movement" ', *Historical Studies*, vol. 6, no. 21, November 1953.

37　'Boke ...', 5/874, prayer CXXI, 2 December 1891.

38　*Bohemia*, Melbourne, 3 December 1891; see M. Cannon, *The Land Boomers*, Melbourne, 1966, p. 34, for an account of Deakin's part in the 'boom'.

39　'Clues', vol. 3, 3/287, no. 521, 5 December 1891.

40　T. M. Chambers to Deakin, 15 May 1893.

41　Diary, 10 August 1891; for an account of the tense situation in Queensland, see S. Svenson, *The Shearers War, the Story of the 1891 Shearers' Strike*, St Lucia, 1989.

42　Diary, 6 September 1891.

43　'Boke ...', 5/873, prayer CXX, 28 November 1891.

44　C. Pearson to Deakin, 16 August 1892; quoted in Tregenza, *Professor* ..., p. 230.

45　'Boke...', 5/875, prayer CXXVII, 30 January 1892.

46　Deakin to Charles Dilke, 11 December 1891.

47　'Boke ...', 5/876, prayer CXXIX, 13 February 1892.

48　'Links', 3/5, no. 50, undated, c. 1885.

49　'Boke ...', 5/878, prayer CXXXV, 15 May 1892.

50　This gave it power to make bank notes temporary legal tender to avoid runs on issuing banks, and allowed for the suspension of cash payments in an emergency: G. McMinn, *George Reid*, Melbourne, 1989, p. 84.

51　Deakin to C. H. Pearson, 18 March 1893; quoted in Tregenza, *Professor* ..., p. 235.

52　La Nauze, *Alfred Deakin*, vol. 1, p. 138.

53　Deakin to H. Parkes, 23 May 1892; Deakin to Josiah Royce, 5 June 1892.

54　La Nauze, *The Making of the Australian Constitution*, p. 91. The 'Quick formula' was a measure of Enabling Acts outlining a statutory procedure for each colony, whereby a convention would be followed first by discussion in the legislatures on the proposed Constitution, then by a referendum.

55　G. Serle, 'The Victorian Government's Campaign for Federation 1883–89', in A. W. Martin (ed.), *Essays in Australian Federation*, Melbourne, 1969.

56 *Australian Cyclist, Tourist and Traveller*, 20 July 1899; see La Nauze, *Alfred Deakin*, vol. 1, p. 158, for a summary of Deakin's strenuous organisational work during 1893–4, first with the A.N.A. Metropolitan Federation Conference, then in linking up with Barton's organisation in N.S.W.

57 Deakin to the Federation Conference, 3 August 1894, La Nauze papers, series 5248, N.L.A., reported in *Evening Standard*, 4 August 1894; R. S. Walpole, 'The Fighting Agencies in Federation—Victoria', in *Australian Review of Reviews*, 15 June 1898, pp. 707–10.

58 J. Roe, *Beyond Belief*..., p. 94, p. 119.

59 'The Gospel of Buddha', *Australian Herald*, December 1895; 'Boke ...', 5/901, prayer CCXI, 12 May 1895.

60 'Boke ...', 5/901, prayer CCXII, 12 May 1895.

61 'Clues', vol. 4, 3/286, no. 607, 7 April 1893.

62 'Clues', vol. 1, 3/283, no. 607, 7 November 1885.

63 'Clues', vol. 4, 3/286, no. 635, 15 July 1894.

64 'Boke ...', 5/901, prayer CCXIII, 24 May 1895.

65 Ibid.

66 Ibid., 5/861, prayer LXXXVII, 11 October 1890.

67 Diary, 3 February 1895. The agreement included Reid's 'amendments': the provision of a simple majority instead of three-fifths at joint sittings of the two Chambers to resolve deadlocks; the right of either Chamber to present a constitutional amendment to the electors; a capital site within N.S.W. but at least 100 miles from Sydney; and the limitation of the 'Braddon clause', whereby three-quarters of the federal customs revenue was paid to the States, to a period of ten years: La Nauze, *Alfred Deakin*, vol. 1, pp. 182–3.

68 'Boke ...', 5/906, prayer CCXXIV, 4 March 1897.

69 Ibid., 5/906, prayer CCXXIII, 6 March 1897; Diary, 22 March 1897.

70 La Nauze, *Alfred Deakin*, vol. 1, p. 168.

71 'Boke ...', 5/845, prayer XLVII, 12 August 1888.

72 La Nauze, *The Making* ..., p. 157.

73 McMinn, *George Reid*, p. 66, p. 131; *V.P.D.*, vol. 87, 28 July 1897, p. 802.

74 Diary, 10 April 1897; La Nauze, *The Making*..., p. 144.

75 Ibid., p. 213.

76 McMinn, *George Reid*, p. 67.

77 R. Ely, *Unto God and Caesar*, Melbourne, 1976, p. 33.

78 *Official Report of the National Australasian Convention Debates*, Parliament House, Adelaide, 1897, 22 April 1897, p. 1185.

79 Ely, *Unto God* ..., p. 69; see also J. Rickard, *H. B. Higgins: The Rebel as Judge*, Sydney, 1984, on Section 116, and W. W. Phillips, *Defending 'A Christian Country'*, St Lucia, 1981, p. 259ff., on the 'recognition' controversy.

80 Ely, *Unto God* ..., p. 73; Deakin, *The Federal Story*, p. 95.

81 Deakin to Herbert Brookes, 21 May 1897.

82 Deakin, *The Federal Story*, p. 3.

83 Ibid., p. 179.

84 Diary, 15 March 1898.

85 La Nauze, *Alfred Deakin*, vol. 1, pp. 173–5; see also F. Cusack, *Bendigo: A History*, Adelaide 1973, pp. 184–5, and H. L. Hall, *Victoria's Part in the Australian Federation Movement 1849–1900*, London 1931, p. 122.

86 Deakin, *The Federal Story*, p. 179. Among other acts of kindness, Deakin, at the request of Gay's partner Mary Sampson, obtained leave of absence for her from the Education Department so that she could be with Gay in his last hours; see Mary Sampson to Deakin, 17 November 1897.

87 B. Wise, *The Making of the Australian Commonwealth* . . ., p. 338.

88 Ibid., pp. 173–4.

89 Deakin, *The Federal Story*, p. 96.

90 La Nauze, *Alfred Deakin*, vol. 1, p. 174.

91 Ibid., vol. 1, p. 172.

92 Deakin, *The Federal Story*, p. 97.

93 Ibid., p. 173.

94 'Clues', vol. 2, 3/288, no. 341, 18 May 1889.

95 Deakin, *The Federal Story*, p. 37.

96 Ibid., p. 66.

97 Ibid., p. 32.

98 Ibid., p. 34; on physiognomy, see 'Clues', vol. 2, 3/288, no. 268, 28 July 1888.

99 Deakin, *The Federal Story*, p. 27.

100 Ibid., p. 55.

101 L. E. Fredman (ed.), *Sir John Quick's Notebook*, Newcastle, 1965, p. 40.

102 La Nauze, *The Making* . . ., p. 193.

103 *Official Report* . . ., (Adelaide), 30 March 1897, p. 297.

104 Quoted in La Nauze, *Alfred Deakin*, vol. 1, p. 179.

105 La Nauze, *The Making* . . ., pp. 91, 161, 244.

106 'Boke . . .', 5/910, prayer CCXXXIII, 4 June 1898.

107 La Nauze, *The Making* . . ., p. 190; R. White, *Inventing Australia*, Sydney, 1981, p. 111.

108 J. R. Seeley, *The Expansion of England*, (1883), London, 1895; C. H. Pearson, *National Life and Character, A Forecast*, London, 1894; see also G. R. Searle, *The Quest for National Efficiency*, Oxford, 1971.

109 *Official Record of the Debates of the Australasian Federal Convention*, (Second Session), Parliament House, Sydney, 1897, 10 September 1897, pp. 331–2.

110 *Official Report* . . ., (Adelaide), 30 March 1897, p. 302.

111 *V.P.D.*, vol. 66, 16 July 1891, p. 436.

112 Deakin, *The Federal Story*, p. 162.

113 Deakin to Edmund Barton, 7 June 1900, Barton Papers, N.L.A.; Diary, 11 July and 22–26 August 1900.

114 'Points for Reflection', 14/517, 26–27 September 1900; Deakin to Edmund Barton, 24 October 1900.

115 Deakin to Edmund Barton, 29 August 1900.

116 La Nauze, *Alfred Deakin*, vol. 1, p. 208; J. A. La Nauze, *The Hopetoun Blunder: the Appointment of the First Prime Minister of the Commonwealth of Australia December 1900*, Melbourne, 1957.

117 Loose notes, 14/519 [back], undated; London *Morning Post*, 5 February 1901.

118 There was indeed a faltering note in Deakin's letter to Kingston on 22 December. Although he had previously made up his mind not to join under any circumstances, now 'everyone here condemns the policy & I am fairly puzzled at present as to what we ought to do.' Turner and others argued that their influence on a Protectionist policy could best be exercised from the inside, and so they ought to join: Deakin to C. C. Kingston, 22 December 1900.

119 Loose notes, 14/519 [front], undated, inscribed on Pattie's old 1885 calendar.

120 Deakin to Edmund Barton, 20 December 1900.

121 Ibid., 21 December 1900.

122 Diary, 31 December 1900.

123 Deakin, *The Federal Story*, p. 173.

124 A. Deakin, *The Crisis in Victorian Politics 1879–1881*, Melbourne, 1957, p. 59.

125 Ibid., p. 60.

5

Gospels and Gospels

For a man lives what he desires, and what lives is his delight, and whatsoever is lived passes with joy and with light, with the comprehension of the mind.

Emanuel Swedenborg,
Apocalypse Revealed

We have traced the life and career of Alfred Deakin thus far to the eve of the inauguration of the Commonwealth and the beginning of the new century. From this point, a combination of health problems and other factors such as the extreme factionalism of the early Commonwealth Parliament would make him a less effective leader than his early career might have promised,[1] although there were more triumphs for Liberalism to come. Through an alliance with Labor, the first two Deakin ministries produced an impressive list of social legislation, liberal in character, making Australia at its day among the most progressive societies in the world.

It is necessary now to leave the narrative mode temporarily, and to retrace some ground in a survey of two specific genres in Deakin's private writing, the 'Gospels' and what I have called the experience narratives, that attempts to place them in an appropriate context of Deakin's energetic literary activity. Considered together, they illustrate the evolution of Deakin's beliefs and concepts from his late teens, when he produced a precocious gospel ascribed to the Puritan moralist John Bunyan, to the eve of Federation, the hour of his greatest political triumph, when he was writing and thinking about Islam's 'seal of the Prophets', Mohammed. In the next chapter, the examination of specific genres concludes with a consideration of some of the 'out of body' experience narratives, most of which Deakin penned during the troubled 1890s.

As Deakin's political star rose, a toll began to be exacted, in health, and in diminishing hours of leisure. Away from the world of politics which he stepped into and out of with such definiteness, there were treasured moments with family, Pattie and his three daughters, his sister Katie and a few close friends at Ballara, his haven at Point Lonsdale. For the most part these stolen hours were spent in solitude, with books, writing and meditation. This habit of private study and prayer, together with a strong urge to write, was to yield during half a century a large and eclectic, yet curiously systematic collection, most of it in one way or another about religion and spirituality. Amid the mass of prose and verse that came from his prolific pen, two modes seem to bear an intimate relation to the expressive dimension of Deakin's religious praxis: the prayers he recorded in a special book for most of his adult life, and the occasional manuscripts which he entitled 'gospels'.

About a half dozen 'exegetical' gospels were written before Federation. Their diversity of plot, structure and even form makes it impossible to convey their substance, for they comprise an eclectic collection of treatises, essays and allegory exceeding a million words, composed over several years and put aside at various stages of completeness. Yet they do exhibit consistent general themes, and while they will always remain protean, taken together they reveal a consistency, if not a systematic unity, in their various expressions of the Ideal. The most important gospels were *A New Pilgrim's Progress*, the gospel of Spiritualism, and that of Swedenborg written twelve years later, which was in essence the spiritistic gospel extended in matters of theology and morals; these will command our greatest attention.

The term 'gospel' to Deakin covered a far broader field than the Christian synoptics. While never counting himself a Christian in the orthodox sense, he felt reverence for all sacred works, and especially for the Bible. Over the years he made detailed studies of many of the world's scriptures, along with long journal entries at various times on Jesus and the Bible, on Socrates, Buddha, and on commentators from Schleirmacher to Newman.[2] Nor were gospels limited to sacred works and holy persons, for Deakin believed wisdom might be gleaned also from the lives and thoughts of other, perhaps lesser, 'gospel-bearers', as he rather awkwardly termed them, throughout the world's history.

In broad terms, a gospel related to conduct; yet it was coloured always by the possibility of Revelation conceived as an immediate spiritual illumination. Deakin's belief did not entail a narrowly 'moral' enterprise. His discussions of gospel-bearers and their gospels stress the centrality of this concept of transmundane Revelation, a paradigm which developed beyond the Spiritualistic model of the mediumistic 'channel' to something qualitatively different, yet still related, to the 'gifts' he had seen exhibited 'through' various mediums. This was true especially of the 'higher' phenomena of prophecy and inspiration, for as he became absorbed with the perennial question of how far human efforts and circumstances originate with ourselves, and how much depends on higher powers, so in proportion did the doctrine of a Divine Providence acting through human agency gain increasing currency in Deakin's mature reflections. We have seen this already in the all-important 'signs', for as Deakin rapidly transcended the scientific pretensions of Spiritualism, a broader belief emerged whose central feature was the possibility of direct guidance from Deity through the essential or Higher Self. The fundamental importance of 'signs' in Alfred Deakin's life cannot therefore be overemphasised. They helped determine his marriage and public career, and shaped a private religious faith nourished upon these evidences of a Divine Providence.

Through the gospels Deakin turned his copious reading inward to discover his own Ideal of conduct, thereby linking his study of those who professed enlightenment with his own private aspiration for spiritual enfranchisement. Revelation and the pursuit of the Ideal were intimately related, through morality, so that the moral quality of one's life determines the Revelation one is fitted to receive. The Ideal begins as an improbability, and becomes reality through aspiration fed by inspiration. Deakin believed that a shadow of that primary inspiration, shining through great lives and noble ideas, might be imparted by an earnest reflection on texts. There is an almost Judaic quality in Deakin's reverent attitude to what in his terms were 'sacred' texts, both in his ritual of study and in his assumption that they might render accession to the Inner Light, that Light as he wrote regarding perhaps his greatest exemplar Emanuel Swedenborg, 'which his own mind derived from & shed upon' the Bible during the reading.[3]

The written prayers reveal Deakin's aspiration, particularly during the Federation campaign, to serve as Divine instrument. Some of the ideas supporting this reading of the universe can be found in the gospels. Seen from this perspective they represent the fruits of a process of crystallisation, in which Deakin reflected upon the Ideals of meritorious and unselfish living, of Revelation, of wisdom and the evidences of God's Love. These gospels then, can be understood as periodic expressions of an Ideal whose contours changed over time.

Deakin scorned no revelation, though he ranked them according to the sublimity of their message, and their moral effects. His endeavours to reveal an 'objective' Ideal in the lives and thoughts of great men (they were all men) were inspired by Emerson's *Representative Men* (1883), which had considered six great men from Plato to Napoleon as symbolic types. There are sections on 'Plato the Philosopher', 'Swedenborg the Mystic', and 'Shakespeare the Poet'. 'Representative' men, a notion Emerson derived from Swedenborg whom he greatly admired, are: 'facts that symbolize essences or ideas, men who give temporary form to the grandest and largest potentialities of the creation. Through them we see what all men may one day become.'[4] Deakin's own detailed studies, planned as resources for a projected book, would draw on the 'soul life' of humankind's Revelators, to reveal transcendental influence in the lives of great individuals who had understood and lived by great precepts, and once reaping the fruits of Illumination, had tried to convey them to their fellow beings.

The allegory *A New Pilgrim's Progress* was his first gospel, though Deakin did not adopt the term as title until 1884 with the 'Gospel According to Wordsworth'. What I have called his 'exegetical' gospels, on Shakespeare, Swedenborg, and Mohammed, were imitative of Carlyle in the 'Great Man' view of human history, and of Emerson as a study of the lives and thoughts of a spiritual elite, each of whom 'representatively' expressed some of the 'grandest potentialities' of creation. Idealism declares a religious Ideal, an end of spiritual seeking, to be realised in this world. 'The Kingdom of Heaven is within you' suggested to Deakin how by individual effort, study and prayer, and by Grace, humans might come to understand some of 'life's manifold mysteries' and thereby serve the Light more completely.

A New Pilgrim's Progress: The Medium as Reformer

It seems entirely characteristic of the young Alfred Deakin that the first—and only—gospel uttered through his agency should claim to be that of a great heroic personage, taking the form of a moral and religious allegory. *Pilgrim's Progress* was an early favourite, as was Carlyle's own heavy allegory *Sartor Resartus*. It is difficult for our era to understand Carlyle's appeal to Victorian youth, and to appreciate the heavy style and constant moral exhortation; but to Deakin it was like mother's milk, and his own allegory is redolent of such influences.

A New Pilgrim's Progress is a rather heavy and pompous, yet somehow naively disarming tale of some 260 pages which departs radically from its famous predecessor. In many ways typical of 'impressional' literature of the era, yet far more ambitious in its scope, it was claimed as a Revelation, a new 'allegory for modern times' dictated 'through' the young 'medium' by the spirit of the Bedford tinker.[5] As the gospel of mediumship, in its most doctrinaire form a belief regarding a new Dispensation of spirit power for the nineteenth century, it claims direct knowledge of the afterlife, and guidance from a spiritual world. Mediums were regarded by 'religious' Spiritualists as the interlocutors between the spiritual and material realms, veritably the instruments of Revelation.[6]

To the young enthusiast there was little doubt that the spirits of the mighty dead might influence the thoughts of the living, nor that they could augment the faculties of certain persons 'chosen' as mediums. By the mid-1890s Deakin was at least certain that *A New Pilgrim's Progress* contained nothing of Bunyan: 'nothing of his strong personality; none of his power of characterisation, his genius for narrative, or his homely vigour of style'.[7] The first instance of this impromptu mode of composition appears around 1874, the year he joined the V.A.S. and Dr Motherwell's circle. 'A New Year Carol', written two years later was, as he had explained, the result of 'one of those inexplicable visitations of verse' arriving 'without warning as if from without me'.[8] His earliest surviving journal 'Impromptus' (1875–81) sought to catch the spontaneous 'hints & humours' of his moods and thoughts. By 1876 when he commenced taking 'dictation' from the spirit of Bunyan at weekly sittings of Dr Motherwell's circle, this mode of composition was well established.

From Deakin's always prolific pen, other 'inspired' writing continued to flow, most of it in verse, where he appears to have been trying to synthesise his spiritistic ideas with his lingering dramatic and literary aspirations. The 1876 poem 'Footsteps' is described in a late retrospective as 'one of those curious "inspirations" that tho' quite true to my own mood & feeling, floated into me & took possession of me suddenly but only partly in words ...'.[9] 'The Ocean', another juvenile work from his 1877 'Song Sonatas' written for Pattie, was based upon 'an ecstasy which transported me at the time beyond all possible description'. The older Deakin could dismiss these as 'many variations & mixed metaphors illustrating Strife & Suffering as the means & mode of progress',[10] but the experience, like the notebooks, had remained with him.

With his 'development' as medium in Dr Motherwell's circle, Deakin seemed momentarily to link these two ambitions, in his role as 'inspirational' writer. These conflicting aims and some fantasising over fame, along with a studied *ennui*, are illustrated in the figure of 'The Actor': 'who steps late into the theatre crowded expectant & impatient—if its favourite jester. Pale thin absentminded he stares across the din of applause that greets his entrance.'[11]

A more direct record of Deakin's spiritistic activity during these university years survives in *Spirit Teachings Oral Impressional and Automatic* (1908), a selection of addresses given 'through' participant mediums during ten years of Dr Motherwell's circle. Deakin is identified in the preface as 'a gentleman studying for the legal profession, who will be referred to as "Mr A"'. The discretion of the editor W. H. Terry is understandable, since the gentleman referred to was then Prime

Minister of Australia! We are informed that 'Mr A' became a 'good trance speaker and impressional writer', and four of these trance addresses from the year 1875 are included, typical of 'spirit communications' of the era in their air of mystery and lofty exhortation.[12] It seems that the remainder of Deakin's short career of some three years as 'medium' was devoted to receiving Bunyan's 'dictation'.

A New Pilgrim's Progress may therefore be located within an ostensibly 'impromptu' mode of composition. In the preface Deakin, as anonymous author, explains the method of reception. He would sit within a seance circle opened with a prayer, and after a period of meditation, would rapidly write down what had just passed in serial form before his mind, while the others provided 'power'. Written usually with great rapidity 'as, after a short interval of semi-trance, the impressions came pouring in', these ideas were 'passed before my mind in regular order and succession', beginning and ending involuntarily.[13] This partial trance might be compared with that described by Wordsworth in 'Tintern Abbey', or to Tennyson's 'waking trance'.[14] Probably one evening of the twice-weekly circle was dedicated for a full year to the reception of this allegory; it must have been very tedious for all but the most devoted believers.

As a religious allegory *A New Pilgrim's Progress* represents something of a hybrid between Bunyan's Christian epic and mystical works like St John of the Cross's *Ascent to Mt Carmel*. Superficially it is a tale about a soul's travails in its ascent to the City of Reason, and on one level, like *Pilgrim's Progress*, it recounts the saga of the lonely integrity of the ideal Puritan.[15] And like its famous predecessor, it attempts to make universal statements about the religious life; that it succeeds less was due to no lack of enthusiasm on the part of its author (or amanuensis). The protagonist 'Restless' is (like Deakin) a young man of twenty years, but of noble birth, who lives in the City of Worldly Content, one of the three cities on the 'plain'. Becoming dissatisfied with his lot he, like Christian, leaves his wife and children to seek Truth. In one passage with an almost Orwellian flavour, he defies the authority of the god of the people, Ignorance. Gradually he becomes aware of 'recollections long silent', which precipitate an internal conflict. He becomes delirious, refuses nourishment, and falls into a profound trance, from which he eventually awakens recovered.[16] Thus his quest begins, and 'Restless' departs for the City of Sensual Science where he meets Wilful, a young urchin girl later to become his partner.[17] In this new city they are taught only the 'gospel of physical facts', and having thus passed from 'the Pride of Ignorance to the Pride of Science' and found comfort in neither, they continue their quest.[18] Angels secretly lead the two to a small hamlet, 'Faith's Content', where they reside for three years, but when they refuse to read the 'Public Test' of faith, they are banished. They continue along the road of 'Progress' toward the City of Reason, where they meet Honesty and Prudence, who tell how this road was once perilous to travel when 'Honesty was young'.[19]

As the story proceeds breathlessly onward, there are numerous clumsy allusions of this sort to the early days of Freethought. The storyline is jejune, and the constant intervention of spiritual helpers at crucial points lends it a fragile 'Deus ex machina', where spiritual truth inevitably triumphs over spiritual ignorance. The principal characters are rather flat Carlylean heroes. Some passages offer vivid illustration of Alfred's current reformist zeal, as a self-styled 'ultra-radical' both in his Liberal politics and his metaphysics. 'There is no heaven but Reason', Honesty tells the young couple. Ignorance, the god of the plain, is constantly identified with churchiness, as when they meet 'Reformation' and his offspring 'Dissent',[20] proclaiming with rather heavy-handed symbolism that Freethought, the rule of Reason, had arisen from the upheavals of Protestantism. After further trials, they arrive at Reason where Restless learns from a mysterious oriental Sage of his Divine mission; he is fated to become an 'instrument of good'. He secures a position as secretary to a professor, and rapidly earns respect as an independent thinker, obtaining a Chair in his own right which makes him famous, and he writes a book that becomes a textbook 'among the liberal thinkers'.

All the while unseen visitors hover, and secretly influence the two at crucial points along their odyssey. Although now a 'Prophet of Reason', Restless is still dissatisfied. Wilful, who has through the Sage's influence meanwhile become clairvoyant, is his first conscious link with the spiritual world, when he has tentative conversations 'through' the entranced girl, and receives instruction. Eventually they are enabled to leave their bodies, undergoing an elaborate initiation conducted by seven heavenly angels. As each angel speaks in turn and at length, they are made to behold a different vision, on the history of earth's evolution, on the condition of man, on the loathsome though transient agonies of hell. Finally, with the seventh spirit the seven rise together: 'while the first amid a breathless silence consecrated him in the eloquence of perfect prayer, to the task of duty.'[21]

Bunyan's pilgrim also underwent initiation by three 'Shining Ones' after he had lost his burden at the Cross, who testified that his sins were forgiven, and stripping him of his rags, they gave him a broidered coat and a sealed roll, and set a mark on his forehead.[22] His initiation was a sign of salvation; for his nineteenth-century counterpart, the ritual embodied consecration to service. Christian received the messengers, while Restless and Wilful experience an intromission from their bodies, taken up to the 'higher intelligences and nobler hearts' who guide the 'seers of the earth',[23] who in turn receive their inspiration from a yet higher plane, the 'third altitude'. In this celestial initiation, Restless and Wilful discover an almost pastoral universe:

> united in seraphic love, and guided by ineffable wisdom, angelic intelligences, calmly tended and willing worlds, and systems; themselves instructed by still higher beings and subject all to God.[24]

The three-tiered universe, even the ascent to Revelation from the body, are the first clear indications of the influence of Swedenborg, into whose works Deakin was 'plunging' deeply at this time. 'Hell was selfishness', as Swedenborg had taught and Restless saw in this, his first vision. They had seen 'the end, the means, and now the needs of life'. The final lesson was: 'Duty, self-denial, self-consecration, and thus worship, the labour of charity, the service of God, is in it.'[25] After being consecrated to Service in a magnificent aetheric temple, and following an anthem of honour from an assembly of radiant spirits, Redeemer and Redemptress, as they are henceforth known, returned to their bodies.

The remainder of the book is a denouement of selfless dedication and privation, with constant assistance from the 'invisible guardians'. It is difficult not to caricature, though some passages are remarkably eloquent. On the day following his vision, Redeemer was to give the third of a scheduled series of lectures on the philosophy of mind. With the benefit of his recent experience, and to the extreme surprise of his many admirers, the erstwhile 'Prophet of Reason' expounded 'occult' doctrines instead, positing for the first time a personality 'within but distinct from the material frame', capable of leaving its 'shell' and able to exercise all faculties of 'understanding motion and sense.' Then warming to his topic, Redeemer declared 'There is no death', much to the disgust of his 'rationalist' followers.[26]

Following numerous other trials and blessings in a life of selfless devotion to the truths of the spirit, Redeemer and Redemptress receive a further vision prophesying the manner of their death. Redeemer sacrifices himself unselfishly for the good of his fellows. The final scenes give a flavour of the French Revolution, for now the 'spiritual wave of inquiry and reason which he had inaugurated had passed on into the political sphere', and eventually the reign of Reason is extended over the plain.[27] Making a very Socratic exit, Redeemer reminds his devoted followers just before his death: 'Fear for your conscience only, fear not these. Save virtue but forgive men. Follow me.'[28] The guards tear his flesh (it would not do to have him crucified or poisoned by hemlock), so that political enfranchisement follows closely upon spiritual liberation from the god Ignorance.

On internal evidence, and notwithstanding the opinions of its youthful author, the themes are firmly centred in Deakin's own preoccupations in the 1870s. Besides much unconscious self-portraiture, there are constant echoes of recent events like the Paris Commune. There are also numerous parallels with its famous predecessor, in the general structure as a pilgrimage, and the use of archetypal names, as well as several fundamental differences. There is no Valley of Humiliation for instance, or Shadow of Death, and no anti-papalist propaganda. The central message is that Worldly Content and Sensual, that is materialist, conceptions in science and art are a bar to the rule of Reason. 'Graceless' becomes 'Christian', while Restless becomes his own 'Redeemer', hence implicitly rejecting the major Christian tenets of the Atonement and a vicarious Saviour. And whereas Christian was shown the way by 'Evangelist', Restless depends upon Platonic 'recollections'. Most significantly, the Celestial City was reached after crossing the River of Death, while the City of Reason is to be attained in this life. Even the term 'progress', which in the original work denotes simply temporal passage, assumes an evolutionist meaning. Christian's pilgrimage was toward salvation through discovery of Christ; Redeemer sought his gospel of religious reform through Reason. Deakin's later gospels abandoned this naive conception of the power of Reason; yet reinterpreted with the consciousness of a guiding Providence, Reason remained the linchpin of his personal gospel, although his interests became more moral and less metaphysical.

The advent of *A New Pilgrim's Progress* brought the young Alfred a certain fame within the Spiritualist Association. He was seen as a sort of mediumistic prodigy, and in 1878 he became president, aged barely twenty-two. It had been prophesied in Dr Motherwell's circle that he would become a 'great medium'. It is likely that with this precocious success, Deakin came momentarily to believe such predictions, for only this context of frenetic and sustained activity can explain the emergence of *A New Pilgrim's Progress* as a serious enterprise taking more than a year to set down. There is no reason to suppose that the older members, Motherwell, Stow and Terry, believed other than what the 'communicator' claimed—a new Revelation, an 'allegory for modern times'.

For his part Deakin, always searching for his true path of Duty, at this early way-station believed like Redeemer that he had found his calling in mediumship. But another image is almost as prominent—that of the Reformer. At the Eclectic Association and then the University Debating Club, Deakin was on the cutting edge of social and religious debates of the day. The Spiritualism he then embraced taught that if an afterlife could be proven 'scientifically', the grip of the churches over their adherents, the claims of faith, would be discredited. This notion of science as a purifier of religion is a peculiarity of early Spiritualism. It was in this sense that the young Alfred and his colleagues believed Spiritualism to be a new Revelation. Seances, as declared in *Spirit Teachings* ... were meant to fulfil the 'scientific' task of bringing the departed near and blotting out doubts about the afterlife, and of banishing 'superstitious frenzy'. From science, that most rational of pursuits, Spiritualism had 'nothing to fear'; indeed it was regarded as an ally in a process that would sweep away the twin evils of materialism on one side, and theological error on the other.[29]

Together with a scientific Spiritualism, the influences of Theosophy and Swedenborg are also prominent; in his second initiation Redeemer, in 'spirit form', sees a winding procession of white-robed priests who proclaim:

> Welcome first of the new light ... to the last lamp of the old. Thou art the son, as we were the fathers of the great faith. In you the promise of the ages becomes complete, and this day marks the beginning of a new Avatar. Behold![30]

The idea of the descent of an Avatar is another Theosophical borrowing from Hinduism (Avatar is traditionally one of the ten historical manifestations of Vishnu), whence came also the notion of a new 'root race' destined to populate the earth and to rediscover the original 'Wisdom Religion' of the Ancients. And as we shall see, the method of this second initiation, when Redeemer's spiritual eye was opened, bears a marked resemblance to that which Swedenborg had claimed: 'Henceforward into this state you shall enter at will, and behold with all the spirit's power the inner side of Nature.'[31]

An illumination enabling entry at will into the 'inner' side of Nature in 1870s terms came through an unspecified 'development' of the faculties. For Swedenborg, it was achieved through Grace: 'Those who await illumination do not receive it from the Lord', he cautioned, 'but from the spirit of some enthusiastic Quaker.'[32] An ascent to Revelation features in other writings, notably the 'out of body' experience narratives to be considered in the next chapter. He believed always that illumination, like all things, comes ultimately from God, but when he wrote his commentary on Swedenborg a decade later, Deakin had dispensed largely with intermediaries in matters of faith and Revelation. As that other mode of his 'inner' expression, the written prayers also testify, he now dared to ask for an 'illumination of the understanding' directly from the Almighty.

The poetic gospels:
The poet as seer of the human heart

By the time he composed the 'Gospel According to Wordsworth' seven years later, Deakin's outer life had been transformed. In 1884 he was a Minister of the Crown about to initiate pioneer social legislation, and at twenty-eight he was the rising star in the coalition government. The gospels of the mid-1880s focused on the Ideal through poetry: the poet as mystic, as in Wordsworth; as humanist in Shakespeare; and with Dante, the poet as 'seer of the human heart'. They were not elaborated as fully as Swedenborg's, and the frequent reworking of the same themes in various gospels and their sequence confirm Deakin's intention to write a major work, perhaps as a historical and philosophical study, on the Ideal gospel permeating human life and history, taking his cue again from the Theosophical claim that all gospels are parts of one great 'Gospel'.[33]

Redeemer was an archetypal figure, nobility of soul personified. Later gospels defined the Ideal by the limitations as well as the triumphs of their originators. In the Lake District Bard he recognised true genius, along with many serious artistic and personal deficiencies. Deakin's brief essay on Wordsworth looked for the springs of inspiration and the grounding of his faith in Nature as Revealing Agency. He believed that inspiration, springing from all great souls as expressions of their inner spiritual life, was conspicuous in but not restricted to religious reformers, taking as starting point the poet's own assertion that he was 'treading holy ground' and 'speaking no dream, but things oracular'.[34] Wordsworth's conception of Nature as a living unity, his 'rather leisurely' life of quiet contemplation of God and communion with His creation appealed to the poet and the pietist in Deakin. Yet he was aware too that Wordsworth's 'lyre had few strings' and that he sometimes 'found himself playing on the wood'.[35] Moreover Deakin noted his egotism, selfishness, and his extreme political conservatism.

Deakin tells the reader that Wordsworth's poetry was one by-product of his communion with the mysterious 'Presences'; its first fruit was 'guidance on practical life', the next 'happiness and peace', and that poetry was a 'thank offering for what he had received'.[36] These invisible and intangible 'Presences' were not only visible Nature, but, as Deakin suggests in an extremely vague passage, they were the result of preaching a gospel at the 'pulpit of Nature', which had made his contemplation a 'revealing agency' into a transcendent world.[37] In contrast Shakespeare, about whom Deakin wrote intermittently over the next three years, taught a purely natural gospel that shows humankind as complicated mixtures of good, evil, and indifference. Running to over 200 handwritten pages, the 'Gospel According to Shakespeare' reviews all the plays, including the comedies and tragedies and *Troilus and Cressida*. His was a 'gospel according to Society',[38] by no means optimistic and, like Hume, he contends that we are not entitled to credit the Supreme Power with being any better than the world He has created.[39] In this gospel Deakin declares that 'all gospels relate to conduct', and he shared Shakespeare's Hobbesian view that 'within every man lies a savage & slumbers a brute'.[40] Deakin commended his special genius as revealing through his art 'an incomplete moral order & an immature moral Law'. It is this truthfulness to life which 'lifts his ethical theory out of the ruck of theatrical contrivances [,] elevating it into a gospel'.[41] Emerson too had argued against those who would regard Shakespeare as a mere playwright and not as a philosopher.

Following a lengthy general introduction, Deakin proceeds to close analyses of several of Shakespeare's tragedies; he does not seem to have been overly interested in the comedies. In *Hamlet*, for instance, the inherent fascination of the Prince is that 'the tragedy takes place in his intellectual & moral nature.'[42] All comes to naught because the link between 'thought & action, between belief & practice, between duty & performance' had been wanting.[43] *Hamlet* is a play 'too deep for tears' in which 'the sufferer's nobility is the cause of his own calamity.' Retribution is paid out also to others; to the Queen for her inconstancy, and to Laertes for his treachery. However the moral is not to be summed up in any precept or aphorism, and Deakin expressly denies that Shakespeare set out to teach a gospel.[44] But he concludes that Hamlet's major sin, like Brutus, was his 'indecision in the path of duty', a faltering of belief in the Ideal.[45]

Elsewhere Deakin called Shakespeare's the 'opposite gospel' to Swedenborg's. His beliefs about God and immortality were almost wholly derived and traditional, but Shakespeare's unique contribution was his depiction of men and women and the world, what Deakin calls 'Worldly Wisdom & Worldly Experience of the highest type.'[46] Swedenborg's gospel was opposite in that it spoke of these matters from the 'inner' side. Hence as the gospel of society, of man, and of goodness, as he variously terms it, Shakespeare's was purely natural, what had also been termed a 'noble positivism', based upon no Revelation, except of the human heart.[47]

With the Florentine poet Dante, Deakin continues his principal focus on the Carlylean 'great man' theory of historical influence. Dante's was the main gospel of the Middle Ages, the product of a man of 'higher quality' and 'freer intellectual fibre' than the Swedish mystic. According to Deakin he had attempted through his epic allegory a task similar to the Swede's, for his own era, to harmonise his creed with the facts of the universe, portraying the three worlds 'in a relation which within the limits of his belief, he felt they ought to hold to each other'.[48] Unlike Swedenborg he did not claim to be a firsthand witness to the other worlds. Yet adopting the current theology, legend and the Aristotelian learning of his time, as 'true seer of the human heart & true prophet of the awakened soul',[49] Dante had constructed, by poetic vision and religious feeling, a metaphysical universe which speaks of man's relation to his Creator. In this context the term gospel refers to certain universal truths about man, the world, and God.

Deakin goes into great detail in reviewing the *Divine Comedy* and earlier works, and in relating them to Dante's turbulent life. Dante's universe had been no dream, but 'the creed & faith, the religion of ... millions of his time'.[50] If it be antiquated in form and erroneous in fact, Dante's gospel remains nevertheless 'true in its spirit for all time'.[51] Like Virgil he had blended the 'prophet's moral zeal with the poet's power of imagination'. Forged to an unquestioning faith, his genius rendered a vision which if not personal was at least 'true to the knowledge, the belief, & the ideal of his epoch'.[52] The true poet, capable of a deep understanding of the human condition, gives lyrical expression to great truths in epic form. He renders through the transcendent flights of his imagination an image of humanity susceptible of a higher dialectic of life, as in Wordsworth's lines in 'Tintern Abbey', when with:

> *an eye made quiet by the power*
> *Of harmony, and the deep power of joy,*
> *We see into the life of things.*

Swedenborg: The Seer as Moralist

Deakin had planned an extended article or a small volume giving 'a modern rendering of the vital teachings' of Emanuel Swedenborg since at least 1881.[53] The 'Gospel According to Swedenborg', written in about nine months between Parliamentary sittings during 1889–90, is the longest and the most important of the gospels. A work of over 600 handwritten pages in two volumes, it reflects the status accorded to the eighteenth-century Swedish mystic, and his significance to Deakin, most profoundly through his ideas on the nature of morality and on Revelation. In this first (and last) professedly theological work which brought together earlier writings, Deakin rendered account of Swedenborg's system in an erudite, if somewhat undigested and rambling exposition. Among his most literary works, though no more than a preliminary sketch for a larger work never completed, it was a selective excursus through Swedenborg's considerable body of writings, in the form of essays on set topics supported by copious quotations from the mystic's many books, and linked together with numerous lengthy digressions. With this gospel Deakin tried to reach some definitive theological formulation on questions like the nature of religion, on duty and morality and, as he put it, on the relation between 'Creator & creature'. Its major impetus was I believe a religious labour, undertaken partly as a response to the Grand Prophecy.

The gospel was completed around April 1890. As historical document, it is especially instructive when considered alongside the 'Testament' which Deakin composed and had printed five months later. A solemn and didactic twelve-page treatise prepared for the guidance of his daughters in the event of his early death, the 'Testament' seems a strange document for a 34-year-old man in good health to compose, and it may well have been inspired by the medieval Judaic practice of leaving an 'ethical will'.[54] Yet it is sincere, evoking a real sense of adoration for God and His works, for the life of religion, and revealing a tender and protective love for his family. More importantly, it provides a reliable index of the parts of the Swedenborgian metaphysic which Deakin accepted.

Emanuel Swedenborg, (1688–1772), an extraordinarily prolific scientist and engineer, and member of the Swedish Parliament, worked for most of his life as Assessor for the Swedish Board of Mines. His life according to Deakin can be divided into two periods 'laid down for him before he was born', the fifty-five years prior to his illumination, and his last twenty-nine years, when he produced numerous tomes on theology.[55] These he claimed to have been dictated by 'the Lord' who had selected him to give humankind a twofold Revelation: the testimony of the objective existence of a spiritual world, and the spiritual or 'inner' sense of Scripture.[56]

Swedenborg was at the pinnacle of a brilliant career in science, author of over 150 works in seventeen disciplines, member of the Russian and Swedish Academies, an aristocrat and friend of royalty, when his life suddenly took a dramatic turn in 1743 with the first signs of his illumination. Over the next two years he experienced visions, trances, tremblings and other phenomena, which he recorded in a 'Spiritual Diary'. In April 1745 there came a grand vision when the 'Lord God' appeared and commanded him to explain to men the spiritual sense of Scripture.[57] The instructions received from the Lord Himself were dutifully set down and published over the remaining years of his life, beginning with the *Arcana Caelestia*, where he recounts his first intromission into the spiritual world:

> Hence it has been permitted me to hear and see things in another life which are astonishing, and which have never before come to the knowledge of any man, nor entered into his imagination.[58]

Swedenborg believed his Revelation would rejuvenate this world: hence one of his titles, *The True Christian Religion*, where he asserts that 'It has now been permitted to enter rationally into the mysteries of Being.' His influence on Deakin was considerable, and also on the Spiritualist movement through writers like Alexander Jackson Davis, the 'Poughkeepsie seer' whose *Nature's Divine Revelations*, received while entranced, became its 'Bible'. As Deakin points out in this gospel, it was a derivative piece drawing heavily on the ideas of the Swedish mystic.

Since his 'appetite for marvels' had diminished,[59] Deakin's present interest in the psychic realm centred upon the untapped potential of the human mind. Both as seer and prophet, and as scientist and religious moralist, Swedenborg held an unique appeal for Deakin at this time in his life. He represented the best of both worlds: a hard-headed scientist who translated his analytic mode of thinking to celestial spheres without losing the power of discursive reason, and a theologian who incorporated an immediate Revelation with a pious regard for the Bible. Hence a transcendental Revelation was received via the Reason, rather than through an unifying mystical experience like those claimed by Plotinus or Jacob Boehme. This bold claim regarding the rational evidence for another level of Being had been one of the reasons for his early immersion in Spiritualism, and with a continuing commitment to Reason as revealing agency, Deakin now considered the rational character of Swedenborg's Revelation 'one of its peculiarities, & its single greatest value.'[60] His attraction to Swedenborg's religious teaching concerning an objective spiritual world and an ordered and moral universe is evident in Deakin's division of the Gospel into two volumes 'Seership', and 'Ethical System' or alternatively 'Theology', and it proclaims his belief in the function of seership in disclosing the moral purposes of life.

On 6 July 1889, having just penned the closing lines of the incomplete Shakespeare gospel, Deakin turned to his 'Boke of Praer & Prase' for an invocation. The next day he opened a new leather-bound journal and commenced writing the 'Gospel According to Swedenborg'. More than any previous gospel it was an intellectual exercise where Deakin, widely read in the Idealist lineage, particularly Plato, Royce, Hegel and Kant, and in the sacred Scriptures, is shown in some passages at his systematic and literary best. And Prayer LXII, his solemn invocation to God on the previous day, testifies to the religious nature of this labour. He asked for:

> grace & light, that I may be enabled to discharge with fidelity & power the task of seeking for the evidences of Thy being & Thy nature which I am about to undertake. Enable me in pursuing them, to grow in comprehension & certitude, & in setting them forth, to be a means of impressing them upon others. Grant me the intermediate guidance & inspiration of the great mind whose utterances I am about to study, that I may, all else apart & beside, become a vehicle for the diffusion of goodness & truth.[61]

Nowhere in Deakin's writings is there a more direct linkage between study and religious praxis than in this sincere invocation. It also seems highly likely that the date held a special significance. The gospel was commenced on 7 July 1889, on the seventh day of the seventh month, and in the thirty-third year of Deakin's life; so that as with the inauguration of the 'Boke of Praer & Prase', an undefined yet deeply personal kabbala of numbers seems to have played a decisive role in the timing of a major spiritual enterprise.

With important qualifications Deakin accepted Swedenborg's two major claims: direct acquaintance with a spiritual world, and the reception of a new Revelation. This did not extend to the status claimed by the Swedish mystic himself, to be the instrument of a Second Coming and harbinger of a 'New Church'. There are great gaps in Deakin's exposition of certain tenets he found unconvincing. He rejected for instance the doctrine of Correspondences and of the inner meaning of Scripture, both of which remain for the Swedenborgian Church today central tenets of their founder's Revelation. And he could make no sense of Swedenborg's boldest and most cryptic claim, that the Second Coming occurred in 1757.[62] In Deakin's eclectic treatment, the points he wished to emphasise were largely in concordance with his own views.

Deakin's exposition lays great stress upon the gradual opening of Swedenborg's 'spiritual sense', on his scientific method, and on his absolute normality, except for a crisis of short duration during the opening of his inner vision, which had come to him gradually; it was a 'transmutation & transformation' of the doctrines he had been approaching steadily all his life, and thus in Deakin's view 'not in any sense contradictory or unrelated to his former life & mind'.[63] To strengthen this claim he relates similar crises in the lives of Mohammed, Cellini, Bunyan, Charles Lamb and Blake, among others.[64] He assures the reader that Swedenborg's teachings, once he had regained his equilibrium, were the 'healthy outcome of a healthy mind'.[65]

Swedenborg's was thus 'the most powerful' and 'the most truthful' gospel since Mohammed's.[66] According to Deakin this was due to his scientific training and matter-of-fact exposition. Committed to the primacy of personal experience, Deakin seems to strain the meaning of 'science', for surely he did not mean that Swedenborg's transcendent experiences fulfilled the canons of empirical experimentation; rather his usage places great weight upon Swedenborg's analytic method. He had described what he alleged were spiritual facts, Deakin tells us, 'in the dryest & baldest manner & theorise[d] on them dispassionately', where his theological dogmas are applied like 'mathematical groups', and he proceeds from point to point 'as if demonstrating a problem in Euclid'.[67] Yet Deakin was aware too that 'his premises require to be admitted or else his demonstration goes for naught.'[68] Hence we see why Deakin's gospel labours the normality and thorough scientific training of Swedenborg, who appeared to him the 'apostle of spiritual facts', and whose 'sobriety is a guarantee of his veracity'.[69] Even his dullness (and it is considerable) is turned to advantage, for a more impressionable mind, in Deakin's special 'mediumistic' sense of the word, would have been 'capable of soaring higher'.[70] So it is to his credit as gospel-bearer, Deakin maintains at length, that Swedenborg appears 'the plainest of men, without wit, without fancy, without humour, without eloquence, & most assuredly without any trace of imagination'.[71]

In insisting that Swedenborg's visions were not the result of credulous imaginings, Deakin stressed his analytic method and his middlingness, the geniality and equability of his character. In the second volume he renders a similar picture in his selective exposition of his theology, stressing the quality of Swedenborg's personal moral code as he sketched his account of 'man's relation & responsibilities as creature to his Creator'. Not that Deakin regarded his ideas with naive veneration, since attention was called to certain strongly rooted prejudices and preconceptions, like his anti-papalism, and the dogmatic Christian framework of his faith which 'exalts the Bible even above the ordinary Christian standard'.[72] Swedenborg's particular dullness was that of the pedant, and of 'that worst of pedants, the theological'; yet as Deakin insists:

> Notwithstanding his wearisome prolixity, his endless repetitions, his formal jargon, his endless scriptural interpretations, his dull dry-as-dust style of composition, the Divine Light sparkles among his heavy pages & glows beneath his pedantic formalism with a real & lasting lustre ...[73]

Although he dwells at length upon their truthfulness, Deakin admits that ultimately all rests on faith in the veracity of Swedenborg's spiritual experiences. Hence he develops a picture of the man, measuring his life and conduct against the principles he espoused. Swedenborg's seership was for Deakin the 'linchpin' of both his Revelation and his theology, and his direct personal encounters with the world of spirits and angels were the fundamental source of his authority. Writing from the 'inner' side, Swedenborg preached a gospel which:

> teaches directly of the nature of God, which postulates in the most plain & emphatic fashion the immortality of the soul, & is as positive in its declarations as to the conditions of life in the next world as to those in this world.[74]

Again as in the first volume, Deakin sought corroboration in the experiences of others who had claimed to be 'absolute witness[es] to a spiritual world which they actually perceived by superphysical senses', among them Mohammed, Loyola, George Fox, St Paul, St Francis, Bunyan and Jacob Boehme, the itinerant cobbler whose volumes of religious exhortation held for Deakin a 'mystic beauty born of sincerest piety'.[75] Each had received a Divine inspiration, and like Swedenborg, each had suffered a crisis followed by a grand vision which galvanised them to their respective cause. While Deakin's analysis is perceptive, it falls down in lumping them together in one category, contradicting his earlier distinction between 'unifying' mystical experience and the experience of 'rational' mystics like Swedenborg.

Deakin believed that Swedenborg's gospel 'cuts the gordian knot' and that it 'crosses the dividing gulf' between philosophy like Kant's based upon knowledge and the knowing powers, and religion.[76] While he concedes that a leap of faith is required to accept another person's immediate experience, Deakin implies that because of his empirical training and high moral tone, Swedenborg's claims were to be taken seriously, since they were an outward and visible sign, a living testament, to his truthfulness. He argued that his intromissions, while the most dramatic, were potentially no less valid than Swedenborg's other claims, if the truthfulness of the man be credited in his life as a whole. It is an ingenious argument. Better to understand its force for Deakin requires some consideration of the relation between morality and religion in Swedenborg's system.

For Swedenborg as for Kant, the quality of the interior life was the principal truth of human experience. The life of religion is the life of morality. In essence Swedenborg's rational theology, like most eighteenth-century thought, revelled in an almost unbounded optimism about what raw human intelligence could achieve in the realm of religious knowledge. It is one of the fruits of the Enlightenment, for both philosophers believed that 'all religion has relation to life & the life of religion is to do good.'[77] But for the more famous Prussian philosopher there was a rational and *a priori* idea of moral perfection connected with the notion of a free will. According to Deakin, Swedenborg simply went further than Kant's categorical imperative (act as though thy action were to become by thy will an universal maxim of conduct) to demonstrate, through the senses God had opened, the reality of such a maxim 'in its extension beyond the grave'.[78]

Deakin therefore judged Swedenborg's Revelation to be objective and intellectual, coming through the altered and extended field of the mind. However, the vehicle for that process whereby the soul is turned to God was affective, arising from the emotions manifest in contemplation and devotional prayer. In his discussion of these ideas in the second volume 'Theology', it is at times difficult to discern whether Deakin was still expositing Swedenborg's ideas, or speaking in more general Idealist terms of the task of the aspirant. The utility of Revelation, he notes in one passage, is in awakening the religious emotions of 'wonder awe admiration & worship'.[79] A current 'Clue' puts it better, citing as one of the dangers of materialism a tendency to render 'the emotional & sympathetic void of elevation & the moral void of power'. Cryptically he added that it also denies 'personal commerce' (with the transcendental?).[80] Thus Revelation might be achieved by rational means, but for Deakin its true glory was its very numinous quality, the 'evidences' of the Divine Will and the Divine Goodness in the course of events, the intimate communings of deep prayer, the wonder evoked by the fulfilment of prophecies; all these were additional spurs to expand the Ideal:

> The more conscious we become of His presence, the more do we feel His pureness & become awed by His inexpressible majesty & goodness ... the more are we humbled, softened, & at the same time strengthened to erect for ourselves a lofty standard ... of virtue & benevolence. The whole universe is transfigured by this one transcendent truth.[81]

In the 'Testament' to his daughters, contemporary with the gospel, Deakin gave due emphasis to the affective. He confessed firstly that intellectual exposition had been essential to him, but that it was subsidiary, since the chief aim of religion is to secure harmony:

> between life and belief, between intellectual convictions and moral principles ... the mental assent of the few simple truths, great as no other truths are great, which are at the root of religious teaching, [and which] has a transcendent importance.[82]

While he rejected much of what he called Swedenborg's metaphysical theology, one of the jewels of this study which he retained, and which in transmuted form was to assume even greater significance in the new century, was the doctrine of Divine Influx. Swedenborg had derived from Descartes the dogma that 'existence is perpetual subsistence'.[83] From this perspective, his system can be understood as a form of panentheism in which Nature, man, Heaven and Hell are only partial expressions of God, who is in Himself all Goodness and Truth. Deakin describes Swedenborg's central teaching of a Divine Influx thus: 'All life is God—God is the source of all life which from moment to moment flows freshly from Him into its myriad forms, so that without constant Influx, they would instantly cease to be.'[84] While remaining individuals, all creatures in the various worlds are receptacles according to their varying capacities for Love and Goodness, of the primordial Influx, and by its extension, of Truth as they become more like God. As Swedenborg himself phrased it in his enigmatic way: 'Goodness is one and becomes various by Truth.'[85]

For the life of religion and morals, the reception of Influx is related to the Ideal of Unselfish Love. Swedenborg like Kant divided the mind into Will and Understanding, where the true individuality resides in the will. Salvation is a moral attitude, an 'inclination' toward God and our fellow man requiring an act of will, an absolute choice between higher and lower, heaven or hell, which is predicated by the quality and sincerity of one's moral intention, so as to receive this higher Influx of Goodness. Deakin did not concur with Swedenborg completely. Though he could agree that the Infinite suffers with us, since God is ruled by the same laws as all creation and hence all evil is not His, he could not accede to Swedenborg's radical Monism which gives all substance and all individuality to God, thereby reducing man to a 'mere consciousness' and placing the 'responsibility of the mortal to zero'.[86]

However, the most profound and lasting influence of Swedenborg's teachings on Deakin's inner life was his practical ethics. These were embodied in his Ideal of Unselfish Love and the cognate Doctrine of Uses, which Swedenborg claimed gave a modern rendering of the simple yet profound teachings of Jesus, exceeding his injunction to love one's neighbour as oneself, by placing the welfare of one's neighbour first. Again this was related to the affective dimension. Swedenborg wrote that 'a man lives what he desires, and what he lives is the delight of his love.'[87] Swedenborg had adapted this conception from Augustinian theology, where 'delight' refers to the mobilisation of feelings as allies of the intellect; for Augustine this process represented the mainspring of human action, where through a mysterious alliance of intellect and feeling, God working through the individual influences the will. Salvation then depends on one's capacity for 'delight', and conscious actions are the final results of hidden processes whereby the 'heart' is stirred, is 'massaged and set' by the hand of God.[88] This idea, integral to both Augustine and Swedenborg's theology, was enthusiastically appropriated by Deakin with the important proviso that it did not reduce free will. The Ideal of Unselfish Love was to remain central to Deakin's moral life.

It was, however, the question of free will that concerned Deakin most. As bourgeois political radical, the natural corollary to free choice and the need to ameliorate the lot of the masses, was that humans must have the ability to control and adapt their environment. In his personal religion as in his public endeavours, the concept of free will figures prominently. In his lengthy discussion of free will Deakin presented first the antithesis to Swedenborg's views in the French aristocrat and philosopher Rochefoucauld, who argued that even the most noble and seemingly selfless actions of men are due to 'an egoistic feeling which is chameleon like in its manifestations, but single in its spirit of absolute selfishness'.[89] Deakin's lengthy response is in essence simple and direct: Swedenborg taught that we could not cease from the commission of sins, selfishness being the most pervasive and insidious, 'except from an interior & superior love'.[90] True morality springs only from sincere intention. It was a simple and austere maxim that Deakin earnestly tried to apply to his life, the practical and moral coefficient of the spiritual Ideal of Unselfishness.

While he agreed with Swedenborg on the 'absolute inutility for philosophic purposes of the mere knowledge of an objective spiritual world',[91] Deakin also regarded the truth of immortality to be 'the keystone of morals in religion'.[92] What he meant is again best conveyed in his critique of materialism and still earlier of Utilitarianism and the positivist philosophy, which he also considered a gospel, but in a 'dwarfed & stunted' form.[93] With no eternal life and no eternal progression self-sacrifice, the qualities of self-control and devotion to the Ideal would be 'rendered ridiculous', since there would be no ultimate justification for pitching one's conduct and aspiration to the highest key.[94] The inference is clear: with no ultimate reward, we would all revert to the level of the brute acting only for selfish gain. Thus in the Swedenborg gospel considerable space is devoted to a review of the teachings of world religions on personal immortality, which he insisted either redresses the inequalities of earth life, or else 'men are not justly ruled'.[95] Deakin's evolutionism, never a part of Swedenborg's own system, connects this belief with the ideas of free will, cosmic justice and reincarnation. Through successive lives apparent injustices are redressed in an eternal progression, while 'the nascent qualities, the latent capacities & the unexercised powers' inherent in the soul are slowly brought to maturity.[96]

This transformation of Swedenborg's doctrines, who would have regarded them as rank heresies, again illustrates Deakin's eclectic mind: from the Freethought of his adolescence, confirmed by his study of Swedenborg, he derived the proclamation of a future existence; from A. R. Wallace, the idea of an eternal progression extrapolated beyond Darwin's physicalist theory; from Blavatsky and Theosophy, karma (though he did not use the term until later writings) and reincarnation, understood as an extended cosmic mechanism for achieving spiritual maturity. His conception of the Ideal now inclined to questions of morality rather than metaphysics. His current instructions to his daughters aver that the future life is 'doubtless natural in its forms and conditions', and that its sphere is 'probably around us, and already influences, and is influenced by, the natural sphere'; but he added that 'except as matter of proof of its existence the next sphere and its peculiarities are not worthy of much attention while we are in this.'[97]

From Swedenborg Deakin also derived the fundamental belief that 'the moral is that which proceeds from the love of others, & the spiritual is the consciously & deliberately moral.'[98] He continued to believe that elevated beings and Divine agencies exist, through whom God enters human life and human history. Hence a sort of moral dialectic transpires between those higher agencies and beings and the aspirant, who by a purification of intention prepares himself for yet higher inspiration. Swedenborg's practical ethics were based on the simple declaration that good deeds done without good motives are as futile as faith without good deeds, or intellect without morals.[99] This was the meaning behind Swedenborg's claim to be going beyond the injunction of Jesus. Happiness is the corollary of unselfishness, and the moral law is the 'axis of life & the key to creation. It is the very heart of Swedenborg's gospel.'[100] Deakin regarded this a 'code for use' as thorough as the New Testament, yet adapted to the needs of the modern world. In an eloquent passage he warned his daughters:

> Apart from God life is selfish mainly and sensual mainly—narrow, hard, harsh, and discordant ... Sheer selfishness is hostility to all other life ... Unselfishness without God is at best partial and spasmodic or despairing and ineffective. Without God there could scarcely be a Divine order conceived or a future life trusted in. Without something beyond us answering to the better impulse within, and without some confidence in the final success of the unselfish principle which we wish to obey, there is practically nothing to be hoped for or striven for.[101]

It was an Idealist gospel through and through—the good person is made better by the intellectual apprehension of Divine truths, and as these become incorporated into his character, influencing his moral nature, so he becomes receptive to higher and deeper truths.[102] Deakin like Swedenborg exalted Duty. With the important provisos of capacity and opportunity, humankind's duty is to work toward the best and the highest, to effect the Divine will as it is progressively revealed. In the light of the evolutionistic framework of his era Deakin could conceive a slow and fitful but steady progression of the soul. In the gospel as elsewhere, he considered Duty the highest Ideal within us:

> The obligation of Duty, of obedience to the highest, is the most imperative of all our obligations, & in fulfilling that, we are certain that we thus discharge our part in the world. There is no uncertainty on this head.[103]

Morality then was the very heart of Swedenborg's gospel. Like Kant, and according to Deakin and others, long before him, he believed that the truly moral are those deeds which spring from a 'good will'. If his account of the spiritual world can be accepted, Deakin declares, there need be no further discussion on the problems of morals since 'the moral law can be deduced with absolute certainty from the facts before us.'[104] For Swedenborg the spiritual was always 'the enthusiastic, the inspired moral'.[105] We can see the absolute force of this view in Deakin's advice to his daughters a few months later in a passage that, but for its evolutionism and its more agreeable style, might have come straight from Kant:

> The one and only concern of man is moral, for this alone can secure at once the happiness and progress to perfection of the whole race; the two aspects of the one ideal which makes life worth living, confers dignity upon humanity, and indicates the purposes of creation. The implications of morality are the existence of God and immortality, two dogmas which we are bound to believe apart from proof, because morality demands them, though they have the highest warrant of faith as well, since they win the consent of our whole nature, and although much can be advanced in their behalf as purely intellectual hypotheses.[106]

No system could have been better suited to Deakin's character and experiences than Swedenborg's at this time in his life. He had seen much, but was dissatisfied with all but 'the bare facts' of Spiritism. His experiences with prophecy and politics, especially the Grand Prophecy, had convinced him that there is a greater Will involved in human affairs. Yet he remained perplexed about the relations and the responsibilities these implied. With what Deakin called a 'direct & communicable' standard, Swedenborg had provided one answer. His seership was rational, hence more trustworthy than the enigmatic utterances of previous prophets and mystics. There were not the apocalyptic visions of the Old Testament prophets, nor the 'cloudy glories' of William Blake. Guaranteed by its 'strictly natural & scientific character',[107] Swedenborg's Revelation had consisted simply of what his spiritual senses had disclosed to him, made possible like all things by the Divine Influx.

Hence the 'Swedenborgian' elements of Deakin's lifelong faith are here apparent: personal Revelation, a purified Reason as illuminating agency, and Providence. Implicit throughout Deakin's lengthy exposition was the assumption that Swedenborg had been prepared for his illumination both by his intellectual training and by his moral fervour. Swedenborg's practical religion taught devotion to an Ideal exemplified in Unselfish Love. On the transcendental level his gospel affirmed the reality of a future life, the rule of law, and a Divine Justice throughout the Kosmos. There is no doubt that during this labour of eight months, Deakin, so recently shown the Grand Prophecy himself, longed in his depths for just such a direct Revelation as Swedenborg had claimed. There are several parallels between their lives, but the most important was their shared belief that a prayerful, productive and moral life is the pathway to illumination. Deakin's paradigm of Revelation was now firmly linked to a meritocracy of moral intention.

'Islam': The Preacher as Prophet

In the latter half of the 1890s, Deakin produced a great rush of writing, including the *Federal Story* and *Crisis in Victorian Politics 1879–1881*. We have already considered 'Personal Experiences in Spiritism'. A brief acquaintance with 'mind cure' resulted in 'Seven Lessons' which has affinities to Christian Science, being a kind of do-it-yourself manual to better health through the affirmation of the Divine nature within.[108] 'Seven Lessons' was never published; it was very much in the style of what William James called 'The Religion of Healthy-Mindedness' which enjoyed great popularity around the turn of the century, when not only James' *The Varieties of Religious Experience*, but books like Mary Baker Eddy's *Science and Health* and R. W. Trine's *In Tune with the Infinite* were popular bestsellers. Eddy, the founder of Christian Science, went furthest in denying the reality of ill health. We note that from this time, the question of health assumes increasing importance in Deakin's outlook, and that his faith in heterodox healing techniques was now turning, like his religion, to a greater reliance on personal resources.

Finally, during the same period he wrote at least two further gospels. The 'Essay on the Modern Gospels' (1896) repeats or expands previous themes, and it seems to have been related to his unsuccessful push to have Scripture reintroduced in State schools. Characteristically, Deakin left his musings incomplete and begging a number of questions. This somewhat directionless essay does not specifically address the question of children's spiritual development, but it expatiates at length on the positive influence of gospels throughout the history of humankind and on the value of religious education to moral development, supporting the inference that it was written for the specific purpose of clarifying his ideas.[109] Far more revealing of Deakin's attitudes, and more interesting in its speculations, is 'Islam', a treatise of 150 pages written in 1897. It makes an instructive adjunct to Swedenborg's gospel, since it focuses on the personality of Mohammed and the nature and method of his Revelation. Deakin did not consider Islamic theology, and consciously bypassed its history, intellectual and artistic flowerings, and the 'relation of religion to race'.[110] Instead he wished to consider Islam 'only at its source, to enquire into the origin of this mighty human agency' just prior to and during Mohammed's life. His declared method was to 'study the *man*' and by a simple subtraction of the state of things he left from those he found, to determine 'what it was he added', relying upon Mohammed's own words and speeches.[111] Since Deakin could not read Arabic, his methodology seems suspect, and how far he succeeded in his aim is not clear. But this focus of attention on the Revelator is consistent with previous gospels.

Deakin always admired Mohammed. His appeal was a simplicity of faith, his capacity as preacher and the directness of his message, in this the 'purest of all forms of monotheism'.[112] In a long journal written eight years previously, he had described the Koran as 'instinct with energy & insight, with heat & light, with fire of conviction & flame of aspiring zeal'.[113] Thermal metaphors abound: there was a 'burning veracity' fired by the 'intensity of conviction' of the Prophet. His central message was of 'good works & exactly proportioned rewards' where heaven is won by those 'who believe & do good works'. Deakin had much to criticise also in the Koran, like the doctrine of Predestination, its otherworldliness, the 'strictly physical character' of rewards and punishments, and a paradise of 'idleness indulgence & banqueting'. But these were outweighed by the directness and simplicity of Mohammed's pronouncements as to the evidences of God. When confronted with such questions, Mohammed offered no 'Argument from Design' as such: 'he points simply to the sun & to the moon to life & to death & says these prove the existence of God the Creator & Presence.' This for Deakin offered more 'feeling of proof' than volumes of 'thick spun argument.' It was a message 'rich in poetical power & ethical energy & in noble declamation'.[114]

In the gospel of 'Islam', written eight years later, Deakin was still concerned with Mohammed's Revelation, and the manner of its reception. His message, like Isaiah's, had been a command expected and desired, to 'Cry', or in another rendering, to 'Recite'. Deakin noted approvingly that, unlike a modern seer who would have 'cross examined' the messenger, Mohammed accepted both message and messenger as coming from the Omnipotent; it was 'one mighty in power' whom legend identifies as the Angel Gabriel. Mohammed simply 'heard & believed the verdict of his senses'.[115]

As before, Deakin compared Mohammed's illumination with others who had experienced 'ecstatic trances & unutterable despairs' at conversion, among them Swedenborg, Bunyan, Fox and the Hebrew prophets, while Wordsworth had described 'a less passionate & serener trance'.[116] Deakin worked hard, as he had with Swedenborg, to establish the veracity of the psychic experiences. Given its frequent repetition, this theme seems crucial to Deakin. Just as it had been Swedenborg's 'dullness' and analytic mode of thought, so with Mohammed it was his fervour and 'moderation' in the way of paranormal experiences that Deakin judged the most reliable indices to his veracity. Mohammed had seen his angel only twice, and with the night vision of the Temple of Jerusalem, these were the total of his experiences over twenty-two years. In Deakin's day, comparative studies of religion were still novel, even radical, and Deakin, like Garth Wilkinson, did not share the confident assumptions of most other commentators as to the superiority of the Christian religion. In yet another comparison he surveyed similar experiences from Ezekiel to the 'modern seers' of Spiritualism like the Reverend Stainton Moses and A.J. Davis, where invariably a 'storm of stress of body & mind' seemed to usher in 'the still small voice of objective inspiration'.[117] He linked the emotions once again with 'true prayer' and individual aspiration. By prayer he did not mean 'the parrot-like repetition of pious phrases'; on the contrary:

> The intensity, the emotion, the concentration of will & wish in supreme effort of aspiration is true prayer, shaking the physical frame when it becomes convulsive, tearing the veil away from self-righteousness & conceit, when it is sincere. Calm it may be, but deep, potent it always is in one way or another ...[118]

Mohammed's inspiration was 'a state of his own mind, or mind & senses, in which he believed himself to be spoken to by some invisible being in the Arabic tongue'. Deakin concluded that Mohammed had claimed simply 'to have received a spirit communication'. He received his Suras not directly from God, but through an intermediary, and except for these two or three occasions, he had neither seen nor heard a voice: 'but simply felt flow into him, as if from an outside source, a certain communication which he remembered & repeated'.[119]

There is more than a mere similarity in the language and concepts in such passages which invites comparison with Deakin's own early 'dictation' and literary inspiration; indeed, there appears to be an identification of his experiences as a type with those of religious geniuses throughout history, though of course lacking their intensity or clarity. Deakin spoke thus as something of an *insider* in matters of inspirational writing. This is always implied rather than stated, but it is particularly noticeable in his discussion of the source of Mohammed's message.

Deakin insists there is nothing in the Koran that could not have proceeded from Mohammed's own mind; it needed no 'external agency', only, he adds in seeming contradiction, 'an impulse which appears to be external to explain its contents'.[120] Whatever he meant, and Deakin is maddeningly vague at such junctures, one is struck by the similarities with the descriptions of his own experiences. While there is no direct mention of his own 'impressional' gospel according to Bunyan, its ambience is everywhere apparent. Mohammed was not an 'introspective psychologist' but an 'unlettered Bedoin of the 6th century'.[121] Whatever the source of the 'impulse', Deakin clearly believed it had been external in some undefined way. 'Where the normal action of his mind ended, & where the abnormal began' one could not measure except by the Koran, his sole production. Not so easily explicable was: 'the immense accession of certainty, faith & force which he derived from his first revelation, & which was renewed frequently after in his trances'.[122]

Deakin suggests that the miracle of that 'impulse' lay not only in the contents of the Koran but also in that immense faith which made an illiterate man capable of producing a master work which has become the inspiration of millions. Deakin's closing line: 'There is no God but God, & Mohammed is one of his prophets', while not at all Islamic, is a succinct aphorism for Deakin's own belief on the nature of gospels and gospel-bearers.[123]

These then were the elements of the Ideal as Deakin presented them in his gospels from late adolescence to middle age. The images implied throughout leave little doubt as to Deakin's religious Idealism, whose fundamental orientation, already evident in *A New Pilgrim's Progress*, was modified later with the addition of a coherent system of morals and a belief in Providence. A total belief will always escape 'reconstruction', and especially the ephemeral relations between reflective thought, religious faith and political action. Yet through such tracts we can discern the strength of Deakin's conviction regarding a Divine government and especially at this period, a Divine provenance for the inauguration of the Commonwealth of Australia. The next decade, with its hard politics, exhausting work and dwindling allegiances, would bring far less elation to the task Alfred Deakin had set for himself, to help make the Ideal a reality—the building of the Commonwealth.

Notes

1 The financial difficulties of the late 1870s had much to do with the conservative resurgence of 1880, which eventually produced the 1883–90 coalition: Berry-Service, then Deakin–Gillies. The budgetary difficulties in the 1890s destroyed the coalition and eventually produced a fresh polarisation, the Labor Party and the Deakinite Liberals: G. Bartlett, 'The Political Orders in Victoria and New South Wales 1856–1890', *Australian Economic History Review*, vol. 8, no. 1, March 1968.

2 These include 'Islam', 3/25, 1897; around 1904 what I have called a Research Notebook on Islam and Hinduism; Lady White Notebook II, La Nauze papers, series 5248, N.L.A.; and 'Ten Letters', a study of the ideas of Plato and Epictetus, 5/201–610; in the 'Gospel According to Swedenborg', 2 vols., 5/1173–4, 1889–90, Deakin reviewed teachings on the afterlife from ancient Egypt through medieval Christianity. As late as 1912, Deakin wrote a further commentary on Islam and on 'Jesus the Healer', in 'A Ragged Re-Examination of the Ultimate' [reverse side], pp. 1–38; copy in La Nauze papers, series 5248, N.L.A.

3 'Gospel ... Swedenborg', 5/1173, vol. 1, p. 95; Jacob Neusner's comments about the proper study of Torah approximate Deakin's views on the illumination available through texts: 'Study becomes *ritual action* when it is endowed with values *extrinsic* to its ordinary character—that is, when set in a mythic context. When a disciple memorizes his master's traditions and actions, he participates in that myth. His study is thereby endowed with the sanctity that ordinarily pertains to prayer or other cultic matters. Study loses its referent in intellectual attainment. The *act* of study itself becomes holy. What matters is piety—piety expressed through the rites of studying.' This notion of study as ritual action, though relating to a far different context, helps to illustrate the process Deakin called 'gospelizing': Jacob Neusner, *The Way of Torah*, North Scituate, 1979, p. 68. The status of another production of this period, the 'Testament' written in 1890 for the guidance of his daughters in the event of his early death, resembles the Judaic practice of leaving an 'ethical will', where the legator would divide not his earthly property, but his highest ideals, asking his heirs to carry out those ideals: ibid., p. 87.

4 R. W. Emerson, *Representative Men* (1883), Malibu, 1980, p. xii.

5 A. Deakin [anonymous author], *A New Pilgrim's Progress, purporting to be given by John Bunyan, through an Impressional Writing Medium*, Melbourne, 1877. The discrepancies between his work and Bunyan's epic were patently evident to Deakin, who admits in the preface: 'As to the personality of that intelligence, each must judge for himself, the only proviso being that critics consider the, I fear, too pronounced peculiarities of another style, and the superficial colouring naturally imparted to all which has its passage through an individual mind': 'Personal Experiences ...', 5/1423, section XIII, p. 9.

6 The schisms during the 1870s between Melbourne 'Religious' and 'Progressive' Spiritualists, indicated by the exclusion of 'Progressive' from the title of the association after 1873, have been touched upon in A. J. Gabay, 'The Seance ...'; Janet Oppenheim has analysed the differences for the English movement in *The Other World...*, pp. 86–7.

7 'Personal Experiences ...', 5/1423, section XIII, p. 9.

8 Ledger, 3/292, 1 January 1876.

9 Foolscap A3 Notebook, 3/294, Notes for 1876, 1910, p. 47.

10 Ibid., Notes for 20–27 January 1877.

11 Ibid., Notes for 1876.

12 W. H. Terry (ed.), *Spirit Teachings. Oral, Impressional & Automatic*, Melbourne, 1908; the preface states that Dr Motherwell's circle ran for twenty years. The evidence for Deakin's short career as medium rests on this production, *A New Pilgrim's Progress*, and scattered 'trance' addresses recorded in the *Harbinger of Light*, e.g., 1875, p. 796, p. 828, p. 838 on 'Inspiration', p. 844 on 'Communication'.

13 Deakin, *A New Pilgrim's Progress*, preface.

14 William Wordsworth's 'Tintern Abbey', and A. Tennyson's 'In Memoriam' penned over seventeen years after the death of his friend A. H. Hallam, were in their ways crucial factors in the popularisation of abnormal states in the Romantic era. Tennyson described a 'waking trance', while Wordsworth claimed 'communion' with the 'Presences', Nature as Revealing Agency.

15 John Bunyan, *Pilgrim's Progress*, Ringwood, 1978, p. 13.

16 Deakin, *A New Pilgrim's Progress*, p. 8. Although Deakin's reading lists from these years have not survived, he must have drawn from Draper's *Conflict of Religion and Science* and from the accounts of Mohammed's illness and subsequent recovery to become Prophet, a pattern repeated by many shamans and mystics; what seems noteworthy is the precocity and range of his reading indicated by such passages.

17 Ibid., p. 13; 'partner' is Deakin's term; perhaps it was another radical idea he was giving voice to, since he and Wilful (later Redemptress) never marry.

18 Ibid., p. 16. Though somewhat ambivalent and inconsistent in its allegorical purposes, the descriptions and even the themes formed part of a 'spiritist' genre of the period. Compare Deakin's with the vision of an Australian 'clairvoyant' in the same era: 'We arrive at a superb city, where there are myriads of spirits teaching; and vast numbers passing out and in, all enjoying their heaven. What a land of exquisite loveliness; words are not sufficiently expressive to speak of it. The surrounding magnificent mountain scenery of matchless rainbow colouring, gorgeous flowers and grand mansions, are all entirely beyond description. It is a glorious city of learning and instruction, with many pleasant winding streets. Mighty bands of teachers are here. My Guide says, it is the Wisdom City. On! further on! and we are again nearing the Bright City; in its effulgence it seems unapproachable. Pure beings are at the gates. Multitudes of very ancient spirits are here gathered together ...'. This tedium meanders along for another six pages. Though it does not approach Deakin's command of language, the themes are similar, and were drawn probably also from *Pilgrim's Progress*. Miss Milne, in J. Curtis, *Rustlings in the Golden City*, Melbourne, 1888, pp. 186–7.

19 Deakin, *A New Pilgrim's Progress*, p. 33.

20 Ibid., p. 36. See 'trance' lecture by 'Mr A's control', which incorporates the Reformation theme: *Spirit Teachings* ..., pp. 32–6, 22 November 1875.

21 Deakin, *A New Pilgrim's Progress*, p. 133. For a remarkably similar scenario in the initiation by 'Six Grandfathers' of a Sioux shaman, see John Neihardt, [compiler], *Black Elk Speaks, Being the Life Story of a Holy Man of the Oglala Sioux*, Lincoln, 1971, especially 'The Great Vision', pp. 20–47.

22 John Bunyan, *Pilgrim's Progress*, p. 69.

23 Deakin, *A New Pilgrim's Progress*, p. 122.

24 Ibid., p. 123.

25 Ibid., pp. 129–30; this passage confirms Deakin's early introduction to the ideas of Swedenborg; for Deakin's discussion of his Ideal of Unselfish Love, see 'Gospel ... Swedenborg', 5/1174, vol. 2, p. 131.

26 Ibid., pp. 136–8.

27 Ibid., p. 254.

28 Ibid., p. 258.

29 The control of 'Mr A' (perhaps Bunyan) in a trance address the previous year had called science 'the plough that will prepare the ground' so as to break up 'the thick crust of ignorance and error which has so long lain fallow.' In this revelatory paradigm, Reason is proclaimed as revealer of the nether spheres: *Spirit Teachings* ..., p. 35.

30 Deakin, *A New Pilgrim's Progress*, p. 170.

31 Ibid., p. 171.

32 'Gospel ... Swedenborg', 5/1174, vol. 2, p. 242.

33 For a discussion of the original 'Gospel' of the Ancients, and the relationship of a Great White Brotherhood to Theosophy, see Jill Roe, *Beyond Belief* ..., pp. 128–9 and passim.

34 'Gospel According to Wordsworth', 4/408 ff., 12 April 1884, p. 5.

35 Ibid.

36 Ibid., 4/496.

37 Ibid., 4/408, p. 7.

38 'Gospel According to Shakespeare', 3/26, was commenced on 12 September 1886, with a pause from 22 January 1887 when Deakin left for England, and resumed intermittently from 4 November 1888 to 6 July 1889.

39 David Hume's argument of the Problem of Evil is discussed in the 'Gospel ... Swedenborg', 5/1174, vol. 2, pp. 224–5.

40 'Gospel ... Shakespeare', 3/26, September 1886, pp. 154–5.

41 Ibid., p. 158.

42 Ibid., 11 November 1888, p. 340.

43 Ibid., p. 345.

44 Ibid., pp. 351, 165.

45 Ibid., p. 351.

46 'Indian & Colonial Diary', 4/1, 6 July 1889.

47 'Gospel ... Shakespeare', 3/26, p. 157.

48 'Gospel ... Swedenborg', 5/1173, vol. 1, p. 2.

49 Ibid., p. 4.

50 Ibid., p. 198.

51 Ibid., p. 4.

52 Ibid., p. 219.

53 'Impromptus', 5/1508, 16 October 1881, p. 115.

54 Neusner, *The Way of Torah*, p. 87; see note 3 above.

55 'Gospel ... Swedenborg', 5/1173, vol. 1, p. 26; for an engaging account of the life and thought of Emanuel Swedenborg, see George Trobridge, *Swedenborg Life and Teaching*, New York, 1976.

56 'Gospel ... Swedenborg', 5/1173, vol. 1, p. 93.

57 Trobridge, *Swedenborg ...*, p. 97.

58 Ibid., p. 85.

59 'Personal Experiences ...', 5/1223–4, section III, pp. 1–2.

60 'Gospel ... Swedenborg', 5/1173, vol. 1, p. 93.

61 'Boke ...', 5/851, prayer LXII, 6 July 1889.

62 Ibid.; for discussion of Swedenborg's claim that the Judgement came in 1757, see Trobridge, *Swedenborg ...*, pp. 117–20; on the New Church in Australia, see I. A. Robinson, *A History of the New Church in Australia 1832–1980*, Hawthorn, 1980.

63 'Gospel ... Swedenborg', 5/1173, vol. 1, p. 56.

64 Ibid., p. 71.

65 Ibid., pp. 79–80. The crisis lasted from April 1743 to 1745.

66 Ibid., p. 8.

67 Ibid., p. 11.

68 Ibid., p. 10.

69 Ibid., 5/1174, vol. 2, p. 331.

70 Ibid.

71 Ibid., 5/1173, vol. 1, p. 10.

72 Ibid., p. 8.

73 Ibid., 5/1174, vol. 2, p. 331.

74 Ibid., 5/1173, vol. 1, p. 1.

75 Ibid., p. 3.

76 Ibid., 5/1174, vol. 2, p. 8.

77 Trobridge, *Swedenborg*..., p. 111. Kant, who grudgingly acknowledged the similarities between Swedenborg's moral system and his own, believed that a kind of practical knowledge regarding God's existence and nature could be derived from morality (hence the title of his principal work on morals *The Critique of Practical Reason*). God and Immortality are necessary so that all morally good men are to be happy and morally wicked men are to be unhappy, which is not the case in this world, but will be in the next.

78 'Gospel ... Swedenborg', 5/1174, vol. 2, p. 327.

79 Ibid., 5/1173, vol. 1, p. 14.

80 'Clues', vol. 2, 3/288, no. 324, 25 April 1889.

81 'Gospel ... Swedenborg', 5/1174, vol. 2, p. 88; for an argument on the numinous quality of religion, see Rudolph Otto, *The Idea of the Holy*, (1917), New York, 1958.

82 A. Deakin, 'Testament (prepared for the guidance of his daughters)', 19/356, 7 September 1890, p. 3.

83 'Gospel ... Swedenborg', 5/1174, vol. 2, p. 352.

84 Ibid., p. 209. Panentheism is the theological doctrine, differing from Pantheism in that Nature, man and the universe are only partial expressions of God, who remains the Source of all Being and Goodness. See F. C. Happold, *Mysticism, A Study and an Anthology*, Ringwood, 1967.

85 'Gospel ... Swedenborg', 5/1174, vol. 2, p. 47.

86 Ibid., p. 226.

87 E. Swedenborg, *Apocalypse Revealed*, 2 vols., New York, 1962, vol. 1, p. 92.

88 Peter Brown, *Augustine of Hippo*, London, 1967, p. 154.

89 'Gospel ... Swedenborg', 5/1174, vol. 2, p. 313.

90 Ibid., p. 314.

91 Ibid., 5/1173, vol. 1, p. 13.

92 Ibid., p. 110.

93 In an 1881 journal, he called Utilitarianism a 'religious positivism, [hence] a religion— but in a dwarfed & stunted form': 'Impromptus', 5/1508, 29 October 1881, p. 119.

94 'Gospel ... Swedenborg', 5/1173, vol. 1, p. 111.

95 Ibid., p. 110.

96 Ibid., p. 111.

97 Deakin, 'Testament', p. 6.

98 'Gospel ... Swedenborg', 5/1174, vol. 2, p. 76.

99 Ibid. p. 14.

100 Ibid., p. 3.

101 Deakin, 'Testament', p. 1.

102 'Gospel ... Swedenborg', 5/1174, vol. 2, p. 71.

103 Ibid., p. 175.

104 Ibid., p. 9.

105 Ibid. p. 39.

106 Deakin, 'Testament', p. 6.

107 'Gospel ... Swedenborg', 5/1173, vol. 1, p. 14.

108 'Seven Letters', 5/108–114, circa 1898–9.

109 'Essay on the Modern Gospels', 5/685–814, circa 1896.

110 'Islam', 3/25, 1897, p. 13.

111 Ibid., p. 15.

112 Ibid., p. 7.

113 'Links', 3/5, no. 69, 21–23 March 1889.

114 Ibid.

115 'Islam', 3/25, p. 52.

116 Ibid., p. 59.

117 Ibid., p. 61.

118 Ibid., p. 48.

119 Ibid., p. 65.

120 Ibid., p. 70.

121 Ibid., p. 65.

122 Ibid., p. 117.

123 Ibid.

CHAPTER

6

Out of the Body

Upon a lucky night
In secrecy, inscrutable to sight,
I went without discerning
And with no other light
Except for that which in my heart was burning.

It lit and led me through
More certain than the light of noonday clear
To where One waited near
Whose presence well I knew,
There where no other presence might appear.

St John of the Cross

From around 1888, in the waning days of 'Marvellous Melbourne', there appeared among Deakin's 'Clues' and other journals occasional narratives, parables, and similar 'fictive' writings, generally untitled and seldom exceeding 500 words, which share as common subject matter what in modern parlance are referred to as 'out of body' experiences. Visions of judgment, ontological displacements and similar experiences that assault twentieth-century consensus reality crowd the pages of this narrative genre which, though small in volume, is relevant to any consideration of Deakin's private spirituality, especially when viewed against the backdrop of his concurrent gospels.[1] The thirty or so experience narratives that survive relate variations of an heightened experience in which a protagonist is either transported to an alien though beatific region of the Kosmos (Deakin's term), or else a sudden disjunction in the pattern of the world shows him things as they really are, and he is in the process impelled from his body, with the identity of self or selves thrown into some doubt.

The liminal zone where 'the two worlds meet', the traffic between divine and secular, between the mundane self and its highest expression in the Ideal, was a constant source of fascination to Deakin; it reappears throughout his writing in different forms. Nowhere is that fascination more vividly expressed than in these narratives, the bulk of which spanned the troubled 1890s. Gradually, they refer less to illumination, and more to an escape from a body racked with ailments and a life beset with worries, and they place a greater value on the power of prayer. Hence it could be argued that they reflect a process over time, expressing in literary form an attendant frustration with mundane matters and a desire for *moksa*, liberation.

In the long march to Federation we saw something of Deakin's religious beliefs in action, largely through his petitions to Deity. The 'silent student' and spiritual aspirant found expression also through the gospels. Now we briefly examine the man from another side, as it were, of his literary corpus. Some of these narratives are undoubtedly stories; in others, the ontological status of the experience remains ambiguous: they may relate a 'real' experience, be purely imaginative, or yet serve as refracted accounts or composites of such 'real' experiences. Hence they are 'fictive' but not necessarily fictional, and at the least they declare fervently for that immediate experience of transcendance whose attainment had been an article of faith at least since his introduction to Swedenborg, and probably long before. It may be that the two concurrent genres comprised as it were two sides of the same story, the 'gospels' engaging Deakin's Enlightenment belief in the capacity of Reason to comprehend great truths, with a Victorian compulsion to make knowledge serve moral ends, while the 'fictive' narratives expressed through a literary mode his fervent aspiration to reach the Ideal. Just as the inscription of prayers recorded a process of praying, not just the words, some of these 1890s narratives may have even been spiritual exercises to promote or induce such an experience of transcendence, based on his current paradigm whereby the Higher Self reveals its true essence only when separated from its 'muddy vesture of decay'.

It is the changing context of belief which these narratives suggest that is of greatest relevance to this study, and what they can render of Deakin's conception of an essential or 'Higher' Self, and his attitudes to the body and health, particularly in the later narratives. We now consider samplings from this mode of expression, in more or less chronological order, to conclude with a close analysis of one story from 1892 given in its entirety, an untitled narrative I have called 'The Thoughtful Idealist', which illustrates important influences in Deakin's essentially religious and progressively more mystical world view and ethos.

'The Theatre', a gothic 1888 tale written in the first person after the manner of R. L. Stevenson, illustrates some of the Kantian and Hegelian themes Deakin was then studying. It begins in vraisemblance to Deakin's own life: 'I am never a close observer of the total scene around me ... Now that I have become absorbed in politics & business ... concerned chiefly with the real instead, as of old, with the Ideal ...'. This prelude prepares the reader for a transformation in the scene, as the protagonist stresses the ordinariness of the crowd, ranging from 'money & the vulgarity that apes money' to the 'sober clerks & fat shopkeepers' in the upper circle, as he entered the theatre to see 'The Lady of Lyons'. The play commenced, and the protagonist, musing now on the illusion created by the actors, discovered suddenly that he could see 'under the mask of flesh & bone' as he had under the mask of paint and dress. He saw first 'a curious complex life that seemed to be made up of lives', and as this monistic vision changed the apparition, he now saw, was 'merely mechanical', and actors and audience alike were revealed as 'automata'. As his gaze was 'gaining & not losing its keenness' they too became shadowy. Rising from his seat with a choking sensation of terror, he found himself free to pass not only through the 'phantom crowd but the phantom walls that surrounded me'. Earth could not 'sustain' him:

> my feet sank through the flagging. I struggled among graves, among mines, among profound strata, all were solved & resolved itself [sic] into vapour & then into light; not warm, not quickening, with the grey even lampless glowless sphere in which were neither sun nor stars nor planet nor mind, except my own, & this was driven out trackless & beaconless upon the vast & everlasting void.[2]

In an instant he found himself abruptly back inside the theatre; speaking again in the present tense the writer notes that, although he has since 'slept & awakened into my old dream' of politics and business, a 'shadow' sometimes seizes him still when he recalls how 'once I awoke & saw [them] not as they seem but as they are'.

Notwithstanding the references to his own life and the use of the first person, the 'Theatre' is a story probably inspired equally by his current reading of Hegel and R. L. Stevenson, self-consciously literary gothic, and with religious themes implicit. In stark contrast are the 1890s narratives where explicit religious themes and the prominence of Swedenborgian and other mystical concepts reflect a deeper commitment to a personal faith. Two of these will give their general mood. With an untitled 'vision of judgment' recorded in 'Clues' in 1894, the disjunction of a 'normal' reality is no longer experienced in an ambiguity and subsequent reaffirmation of identity, nor only on the mundane sphere. In facsimile of Swedenborg's experiences, even in the structure of the scenario, it concerns a soul who suddenly finds itself in the environment of 'the Lord & Soul of All':

> Was I waking or dreaming when just at the seaside at the close of the year & in the early dawn, it seemed as if I had died, or my spirit had been set free & soared up somewhere in the illimitable where there was a sense without sight of myriads of spiritual beings, bright & free, lofty & rejoicing, & beyond them an intense white radiance, spreading down billions of leagues from the Lord & Soul of All, beheld only as a Heaven of unquenchable living Light into which or before which I floated like a dark atom of earthy substance into the infinite blaze of Divine Glory.[3]

Then a 'trumpet tongue' pronounced his name and he 'stood erect for judgment'. A vivid and emotional narrative describes the mixture of terror, ecstasy, and shame that attended this momentous experience: '... [N]othing was falsified, obscured or palliated' as he was followed into 'every crevisse of desire' by the 'awful searchlight of an unfathomable flood of Purity & Truth'. The revelations of 'pettiness, grossness & guilt' were many and terrible, but instead of the expected judgment, there descended an 'ineffable pity', so that returning to his body his 'eyes & cheek' were wet.

It might be speculated that in these dark days in economic fortunes and federal prospects this narrative, written in the first person, represents a dramaturgical expression of shame and a desire for forgiveness, even for retribution.[4] Images of judgment and failure figure prominently in other writings of the period, prompted no doubt partly by his regret at having lost his own and his father's savings in the general speculative rush that precipitated the depression. Alternatively, it might stand as purely literary excursus.

The Beethoven symphony began and 'with its beginning, the outer world was ending'. So commences an untitled narrative of July 1901, bearing many resemblances to the 'Theatre' story penned thirteen years before. As the music soared the audience, the concert hall, and the surroundings disappeared, and '[b]efore I could realize what was transpiring, I was in a vortex, sucked upwards as if out of the body.' He described a remarkable transformation where, sloughing off his old self as a snake sheds its skin, he found himself in a radiant new form 'quivering with energy, sensibility ... palpitating delicately, unfolding as if in rapture'. Luxuriating in this exotic environment, he expanded past 'choruses of ecstatic soul companions', and in company where he was alone and yet not alone, he asked:

> Where was I? We dived or swam or soared upon the surf, like south sea islanders in their ocean sportiveness. Before us & among us, there rose boiling geysers of light, colours, odours, melody blended translucently in the most exquisite arabesques, traceries, fountains & forms of architectural majesty, massive as of Titan, reared & flowing into rarest filligries of fantasy, from thousands of cupolas, minarets & towers, gardened ... with fresh & flower enriched landscapes.[5]

These elaborate reveries ended abruptly and he was received again in the salon's 'white pathless & feckless polar solitudes'. The symphony was over.

In these later narratives, the experience is transient and ultimately edifying, though his relative remoteness from Swedenborg's conceptions is evident in the 'Beethoven' ecstasy. One important difference between 'Beethoven' and the 'Theatre' transport of thirteen years previous is the diminishing emphasis on the 'real'; it conveys instead an exaggerated sense of carefreeness, of joy and insouciance, qualities that his deteriorating health could by this stage allow him to achieve only in imagination. The marine metaphors seem significant; not only do they indicate that they were composed by his beloved Victorian seaside, but also because water featured as a common symbol for the psyche and the unconscious in occult literature, and Deakin frequently employed the image of the sea in this way, especially in his poetry. It is tempting to ascribe this experience simply to a rush of imagination, a personal aesthetic response to Beethoven's powerful music. Yet the vivid exotica of his momentary release contrasts with the bleakness of the images in the salon, conveying well the sad reluctance of his return. When considered in context, such images speak of a very real desire to transcend the cares of the material world, even if only in imagination; similarly the 'vision of judgment' has close resonances with his recent study of the Swedish mystic, in a desire for expiation and forgiveness, and in the scenario of an immediate intromission from the body.

Upon losing consciousness, either through an external stimulus or sleep, Deakin's spirit soars upward to a better world of 'Living Light', or to an exotic spiritual environment similar to Swedenborg's 'Spiritual world' or to that region described as the 'Summerland' by Spiritualists. His journey seems to be inward in some sense, and in both narratives he bypasses myriads of spiritual beings. Whereas in the 'Beethoven' ecstasy he is content to bathe in the suffusing light and radiance, in the 'vision of judgment' narrative seven years previously, emulating Swedenborg he enters the environment of the 'Lord himself' where a profound ritual drama is enacted as every thought, word and deed is revealed by the 'awful searchlight'.

The elements of these narratives illustrate Deakin's eclecticism. The silent communication with the Lord, a commonplace of Swedenborgian-type literature, and the expected moral judgment unfold as a reaffirmation of God's Love and Understanding, which confirms salvation in Swedenborg's terms as being an individual quest based on moral application. Like Spiritualism, this implies rejection of a theological hell. Vivid and contrasting imagery is used to render a sense of immense scale, and to juxtapose the material and the Ideal, as with the Old Testament image of the 'trumpet tongues' of the angelic herald, and the white radiance spreading down 'billions of leagues' into which he, a 'dark atom of earthy substance', a mere speck with all its 'pettiness, grossness & guilt' in full view, is received into the Divine Presence. Yet like Swedenborg he is permitted to ascend beyond the realm of the bright spirits 'to the Lord himself'. Thus Deakin sees himself in some sense 'chosen', at least potentially. Predictably, he finds himself unworthy, and perhaps arguing for lack of free will, offers as feeble justification that circumstances had made him what he was. Instead of the awful judgment there comes an 'ineffable pity', a love and understanding of the human condition from the Most High.

Analysed in dramaturgic terms, this complex tableau implicitly rejects the nebulous phenomena of Spiritualism for the Divine revelation offered by Swedenborg, where the benevolence of God is revealed despite his unworthiness and ignorance. Deakin acts out the Swedenborgian part of an unworthy though sincere seeker who has a direct experience of a transcendent reality. And this may be a clue to the status of such writings—as I have suggested, given his aspiration for certitude of God and His Ways, these may have been spiritual exercises, where in meditation Deakin imagined how such an experience might unfold; perhaps it was even an attempt to induce it by visualisation.[6] At any rate, although this revelation never seems to have been vouchsafed to him, at least not in the dramatic apocalyptic manner he envisaged, he did believe it would come by dint of effort and a moral intention of holiness, a precept common to Swedenborg and Kant, which Deakin made his own.[7]

Around the time the 'judgment' narrative was penned in 1894, Deakin was subject to recurrent bouts of 'English cholera', a type of dysentery, and he suffered from serious eye strain from too much reading. He had only recently completed a 'Testament' for the guidance of his daughters. Though it is unlikely that he was really preparing for death, he was thinking much and writing about death. By 1901 when he penned the 'Beethoven' ecstasy he presented a self casting off 'its past of weakness & weariness & detail with the physical selves in which it lived, outworn & saturated with ailments' for a new and radiantly healthy Self. It is certain that the condition of his frail constitution, frequently overtaxed by the rigorous demands made upon it, influenced Deakin's outlook considerably. Federation had been only recently won at great cost of health, and his deteriorating physical condition was on his mind, as evidenced by his 'mind cure' manual and his current study of Stoicism. When he wrote that the thought of death had ceased to trouble him early in life once he realised the utter instability of all life, including his own, this was based on the experience of a sickly childhood; but thoughts of sickness, and thoughts of death, not as a morbid fear but as a constant awareness were ever present. Certainly some of these images are extreme. Deakin's talent for the dramatic phrase, and his mastery in recording emotional states through language, added to a private dimension of meaning, lends to these descriptive narratives an imagery of release, evolution, liberation, spiritual wholeness. But it does not make for a final judgment on the nature of the account.

Before turning to a close analysis of the 'Thoughtful Idealist' it is instructive to look at a final example of the genre, almost his last, in which there is again a desire for escape from physical ailments, and now also from the severe strains of high political office, and where the resolution of conflict comes not by transcendence, but by a kind of immanent spiritual Truth received through the Higher Self. The 'M.S' (Modern Saviour?) was written on 10–13 April, and expanded on 12 June 1904. Commenced in the first, it was then altered to the third person. The opening lines dramatically introduce the theme of strain so evident at this time in his outer life, when Deakin had recently lost a tenuous grasp on power with the defeat of his first ministry:

> The M.S. told of strife & strain—a strife within & without each aggravating the other—until this world was like a whirlpool—until life & mind were absorbed in the one struggle to make multitudinous details minister to dead dreams.[8]

Probably there was no intentional play on words in the use of the verb 'minister'. What is curious about this piece is not only the tension observed in other 'non-fictive' writings of the period like the journal 'Personal Equations' in its urgent sense of escape, but also the peculiar throwback scenario, in its remarkable general resemblance to his first gospel *A New Pilgrim's Progress* penned some thirty years before. Like 'Restless' (and Bunyan) the protagonist in this narrative speaks of the 'plains', and he ventures out of the city and into the country to search for Truth. But there is no companion for his quest, it is not an allegory, and even its status as story is uncertain. The narrative is very prolix, with fulsome word pictures of the verdure and terrain which strike a Wordsworthian tone. Like much of Deakin's later private writing, it retraces old ground, and shows only fleetingly the confident journalistic style of former years.

Many things happen to the 'M.S.' as he continues his retreat into Nature: he avoids the 'hereditary foe' in a tiger snake,[9] sees a lyrebird, and comes finally to a 'natural temple', a 'Stonehenge' bounded by granite boulders, where he drops to the ground. Then, once he has stilled his thoughts, he gradually comes into contact with something deep down within himself, a 'soundless echo'. It was 'as if he listened to the central earth at a far aperture', and his spirit responded 'as it could [,] in prayer'.[10] There were 'no words no signs', but as if 'tranced himself' the 'M.S.' was reduced to a mere observer as he felt an influence descend upon the field of his consciousness and was made aware of a sublime hierarchy, and he understood more than he could describe:

> He prayed to God—no definite name known Theology or Metaphysics or private conception—no idol human made—but just to God—towards God—towards the Highest & there came reply ... Taking his instruments out of his hands it touched the chords that he was wont to use but with another & a nobler hand—So that his mind spoke to himself at bidding of some other upon whose larger endowment perhaps a higher yet as upon that higher again another breathed [;] far up towards the Highest went the throng repeating as each could expressing as it might the innermost Divine vouchsafed to it until it reached him prone upon the ground with tidings from the Highest. So it came—[11]

This passage strains linguistic description; it again declares the Swedenborgian doctrine of 'Influx' channelling inspiration to the mundane world from the Highest, an idea now melded to modern ideas about the psychology of the unconscious, and it bears resemblance to 'Redeemer's' initiation described nearly thirty years before. From this point the narrative abandons the mystical tone, and it resumes a familiar form as a disquisition on God and the nature of morals, on Jesus and Buddha, and on unselfishness. This added reflection, framed into the story as paltry fragments reduced to speech of what the 'M.S' had been permitted to understand, is probably the section added in June. The experience, if it was such, was not of a transcendence of the material plane; it was instead like 'a film that unrolled before his inner gaze',[12] totally beyond words. Hence rather than being an 'out of body' experience, it was an ineffable awareness arising within himself, yet not without assistance from another region. This narrative serves to illustrate the shift over a decade in Deakin's ideas about the sources of inspiration, for now it was no longer necessary to transcend the body since illumination might come from, or through, deeper levels of Self.

After some twelve further pages, the 'M.S.' reaches a conclusion familiar to other introspective journals of the period, that a gospel cannot be 'said or sung except by suggestion', that it must be lived. 'Live your gospel be your miracle act your revelation'[13] urged the 'M.S.', since to attempt to write it down is to fail, and in a phrase that suggests that this was more than a literary exercise, he added: 'the attempt has been made & has failed.'[14] It closes with the 'M.S.' satisfied that he had received a revelation: 'Deep within flickered a profound resolve by whose light he felt he would presently be able to find & keep his life's pathway.'

We note that the 'M.S.' experienced a *moral* revelation. Whether it was simply wishful thinking, or whether it describes a real experience, we can never know. Yet perceivable changes at several points in the psychological distance between the author and his narrative, and the tenor of the closing lines, support the view that this narrative might well represent an actual record appropriately embellished, or a retracing of an episode from his young manhood, when Deakin seems to have enjoyed unnumbered 'aesthetic' encounters. This inference is strengthened by its similarities, though with gravely attenuated tone, to the adventures of 'Restless' some thirty years before. His was the joy of the satisfaction of the Spirit 'than which nothing comes closer to the heart of things.'[15]

Perhaps Deakin's best crafted story, in the earlier mode of transcendent Selves, was written in June 1892. It is given here in full:

The thoughtful Idealist who, returning home from his professional visits to his patients, enters in a brown study rather surprised that his maidservant walks at him so unconcernedly as to compel him to step suddenly aside & stare after her in speechless surprise, who going upstairs calls his wife without receiving an answer, though he thinks it must be her step that he hears in his dressing room, enters his study & throws himself into a chair—musing on the mutability of ideas & the impermanence of things, despising the physical & thinking as a physician how tyrannous the body is, how gross in its needs, limited in its powers, given over to decay & disease, a clog upon the mind, a veil athwart the perceptions, a weariness to the spirit, a nest of pains & privations & distracting desires—He notices that the bell rings frequently, & that patients apparently enter, who are shown into the waiting room, but none of whom are announced to him although the maid saw him enter—

Shaking off his inertia, he walks to the window, hearing the sound of wheels before ringing his bell, when to his utter amazement, he beholds his own buggy drive up, & handing the reins to the driver, a man stepping out, almost his own image, a little shorter, a little more stooping, with a less alert air than his, & with a different & weaker profile— but dressed in the identical clothes & with the same light shuffle of the left foot when ascending the steps of the house—He remains paralyzed for a moment, trying to think who it can be, when he hears his step outside, & in another minute enters the older, wearier copy of himself who instantly sits down, as he was accustomed to do, on the professional chair, & taking his notebook, made a hurried entry or two in the crooked writing & with the peculiar abbreviations characteristic of himself—This last observation reduced the silent observer, of whom the double took no notice whatever, to a stoney stupor, which was deepened rather than relieved as the patients came in, & one after another, ignoring his presence, rehearsed their complaints & received their prescriptions, each of them addressing the man at the table by the name belonging to the onlooker, & each of them greeted by him in a voice which was feebler & thinner than the onlooker's, & in which the words were rather slurred together in an unfamiliar way—None of the patients appeared to doubt the identity of the doctor before them, who indeed not only had the trifling little habits belonging to the real man who stood transfixed at the window, but prescribed as he would usually have done under the circumstances, though the observer was too confused to follow him closely—The back of the head & its shape, & the back of the pretended doctor seemed strange, & there was an absorbed short sighted look about him that attracted remark. Setting this aside, the double in the armchair might have been mistaken by the other at the window for his own reflection in the glass. As he cast his eyes down to compare his feet, he noticed with a shudder that he cast no shadow himself, while the chair before him cast its shadow clearly forward upon the carpet beyond—

Then he realised, & almost fainted as he did so, that he was a spectre, an invisible, a nameless something outside of life & beyond the world, & yet a silent witness, a spectator not an actor, an exile from the flesh & from his kind—The keenness of his dismay broke the spell which chained him to the spot, & he sprang forward with outstretched hands to the just-retreating patient, crying 'Don't you know me?' at the top of his voice—The woman paused, turned & said 'Did you speak, Doctor?'—The man at the table looked up rather dazed but said quietly 'No Madam'—The patient, an old friend, cast a puzzled glance around the room, passing over the spot where the beseeching man stood, looking through him with unbeholding & unrecognizing eyes, gave a little shiver, a quick bow, & disappeared. The two were left together, the body writing calmly at the table, the mind trembling, fascinated, but with growing determination, standing near the door, turning right around, the unhappy creature walked to the desk & brought both his hands down on the shoulders of the one who was writing—The pen spluttered, the man shook himself lightly, paused an instant, & then sat back & bit his pen as if he had forgotten the end of the phrase—But there was no sign of consciousness of the presence, though it roared in his ear 'Who are you'—'Who are you', & 'Who am I?' More than laying down the pen, & leaning back in the chair, the man of flesh & blood seemed to be thinking of something, while the figure beside vainly endeavoured to clutch him or his attention. There was a sound of little feet upon the stair, & the laugh of a young mother with her brood invading the consultation room to bring him to lunch—The children entered & flung themselves as one into his arms, crying 'Father', while the happy wife stooped over him to kiss his brow, saying 'Lunch, dearest'—When, with an agony unspeakable, of crucifixion, of the tortures of the damned, the impalpable one flung himself upon & into the body from which he had been displaced with an intensity of will & fury of desire that almost stifled him. As the intruder vanished, he felt the warm blood flowing in his veins, the warm kisses upon his face, & knew that his body was his own again. He clasped them convulsively to his bosom, while his wife hurriedly bathed his forehead with scent & his children stood back frightened with wondering eyes. 'What was it, dear?' said his wife anxiously—He put his hand upon his heart & said in a strange husky voice 'A momentary something.' 'Two of your patients told me how absent you were this morning' said she. 'Yes, dearest' he replied in his natural voice, looking carefully around him, when nothing met his eye. 'I was absent ... for a little ... absent ... that is the right word.' Who had been present he never knew.[16]

This is a more mannered piece, a set short story written in the third person with plot, climax, denouement and final twist of irony. The vivid confrontation between the two main 'characters', representing 'Materialism' and 'Idealism', or something of that order, illustrates also a philosophic intent in the confusion created by the plot. Some doubt is thrown upon everyday reality and the common notion of a self, which Deakin, a wide reader of Hindu thought and Theosophy, held to be fundamental illusions. The gross physical being and its environment are rendered unreal by the emergence of a 'double' who becomes a dull and unwitting foe in the existential battle that follows. Rather than being a strict 'disembodied spirit' story, a 'higher' and didactic purpose is disclosed in the contrast between the 'real' and the 'ideal'.

Written four years after the 'Theatre' narrative, this story also presents Hegelian ideas. The battle between the 'real' person and the 'impostor' may symbolise the continuing struggle between the 'real' world of mind and consciousness, and the 'false' world of matter. The absent-minded, preoccupied Doctor enters musing the 'mutability of ideas' and the 'impermanence of things'. Again we note references to the grossness and tyranny of the body, and to 'pains, privations, & distracting desires' as vexations to the spirit. After a moment of terror, and some astute comparisons between himself and the pretender, the 'spectre' fights to regain sovereignty over his body. The description of the other—more aged, stooped, myopic, shorter and with a weaker profile—shows a trace of vanity, but it also dramatises effectively how different our self-images are to the actual, that is to the physical actual.

The impostor, 'trapped' by habits and mannerisms and the routine of a lifetime (and there is a suggestion of this at the beginning) exists in an unreflective, mechanical life, the very opposite to the Ideal Deakin cherished. Hence he mirrors Deakin's awareness, and despair, at the distance from the Ideal which professional life afforded. He too longed to know the real, to pierce through the phenomena to the essence of things. We have seen in prayers his sense of being 'cribbed, cabined & confined', trapped by habit, manner, routine, detail and responsibility. Having recently been forced back into practice as barrister, Deakin's heart and mind, like the 'body', were petrified and rendered unable to transcend the mundane world into the 'inexhaustible mysteries of life' where his Inner Light bid him enter.

Apart from its finished quality and the vivid and terrifying scenario, the 'Thoughtful Idealist' is of greatest interest for its philosophic dimension and its levels of meaning. Following his moment of bewilderment and terror, there comes a determination by the 'mind' to recapture the 'body' from the 'impostor'. At least three entities are implied here, and this ambiguity of concepts suggests that they are archetypes. At last, spurred by the sight of wife and children, the 'impalpable one' by a supreme effort of will flings himself 'upon & into' the body, and following his 'agony' and 'crucifixion', the warm blood and warm kisses tell him his body is his again. These images of warmth, love, life, and activity contrast with the invisible, impalpable, silent spectre, and they give a hint of moral struggle, although the story is about the 'True' rather than the 'Good'. Moreover, they reveal a further ambivalence in that the body—a necessary medium for the experience of human affections—is not simply rejected as a dull impediment. The story also incorporates psychic concepts, as when the patient to whom the terrified being cries in dismay, perhaps because she is a friend, senses a 'something', and gives a 'little shiver', a common index of spirit presence among Spiritualists, as she passes over the spot where he stands. And theosophical ideas are evident with the spiritless 'shell' of the impostor who merely reacts. Although it writes and prescribes well enough, there is a sense of dazed stupefaction, of sloth about its activity. The mind on the other hand, wherever it is, is alive, anxious, 'beside itself' with fright.[17]

Among the questions the story explores, then, is what constitutes our identity. One by one, the common indices of our 'self', body, habits and mannerisms acquired over a lifetime, professional status, dress, even the recognition of others, are eliminated. What is left in the end Deakin seems to say, are only Love and Will— It is Love, of life and of family, and the Will of the 'real' Being, both beyond the world of matter and constitutive of the essential Self, which are in the final analysis 'real'. Here then Swedenborg's supreme principles are revealed, who like Kant divided the human mind into Will and Understanding, motivated in its highest expression by Unselfish Love. Reunited again, the doctor agrees that he was indeed 'absent'. His final line: 'who had been present he never knew', reinforces the notion that rather than being about spirit possession, this well-crafted story operates on at least two levels. The ambiguity of language and identity, of 'self', 'body', and 'other', provide the elements for a Swedenborgian psychodrama where Love conquers all, and through the action of the Will, renders all things possible.

We will be faced again, and through a far less ambiguous genre, with the proposition that Alfred Deakin had a capacity for powerful private experiences, whether aesthetic, religious, or mystical, which he carefully recorded and reflected upon, sometimes at length. It must be granted that the experience narratives may not have been about actual experiences. But when Deakin wrote in other journals of having been hundreds of times 'witched out' of himself by a nature scene, it signified to him no empty metaphor. Dream and 'near-waking' experiences also assumed great importance at times.[18] A Beethoven concert, even a magnificent sunset were enough to take him, by his own accounts, to regions far removed from the mundane sphere. Even allowing for his romantic Wordsworthian view of Nature, there are qualities in some of these 'stories' of bliss, joy, carefreeness, moral purity, health, a belonging and absolute certitude of God and His ways, that by middle age Deakin felt to have been extinguished in his 'outer' life.

By public accounts Deakin appears a man of great kindness and presence, with a voluble energy and wry humour; in private moments, he reveals a depth of religious feeling, even of poetic rapture, that could easily be interpreted as giving a valve of release from the extraordinary tensions of being Prime Minister of the Commonwealth. But this would be reducing the significance of such experiences, even if vicarious, to this deeply religious man. Writing was an activity central to Deakin, in his private meditations no less than in his public life. Whatever the reasons behind his feeling of 'aloofness' in later life, they were clearly linked in some way to his moral intent and his singular sense of Mission. All that we know about Deakin's concerns, his careful noting of vivid dreams, his recognition of signs in the course of events, his written petitions, his endeavours to uncover spiritual Truth through the earnest study of the world's Gospels, make it very unlikely that some of these narratives at least, were merely exercises in imaginative literary fantasy.

If there was one unifying theme in all Deakin's private prose, it was, as he would have put it, 'the question of the Soul'. The possibility of transcendence and enlightenment were items of faith for Deakin, suggested most vividly by this narrative genre. Following Swedenborg and a long line of mystics 'ancient and modern theosophical',[19] he believed this release to be desirable and even necessary for individual development, whether coming through 'out of body' release and transport to another realm, by an 'illumination of the understanding', via auditory or visual phenomena, or other esoterica. For Alfred Deakin such experiences were deemed necessary also in a largely inarticulated way to the service of race and kind, for they provided the guiding hand his Spirit strove to obey.

The experience narratives confirm the importance to Deakin of mysterious phenomena, and they reflect a strong individualism, since their distinctive character is of a personal consciousness transcending material reality. They also open a new vista on Deakin's 'Spiritistic' experiences, and on his short career as 'medium' in particular. Perhaps ultimately it matters little whether these narratives were accounts of 'actual' experiences, or were explorations of possible encounters with other levels of Being. In the sincere spirituality they evince, they stand as further testimony to the importance of the *possibility* of immediate transcendence in the life and thought of Alfred Deakin.

Notes

1 On consensus reality, see P. Berger and T. Luckman, *The Social Construction of Reality: A Treatise in the Sociology of Knowledge*, New York, 1967; and on peak experiences, Abraham Maslow, *Religions, Values, and Peak Experiences*, Columbus, 1964.

2 Literary Memoranda, typescript, 3/302, 5 May 1888. In this year Deakin read Stevenson's *Memories and Portraits*, and in 1889 he read *Kidnapped*.

3 'Clues', vol. 4, 3/286, no. 622, 17 February 1894.

4 On ethnographic history and the use of dramaturgy, see Rhys Isaac, 'Ethnographic Method in History: An Action Approach', *Historical Methods*, vol. 13, no. 1, Winter 1980.

5 'Medley', 3/296, 'Clue' no. 779, 13–24 July 1901.

6 This is admittedly very speculative, but through his reading of authors like Mme Blavatsky, G. R. S. Mead, and the Hindu mystics, Deakin would have been familiar with the outlines of such ritual magic.

7 A prayer penned on the same day shows the direction of his thoughts: 'Almighty God have mercy upon us for living under Thy unscrutable will in a world whose physical laws are but imperfectly understood, in a society whose principles are undiscovered & subject to spiritual laws of whose existence even we are ignorant. We have need & need of mercy. The greatest mercy would be to enable us to understand, the next to enable us to endure, the best to enable us to overcome.' In this lament, with its implicit belief in 'laws' underpinning the natural, the social and the spiritual worlds, that which we have 'need & need' of, beyond understanding and stoic endurance, is *moksa*, liberation: 'Boke ...', 5/894, prayer CXCV, 17 February 1894.

8 'The M.S.', in 'Medley', 3/296, 'Clue' no. 818, 10–13 April and 12 June 1904, pp. 194–209.

9 Ibid., p. 201.

10 Ibid., p. 202.

11 Ibid., p. 203.

12 Ibid.

13 Ibid., p. 208.

14 Ibid.

15 Ibid., p. 209.

16 'Clues', vol. 4, 3/286, no. 539, 18 June 1892. The classic tale of dual identity, 'The Strange Case of Dr Jekyll and Mr Hyde' by R. L. Stevenson, first published in 1884, has few parallels with Deakin's tale. Stevenson's dolorous obsession with Calvinistic notions of good and evil has little relation to the ontological concerns of Deakin's story. Closer is 'The Secret Sharer' by Joseph Conrad, a short story dealing with a recognised 'mysterious similitude', physical and circumstantial, between the two main characters, rather than questions of identity.

17 For Deakin's discussion of Theosophical 'shells' see 'Personal Experiences ...', 5/1440, section XIV, p. 9.

18 See the record of a 'point of light' experience in Book of Prayers, 5/1014, prayer XXVII, 25 February 1904, and 'Clues', 3/287, vol. 3, no. 497, October 1891, on an experience upon taking chloroform; and on the 'mystic & marvellous aspect of sleep', 'Clues', 3/287, vol. 3, no. 535, 11 June 1892.

19 Autobiographical Notes, typescript, 3/300, 3 August 1904.

7

The Religion of 'the Best'

Come ill or well, the cross, the crown,
The rainbow or the thunder,
I'll fling my soul and body down
For God to plough them under.

R. L. Stevenson

Deakin's encounters with what he termed the 'invisible' were rare. Apart from some undefined raptures and an uncomfortable period as 'impressional writing' medium in youth, two remarkable auditions comprise virtually the total of Deakin's recorded paranormal experiences. The first experience came in October 1899 when, absorbed in prayer on behalf of a friend, Deakin suddenly heard a 'spirit' voice. A decade later, as he awoke by the seaside in the early morning he heard another voice, in that liminal zone of enduring fascination to his inner life, a 'monition' coming from within yet somehow outside his own being, and offering gentle counsel at a time when both his inner world and public career were crumbling.[1]

An increasing reliance upon his own spiritual resources had become a salient feature of Deakin's inner life at least since the Grand Prophecy. He still discerned 'signs' in the course of events, and as the gospels and experience narratives have illustrated, he still held out a hope, at least in imagination, for a sudden and cataclysmic illumination. But these two auditions brought fundamental changes in Deakin's inner life, and the last part of this study explores their continuing, and increasing, spiritual significance to Deakin, and their relation to his other writings and to his political career, as boundaries were diminishing between these departments of his life.

Intimations of a transcendental authority represented by a voice appear first in Deakin's commentaries on Mohammed, whose angelic herald had commanded him to 'Recite!', and in his reflections on the *daimon* of Socrates, the admonitory voice that guided the philosopher's life and ultimately his death. The voices represent a paradigm shift over a decade or so in Deakin's conception of what might be termed the method of Revelation; they also bear marked similarities, since each voice was heard while Deakin was in a slightly dissociated state and, regarded as a rejuvenating spiritual experience, each generated a good deal of private prose. Most importantly, each voice was understood as counsel from a separate Reality, though its source(s) remained ambiguous. The real significance of these auditions lay in their religious dimension, their moral utility and their status as 'signs' and heralds to action. To Deakin, they were clearly 'inspirations' of a different order of experience to the spiritistic phenomenon of 'clairaudience'. The first voice heard in October 1899, along with copious reading in the current psychology of the unconscious, thereafter coloured his attitudes as to the sources of inspiration. The second, coming in a half-waking state in November 1910, prepared the way, after one last important battle, for Deakin's retirement from public life.

Probably the most intimate confidant of Deakin's adult life was Herbert Brookes. They first met in 1895 through Dr Charles Strong, leader of the Australian Church, to whose daughter Brookes was then engaged. In 1897 they were married, but within two years his young wife Jennie died and Herbert was thrown into a despondency from which he slowly recovered, with the generous help of Deakin and the family. The opening of the family home was a rare gesture from Deakin, who maintained a rigid distance from all but a handful of friends, few of them politicians. Brookes, only a few years his junior, soon became a friend and almost a son to Deakin, and later still, business adviser and fellow political worker.[2] When they travelled to England in 1900 to 'defend' the Commonwealth Bill, Brookes accompanied the family. In 1905 he married Deakin's eldest daughter Ivy. An intellectual side to their friendship had grown out of Deakin's efforts to help Brookes regain his equilibrium. Their correspondence dating from 1898 lends valuable testimony to a belief which Deakin, usually self-contained about such things, shared to a remarkable degree with the younger man.

A great deal can be learned from Victorian forms of address. Tom Roberts with artist's licence could address Deakin as 'My dear bon Alfred', or even 'Mon Reverend'. Charles Strong too used gently mocking headings like 'My dear Satrap', but even to so close a comrade in the 'Cause' as Barton, except in one instance, it was always 'My Dear Deakin'.[3] With Brookes, Deakin delighted in informal, even facetious titles. They frequently exchanged and discussed books, and in one letter to 'Rajah' from 'Pedagogue' Deakin advised that 'certain books are to be read as discipline whether you like them or not';[4] he then proffered advice on skim reading. Another letter from 'Plunger' to 'Assayer' discusses mining shares, while the religious side of their friendship is indicated by the letter headed to 'the Master' from 'the Chela', a Theosophical term for a neophyte.[5]

Deakin, like many men, valued another male as confidant, yet his disposition was essentially solitary. The letters formed a sort of agenda for their next meeting. If their language seems overblown, they remind us of the formality of interaction between Victorian men, as in that marvellous phrase where Deakin first invites Herbert into the family circle: 'If you can feel the absence of restraint with us', he felt sure his strength of purpose would speedily return, promising 'no constraint upon your moods and motions';[6] they also show Deakin's practical religion in action, in his kindness and care for the grief of another.

Relations with his early confidante, his sister Catherine, had changed inevitably with maturity. By 1904, during a painful episode with Syme, Deakin would confess that there were 'none upon whom I could lean nor have leant for years'.[7] For companionship, and an outlet for his urge to discuss, not to say preach upon, matters metaphysical, Deakin turned increasingly to Brookes. The energy poured into his counselling of Brookes indicates a repressed need to speak of things Divine to one he could trust, what in one letter Deakin called those 'flashlight views of the faith that is in me'.[8] Brookes for his part was grateful for Deakin's sage counselling, and he openly admired the Liberal leader whose political views and high moral seriousness, if not necessarily his mysticism, he shared.

Deakin clearly saw himself as Brookes' mentor, and delighted with his rehabilitation, became something of a teacher to the younger man. Their friendship was important to both men for different reasons. Brookes was 'the son I never had', and a few days later Deakin expressed the hope 'that I have found a friend— a very rare experience for me'.[9] On 25 August 1899, only five months after Jennie's death, Brookes called at Deakin's office at Parliament House. They had a 'long chat'.[10] He had lent Deakin a volume of selected sermons by the American Episcopalian preacher Phillips Brooks (no relation). A letter from Herbert four days later mentioned a 'vision' Deakin apparently had shared with him: 'If ever you think of things done that you are sorry for (and I take it you do from the vision you told me of)', he commenced, might he not think first of 'the friendly human hand' that had been offered in his own hour of grief?[11] It is unlikely that Deakin was using the term 'vision' in any conventional hyperbolic sense. The chat four days before had evidently proceeded from the American preacher's sermons to more personal revelation. Again it is intriguing to speculate, for if he were referring to the 1894 'vision of judgment', it would throw a different light on the ontological status of that narrative.

Herbert Brookes was a civil engineer by training. A well-read and orthodox Anglican, he was only vaguely interested in the psychic phenomena, and he did not always agree with Deakin's views. The most remarkable of their missives, and the most germane to the present discussion, was Deakin's letter to Brookes on 1 October 1899. This is an extraordinary document, loaded with spiritual significance, for not only does it set out in some detail Deakin's continuing belief in the psychic realm; it is also an irrefragable testament to an esoteric personal experience.

The letter is headed 'Dear Dr Teufels *dk* Junior', literally 'junior devil', an allusion to Carlyle's hero in *Sartor Resartus* which Deakin had recently lent to Brookes, along with *Letters from Julia*, an account of communications allegedly received 'through' the medium W. T. Stead from Julia Ames, a young American journalist, recently deceased, whom he had met only once and briefly.[12] Stead had made his reputation as editor of the *Pall Mall Gazette* and champion of the poor. More recently, he had become a medium for 'automatic writing' by which means he received these messages. After the usual preliminary ritual of assuring the younger man that he was not unduly encroaching upon his time, Deakin argued the merits of Stead's communications. He disagreed with Brookes that the letters seemed to speak with a man's voice, though 'of course she writes *through* a man & to the world'; and he thought her picture of 'the next stage true as far as it goes, & in no particular imaginary'. These observations were by way of introduction, because Deakin then turned abruptly to what he called the 'popular orthodox doctrine of a severance between those we call living & those we call dead'. He rejected Brookes' view that spirits are 'done with this world' after death,[13] a doctrine he regarded as both 'absolutely unnatural & untrue', for the dead live 'in us & we in them' in proportion to our mutual love and sympathy. Just as our joys and sorrows can be shared on the other side, so too, he insisted, 'the converse transmission of joy & sorrow to us is also possible'. How surprised Brookes must have been to read on, for at this point, Deakin outlined in some detail a remarkable personal experience:

> As you know I am not superstitious, nor am I what is termed a 'medium', but I have an impressionable inner sensitiveness which is a great stay to my faith at times—Recently in connection with yourself I have been feeling like a man who using the telephone for his own purposes is while using it compelled to overhear enough of a message which is being sent at the same time from some one else to some other person along another line—Some invisible voice full of love tenderness pity & courage has been calling you in my hearing—I can only surmise that it is either your wife or someone speaking for her—Whoever it is does *not* speak to or through me but is trying very earnestly & devotedly to speak *to you*—Perhaps I have been made to over hear this much but I know no more than what I have told you—The impression it has made & is making in me is very clear & strong & has been many times repeated so that at last I thought it my duty to tell you frankly all about it—[14]

Deakin further insisted: 'I do not receive what are styled "communications" directly or through anyone else & what I have written stands simply on my own testimony as I have here given it to you unreservedly.'

What can we make of this startling and unprecedented revelation, explained by the extended telephone analogy? Who might have 'made' him overhear such a message, and what is he implying as to the nature of his 'telephone'? The message was not specified, though it had been repeated many times. Perhaps Deakin had only heard Brookes' name called out. It is unthinkable that he was simply seeking to comfort Brookes, or to shake him out of his torpor with some fantasy, and he took care to disassociate himself firmly from 'messages' and 'mediums'. So he seems to have regarded the audition as belonging to a different order of experience. Brookes was noncommittal about Deakin's testimony as to his deceased wife, or at least he never mentions it in other correspondence, and his response to this letter is unfortunately no longer extant. The stage had been set for the sharing of this 'telephone' experience, firstly in the unprecedented intimacy of Deakin's confidences a month before concerning his 'vision', then by a discussion of *Letters from Julia* dramatically followed by a similar auditory experience to that claimed by Stead, which it was his 'duty' (to whom?) to share.

Was Deakin acting as Divine 'instrument', as conduit to Brookes? He had heard the 'invisible voice' while using the 'telephone' for his own purposes, and he suggests that the experience was subjective—given through the mind rather than via the ear—an 'impression' received during his meditations. Deakin must therefore have been praying for Brookes when he heard that voice. What strikes one in particular is that even prayers and 'Clues' seldom went into such detail as this letter to Brookes. Hence it is both an unequivocal testament to an unique experience, and a further illustration of Deakin's need for intellectual and spiritual companionship, which the younger man satisfied.

It seems characteristic of Deakin that, in accordance with his Ideal of Unselfishness, a personal revelation should benefit another. In a largely inarticulated way that 'voice' was to assume profound significance in Deakin's fecund inner life, and might well have been understood as another 'sign'. In current journals Deakin went into some detail about his method of prayer; when closeting himself in his study he would attempt to 'tune the violin of the mind into harmony with the best & holiest' as a deliberate effort of the will:

> We must act upon the plane of the will & prayer if we are to make these effective agents. For those who have done & continue to do all that doing can prayer is the use of psychic occult & spiritual forces which strengthen & elevate the mind for its task & bend other sympathetic minds consciously or unconsciously towards the end prayed willed & acted towards ...[15]

Notice the three ascending spheres, 'psychic occult & spiritual'. Elsewhere he outlined a procedure: 'In all my communings, I have first to reach my higher & inner self ... then to elevate my thoughts to Thee & Thine.'[16] Deakin was still thinking about this mysterious audition when three weeks later, writing in one journal on the theme 'all is spiritual', he observed almost casually that when we find ourselves in 'abnormal states of consciousness' we enter thereby 'an abnormal world, not necessarily the true world, any more than this is, but often equally true, & sometimes more true, more profoundly comprehended'. We should see this if we were to 'cultivate our spiritual faculties'.[17]

In a careful balancing of ritual favours after the inauguration in Sydney, it had been agreed that Parliament would sit 'temporarily' in Melbourne until a capital site was decided. It would take twenty-seven years for Canberra to be established. The appointed date for the opening of the first Parliament of the Commonwealth was 9 May 1901. It was a wet and stormy day, accentuated in its sombre tones by the mourning costumes worn by the ladies following Queen Victoria's recent death. The occasion has been immortalised in Tom Roberts' 'Big Picture', whose composition suggests the relative status of the actors. A shaft of light beams down ethereally upon the Duke of York, 'a little bearded man in an admiral's uniform',[18] through a skylight in the cavernous Exhibition Building, as he stands on a large stage crowded by dignitaries and an enormous royal entourage. Beyond them the floor is packed with the members of the various Parliaments. Pattie can be seen standing in the foreground among the invited guests. On the other side, almost lost in the throng, Barton and the assembled ministry wait to be summoned. Indeed there was an embarrassing moment when, after being summoned, they had considerable trouble getting through the crowd to the stage.

From long habit Deakin's diary for this day retained the colonial term 'Assembly' for the lower House.[19] In the evening they attended a State concert at the Exhibition Building. The next day, following the Governor-General's address, Deakin rose first to move the Acts Interpretation Bill 'in order to assert the right of this House to legislate at this stage'. An abiding sense of history and racial continuity, an Anglo-Saxon pride, and something of Deakin's religious Ideal are apparent in this motion. Preceding the formal proposal of the address in reply, it thus established a link between the Commonwealth Parliament and the Parliament of James I, when the right to legislate before heeding the king's speech had first been formally asserted. It was indeed a proud moment for him.[20]

The first half of 1901 was taken up with celebrations and electioneering, as the provisional government ceased to exist on 29 March. The Barton ministry was returned, Deakin winning his new seat of Ballaarat by a handsome 3000 votes. But it was a minority government which depended on fragile alliances to push measures through. Professor La Nauze devoted the greater portion of his biography to explicating Deakin's pre-eminent role in the politics of this first decade of the Commonwealth. For our purposes, it is necessary to bear in mind that political alignments into a Parliament of 'three elevens'—Liberal Protectionist, Freetrade and Labor—would continue, and that all Liberal ministries in the first decade were minority governments ruling with the support of the Labor party. Home in April after the hectic round of ritual, celebration, and electioneering in those first three months, in 'Clue' 771 Deakin posed the apposite question: 'What is the love of fame?' It is a 'superstition' that has many selfish elements, the chief being a 'want of faith ... The eagerness to get published, & if published, to get known & praised, to be recorded at ceremonies, distinguished by titles, commemorated by names & tombstones, sung by poets'; all of this proceeds from 'the implied belief that these are more permanent than oneself ... that its footprint in earth's pathways is more likely to last & to be observed than the immortal & eternal individuality'.[21]

Deakin's health had not fully recovered from the strain of the trip to England, and it continued to plague him as he plunged into the formidable task of helping to realise the 'Ideal' of Federation. In the relative lull of February 1901 he commenced making notes, probably for a projected book on the early Common-wealth to follow his Federation chronicle.[22] The rush of events soon arrested this project which, like many others, remained unfinished. While setting up his own Attorney-General's department, Deakin provided legal opinions for other depart-ments and kept a vigilant watch on anti-federal tendencies. He also took his share of promotional work, addressing mayoral luncheons, A.N.A. meetings and other gatherings. Beyond these party and Cabinet responsibilities Deakin remained active in Temperance, anti-sweating and animal welfare, he regularly attended Directors' meetings of two insurance companies, and maintained links as always through a prodigious correspondence. There was now the added strain of frequent commuting between Melbourne and Ballarat, and the weekly 'letters' he had commenced writing for the London *Morning Post* as anonymous 'Australian correspondent'.

While in London Deakin had made an agreement with the *Morning Post*, a Liberal journal founded by Fabian Ware which favoured Preferential Trade and closer bonds within the Empire, to write weekly articles on political events in Australia. Ware aspired to make the *Morning Post* the leading exponent of Chamberlain's new Empire ideology, where sovereign States would cooperate under the Crown, to be fortified by a mutual tariff preference.[23] Over the next fourteen years he would send these letters, weekly for most of that period, going to extraordinary lengths to hide their authorship, such as arranging to have them posted from Sydney. Incredible as it may seem to the modern reader, Deakin evidently saw no conflict of interest between journalism and his role as prime mover in many of the events he reported upon, firm in the belief that it was to Australia's benefit that Great Britain should be kept informed about events in the Antipodes.

In January Deakin caught a chill and was unwell for a week. Intermittently during 1901 his eyes and digestion suffered. His insomnia was becoming more severe. In July he was suffering from 'English cholera', a type of dysentery, when he was purged and stayed in bed for nine days; it was during this period that he penned the 'Beethoven' experience narrative. In October the Interstate Com-mission Bill was postponed because he was in poor health.[24] Perhaps it was the delicacy of his health that brought Deakin back to his prayer book, after an absence of eight months, on his birthday 3 August, renewing once again his resolve to 'commune' with Deity. Over the next two months prayers came more or less weekly, tapering off until with the crushing demands of 1902, only three were recorded. This reopening of the 'channel', as before, was accompanied by a burst of contrition and a solicitation of Divine favour for national ends, despite serious personal shortcomings:

> Forty five years bring me to my knees, O God! In penitence and shame ... There ought to have been a self built out of so much blessing. Gratitude & humility should have given me a soul. That I am naught alas O God is the ground of all my petitions. Fulfill in me Thy Will.[25]

This prayer seems somewhat histrionic, for Deakin never seriously doubted that he had a soul; yet there was now in this familiar ritual a more fatigued and world weary tone. Prayer no. CCXXXIX, written the next day, speaks more optimistically:

> ... The web & woof of history discloses the Divine pattern thro' the dim light of understanding. The myriad unseen influences of individuals living or called dead & the myriads of unguessed agencies operating upon & among them without which the secret of life cannot be mastered ...[26]

The themes are familiar enough. What is new is a change of structure, another indication of a time of strain, in a blurring of genres. Formerly Deakin addressed his prayers in formal and sometimes ponderous forms, such as 'Merciful Father', 'Great Gracious Providence', 'All Merciful, all Peaceful & Perpetual' and 'Infinite Spirit of Truth, Sincerity & Simplicity', always using the archaic 'Thou'. Though his prayers were still numbered consecutively in Roman numerals, they now generally abandoned the formal tone. Another prayer penned at 4 a.m. a week later opens on a common theme of progress and evolution, much like his 'Clues'. Then, reverting to the archaic language, he asks:

> Aid me & guide me O Heavenly Father to prepare the way for Thy Heavenly Kingdom as a Home for all Thy sons & daughters. Grant me the everpresent conviction that is most effectively prepared for by preparing myself, by casting out pride, petulance, the aim for superiority of place or achievement or activity ...[27]

At Dromana for the Christmas holidays, Deakin was enjoying his 'harvest of reading', and he was presently engrossed in a deep study of the Koran and Plato. The resulting journal, 'Clue' no. 782 composed between 12 and 17 November 1901, reflects an amalgam of Theosophy, spiritism, and mysticism as he searched for the 'Ancient Doctrine' declared or hinted at throughout the *Dialogues*. It seems a thorough job, covering not only the major dialogues, but the lesser like *Alcibiades*, and Plato's later *Laws*, along with the very different Socrates presented in Xenophon's *Memorabilia*. We have seen how 'Islam' focuses upon the means by which Mohammed had received his inspiration. In light of his own spiritual audition two years before, Deakin's attention was captivated again by the psychic and spiritual dimensions in the life of Socrates, especially the relation to his 'voice', the *daimon* or 'divine Sign' from whom the philosopher obtained guidance throughout his life. Deakin believed Socrates' mission to have been confirmed, in the *Apology* and elsewhere, by 'oracles, visions & in everyway in which the will of divine power was ever signified to any one'.[28] In these five pages of notes salted with copious quotations, comprising a brief outline along with opening and closing commentaries, we have what looks like a plan for a greatly expanded treatment, possibly the projected book that would draw on the 'soul life' revealed in the lives and thought of the world's Sages.

No-one would have been more surprised than Socrates, one would think, to be included in a pantheon of 'Associate Saviours'. In Socrates interpreted by Plato and Xenophon, Deakin was seeking evidences of an 'Ancient Doctrine' where we witness again Deakin's eclecticism and, paradoxically, his striving for unifying conceptions. He endeavoured to relate the *Dialogues* to a host of other issues, such as the similarities between Greek ideas about health and modern 'mind cure', and between the doctrine regarding pleasure and pain found in the Hindu *Upanishads* and that given in *Phaedo*, and to other writers like Herodotus. Finally, Deakin advances the Theosophical idea that Plato's source for this Ancient Doctrine, which embraced Reincarnation and the legend of the ancient continent of Atlantis, was derived from Pythagoras.[29] Apart from illustrating an enormous industry, these private researches show how closely they followed Deakin's special interests, reinforcing his view of an universe based on Justice and a Divine will made known to humans in diverse ways.

With the opening of the second Parliament Deakin returned to more mundane matters. On 18 March 1902, in a captivating speech extending over three hours he introduced the Judiciary Bill to establish the High Court of Australia, a measure he considered of the highest importance to an effective federal system. Despite general bipartisan agreement, it was to have a tempestuous passage. It was a tough Parliamentary session made more difficult by Barton's absence at the coronation of Edward VII and the second Colonial Conference. For his part Barton (who incredibly forgot to leave the Commonwealth's cipher book!) was grateful for the congenial environment of London society, and Deakin became Acting Prime Minister. His diary for 8 May noted proudly: 'Presided Cabinet 1st time'.[30] But these five months were to be truly a baptism by fire. His additional responsibilities for External Affairs and as Leader of the House, where he won a crucial fight on the tariff, added to the strain of keeping party discipline and maintaining the allegiance of supporters, and other crises like the resignation of Hopetoun, resulted in Deakin suffering his first breakdown, from nervous exhaustion.

The day 3 September 1902 was especially tough, a 'Day of intense strain' when he thought Federation itself might be in danger.[31] On this day the interim tariff was decided, which was crucial to the union in ensuring the financial survival of the Commonwealth. The 'Australian correspondent' understood that it would be through the financial powers of the Commonwealth that the States would in time be bound to the 'chariot wheels of the central government'.[32] There are some fifty-six pages of parliamentary debate on this day of showdown, when the constitutional device Deakin had initiated in 1891, whereby the Senate might 'request' but not demand amendments to taxation Bills, met its practical test. Now a hostile Senate was repeatedly rejecting the Tariff Bill with 'requests'. A deadlock between the Houses such as Victorians had always dreaded, followed by a double dissolution, seemed inevitable. With the help of the Opposition the matter was resolved for the time being, in what Deakin privately regarded as 'A great victory for the wisest course'. Separating the two questions, Deakin had asked the House to deal with the present 'requests' of the Senate, and to defer for later discussion the larger question of the determination of the House's constitutional rights and obligations.[33] With the Tariff Bill passed, as the 'Australian correspondent' knew, 'the Commonwealth was out of the toils at last, and fast escaping beyond the reach of its enemies'. A few weeks later, with Barton's return imminent, it was an exhausted and relieved Deakin who noted in his diary: *'Prorogation Thank God'*.[34]

Following Barton's return on 12, October Deakin left immediately with Pattie for Healesville, then for a few days to the quiet forests at Gembrook. On 17 November the family went to Point Lonsdale for their annual holiday. Deakin thought he was only 'exhausted in nerve power',[35] but he had in truth suffered a breakdown which was not, as he chose to believe, a momentary phenomenon. His activities over the rest of the year belie a state of nervous exhaustion. Writing late into the night, he would regularly wake at 4 a.m. or earlier to write letters, or be working in the garden from 5 a.m. A more subtle indication of decline appears from around July 1901 with the reversal in the order of two letters in his diary abbreviation for 'Breakfast', an activity which like 'Bath' and 'Office' he recorded with monotonous regularity, and which from now read 'bfkt'.[36] This slight dyslexia, taken with other factors, is an ominous indication of a subtle and gradual degeneration of mind and health. Forbidden by doctors to go to Sydney in December, Deakin had an enforced rest. Yet a prayer recorded five months later conveys still a diminished state, and renders a chilling sense of prevision of a continuing decline: 'God grant I may never be a burden if possible, not even upon the physical care of my loved ones, not upon anyone ...'.[37] His greatest fear, exacerbated no doubt by his recent visit to the dying Duncan Gillies, was to be sadly realised within a decade.

Across the top of the diary for 7 July 1903 appears the large notation: *'22 years ago'*, a remembrance of a ball at the Melbourne Town Hall in 1881 when Deakin had a 'revelation with P', and they had declared their mutual love.[38] This tender notation sits oddly against others for July, otherwise a month of conflicts. Pattie was not well, and his own health was not recovered. There was also a major contretemps between them and her father Hugh Junor Browne. The reason is unknown, although Mrs Browne was accused of causing tensions in their home, and at one point Deakin wrote to Brookes that he merely wanted 'peace'. Whatever its cause, the situation degenerated to the point that Deakin sent his father-in-law a 'legal reply' to one of his letters. By the end of the month there was 'a final irrevocable & angry rupture' not repaired for some years.[39] In the 'Cabinet of captains' too there were serious frictions, between Forrest and Kingston, and also with Lyne, large men with larger egos.

Deakin maintained the discipline of written prayer for most of his adult life, and in various books. Between August 1884 and June 1899, 235 prayers were recorded in the 'Boke of Praer & Prase'. In November 1900 he commenced a second 'Book of Prayers', and in 1903 for some reason he inaugurated another book, running two books of prayers concurrently for a year or so. From 10 September 1905, Deakin's prayers were recorded in the former Research Notebook on Islam, again beginning with Prayer no. I.[40]

With the crushing demands of 1902 as Acting Prime Minister, Deakin had recorded only three prayers. In 1903 there were forty-three. The major distribution of these prayers, heralding once again a greater need for communion, occurs around this period of tension, increasing in frequency with the approach of the inevitable fall of his first minority government. Increasingly, Deakin was concerned with his failing health. In July he relates directly for the first time his awareness of the strain: 'To physical presentiments of failure, I add mental';[41] and one of those gloomy Melbourne winter's days may have prompted an, August prayer where he observed: 'This winter I have for the first time realised age—the beginning of old age, of enfeeblement, of withdrawal of a spent force.' Though only forty-seven years old, Deakin had been living a strenuous life in the front rank of politics for almost a quarter century. Still he had no intention of quitting, for he added: 'What I have to do may be however little it is more important than all I have yet done.'[42]

One crucial issue requiring passage without further delay was the Judiciary Bill. Three years before, with that other radical Liberal 'Charlie' Kingston, Deakin had battled energetically in London against any alteration to the Constitution Bill, especially on the High Court's final authority in interpreting the Constitution. Deakin considered the High Court truly 'the keystone to the Federal arch', though he never viewed himself as a constitutional expert, and his anxieties derived as much from the political as from the legal implications of any delay in its establishment. He had argued with constancy over many years that an Australian High Court was essential to a federal system, principally in 'unfolding the Constitution itself'.[43] He insisted that this could be done neither by the committee of the Privy Council, which had no knowledge of local conditions, nor by investing State courts with federal jurisdiction, who lacked sufficient breadth of vision to rule on national questions. Indeed Deakin's fear was that without the authority of the High Court, the Commonwealth would be in constant danger from what he called 'the forces of provincialism'.

The Judiciary Bill might have passed as hoped in the first session, but for the interminable tariff debate. When it received a second reading in 1903, the mood of Parliament had changed. While the ministry was not exactly blamed for the worst drought in Australia's history, its Judiciary Bill became the hapless victim of straitened times, regarded now as an expensive and not very urgent proposal that could easily wait. This view was held not only by the Opposition, but by leading Liberals like Dr John Quick and the formidable H. B. Higgins. Moreover as the reality of Federation was sinking into the national psyche, it produced a backlash. It took Deakin's threat of resignation to bring some of his colleagues around, and his anxiety is suggested by his acceptance of a diminished High Court, which was to be solely a court of appeal, comprising three instead of the five judges originally intended.[44] The 'Vondel' case and other developments by 'States' righters' had convinced him further that a plethora of constitutional challenges was about to face the Commonwealth. As the 'Australian correspondent' put it after its passage had been secured:

> To the Man in the Street the High Court has been a device of lawyers placed on the Statute Book in the interests of their profession. By provincialists it has been better understood. The local sovereignty of their Supreme Courts was in truth the last and strongest of their entrenchments against Federal developments ...[45]

Beyond the Liberal conviction about an independent judiciary, there was an Australian nationalism that insisted upon a sovereignty of control and interpretation of the founding document of nationhood, with roots deep in Deakin's millenarian view of the future of Australian society and of the white race in the Pacific, evidenced for instance in his later proposal for a 'Monroe Doctrine' in the South Pacific.[46]

With the establishment of the High Court there was now a vacancy in the Prime Ministership. For most colleagues like John Forrest it was certain that Deakin would assume the leadership. But to some radical Victorians, and to Lyne, who had a close working relationship with New South Wales Labor, it was by no means a foregone conclusion. The main political difficulty was that now with a national constituency Deakin could only depend on the support of his own Liberal faction in Victoria. There was also Kingston's recent resignation over the Arbitration Bill. Kingston, a pioneer in the field of industrial relations, had vociferously defended his measure, insisting on its extension to seamen engaged in the coasting trade, and remaining 'obdurate' in Deakin's phrase, on a legal point even after an undertaking that a separate Navigation Bill would be introduced soon to cover this anomaly. On 23 July 1903 he resigned, and the Bill became Deakin's responsibility.[47] With his resignation, and Barton and O'Connor now 'retiring' to the Bench, the end-of-year elections would be contested with a considerably diminished ministry. In September Deakin was wrestling with his divided Duty, whether to push for the highest office and realise his highest ambition, or to support Lyne and thereby ensure the support of New South Wales. That turmoil, the familiar dichotomy between selflessness and ambition, is suggested not only by public events, but most vividly again in that twilight world of dreams and monitions.

On 4 September an ebullient diary declared: *'Re PM Vics rally around me unasked'*.[48] It was a pensive Alfred Deakin who travelled 'solus' by train to Eltham the next day. Though his diary noted his frequent 'Tired' state, Deakin walked from Eltham through leafy Heidelberg (about five miles), where he took the train home to South Yarra.[49] His current mental turmoil is dramatically confirmed by two diary notations entered two days later. On 7 September, in a rare reference to a specific dream, he noted: 'Dream gigantic & heroic figure fell & broke head near Adam St'; and above this entry he added later: 'Lessing's Laokoon & visit to Adam St'.[50] At this time Deakin was reading Lessing's classic essay in aesthetics, where to focus upon the differences between poetry and the fine arts he had employed the 'Vatican group' sculpture of Laocoön and his sons being killed by a gigantic serpent. Deakin clearly perceived a connection between his dream and the image of the Laocoön, and it is worthwhile pausing to consider some of these implied meanings.[51]

Laocoön was a legendary Trojan prince who protested against bringing the Wooden Horse within the walls of Troy. It is this connection, rather than the theme of the sculpture itself, that permits judicious speculation on the jumbled imagery contained in these notes. The recent rupture with the Brownes had an undoubted effect, and though it is not known what transpired in that visit to Adam Street alluded to, it is clear that his parents' home in South Yarra, where his mother and sister still lived, served as a fundamental symbol of home to Deakin. The heroic figure suggests Barton, and its breaking off at the head indicates both the head of the government for whose future he feared, and Barton's health. Ever convinced that facial features mirror the soul, Deakin's pen portrait in the *Federal Story* had spoken of Barton's 'Apollo-like brow', and it was often said that Barton *looked* like a Prime Minister.[52] Alternatively, it could indicate Deakin himself. In any case, the Wooden Horse in Deakin's symbolic Troy was patently Lyne, and behind him George Reid, whose ascendancy to the office of Prime Minister Deakin believed would surely follow to destroy the Protectionist edifice they had wrought. Hence the symbols in this vivid and unsettling dream applied heuristically, disclose significant links with external circumstances. Moreover they declare again that moral combat within Alfred Deakin, between a sincere desire to serve, and a towering ambition for the highest office.

From mid-September Deakin was 'Inclined to stand out' of the political manoeuvring, but he did not withdraw from the fray.[53] He retired, ostensibly for a rest, to Syme's Macedon property Kinnersley, where he wrote several letters. In private discussions with Lyne he had offered his support as private member and promised to deliver the Victorian Liberals. To complicate matters, it appears that Lyne was genuinely opposed to Barton's appointment to the High Court on grounds of propriety.[54] Deakin could have cherished considerably less now than in 1901 the prospect of Lyne as chief, whose only redeeming feature was his constancy as a Protectionist. In these times of fluid allegiances personalities mattered, and there can be no doubt that Deakin's dealings with the Labor leader Watson and with Reid were determined to some extent by his respect for the one and his distrust of the other. His dislike of Lyne did not approach his loathing for Reid, but it is a moot point whether his decision to seek office was dictated more by his opinion of Lyne's capacities, by 'signs' in the course of events, or by his own real ambition. Perhaps it was the dream itself, its recording being unusual, which he interpreted as guidance from the 'invisible'.

On 17 September Deakin unburdened himself to his chief. In a long letter to Barton he argued that with he and O'Connor replaced by men of lesser standing their policy, particularly the tariff, was in danger, and that the ministry could not survive the election. There is a certain sophistry in his words, since Deakin knew them both to have already decided upon the High Court, and he admitted that 'what personal ambition I have must point the same way'. He was not masking his ambition so much as seeking to convince himself by putting the thrust of the argument on Barton's predetermined choice. Since he too was 'a husband & father with impaired health', he understood that Barton was compelled to consider family and financial considerations.[55] Upon returning to Llanarth, his home in Walsh Street, South Yarra, and still undecided, Deakin turned to his book of prayers for guidance:

> LXXIV. Merciful God through some of Thy myriad agencies grant me clear sightedness at this juncture not as to myself or my future but as to the public consequences of my choice sufficient to enable me to decide by them & without the shadow of personal motive ... I commit myself & my act to Thee praying humbly, sincerely & obediently for Thy guidance ... allow me to distinguish enough to follow the course that will be best for my country & Thy cause.[56]

This is among Deakin's most direct prayers, a plea for 'clear sightedness', for a foreshadowing of the possible future consequences, thus enabling him to make the 'highest' choice. With Syme's help the matter was resolved the next day, and the luckless Lyne conceded defeat a second time. Four days later Alfred Deakin became the second Prime Minister of the Commonwealth. His petition to Deity on this day was pragmatic, asking that he might 'discern those things which are necessary for the welfare of the people at large & in which something practical may be accomplished'.[57]

Some of the personal reminiscences in the 'torrent' of congratulations that poured in over the next four days shed new light on Deakin. Ceci Hume, née Lang, recalled how some thirty years ago at a 'carpet hop' Alfred had confided to her, in the middle of a conversation on how to fasten a gentleman's necktie, an ambition of 'one day being able to write "M.P." after your name'.[58] In replying as always in his own hand, Deakin commented, 'I did not remember that my thoughts had been political so long ago.'[59] Christopher Crisp proffered sound advice on health. Deakin should place himself immediately in the hands of three doctors. Furthermore he should 'methodise and placidise' his work by hiring more assistants and reserving himself only for 'top work'. He added, 'if you ate more your insomnia would disappear.'[60] Charles Strong wished him 'a clear brain and big heart and steadfast will'; and closing with a verse from Psalm 72, a song for wisdom in judgment: 'He shall come down like rain upon the mown grass', he signed 'Yours prophetically'.[61] Henry Bannister, a neighbour and friend at Point Lonsdale where Deakin built his beachside haven Ballara, put the 'occult' view; he reminded Deakin of the words of Hudson Tuttle, that writer of 'wondrous power' who said: 'the thoughts of the stars are untongued but they vibrate across the limitless aether and are eloquent to the receptive mind'. It was this kind of abstraction that had generally put Deakin off Spiritualist writers, but he was glad to receive the congratulations of his friend, who explained:

> if a man in your position has the good wishes, the good feeling, the whole souled thought waves of a nation ever pulsating and vibrating towards him in that mystical silent outpouring—which only the truly receptive mind can understand—it must and does help him to carry out his great national undertakings ...[62]

Deakin would require all the help he could muster in the seven months his first ministry was to survive. For the moment he was elated. A November prayer is replete with gratitude for the great task for which Providence had singled him out:

> LXXX. ... Not by merit but chiefly by grace & most of all for want of a more useful instrument for the special purposes of the moment I find myself selected, exalted, used, recovered from illness, buoyed up ...[63]

Alas, neither this buoyant tone nor his recovered health were to remain for long, for those 'special purposes' would require an even greater outpouring of his energies. The elections were approaching, and except for four days in September when he momentarily receded from the stage, Deakin had hardly rested since the Parliamentary session opened in March. Now as Prime Minister he was obliged to be more highly visible, which meant those long train journeys when he always had trouble sleeping. Yet Duty called, and at the end of October, after announcing his policy at Ballarat, Deakin made a whirlwind tour of Sydney and Brisbane. The pace took its toll, and the last half of November saw Deakin in bed with influenza. After twelve days' rest he felt somewhat recovered and decided, against doctors' advice, to tour Tasmania. Three days before his departure, with evident frustration he cried:'Infinite Spirit of Love, Wisdom & Truth Use me! Use me! Use me! My life is passing, my powers are failing, my weaknesses & wickednesses encompass me ...'.[64]

What were the 'special purposes of the moment'? If among these he had counted the resolution of the three groups—Liberal Protectionists, Freetraders, and Labor— and their various permutations into two, Deakin was to remain disappointed. Although the Liberals won office again the 'three elevens' continued, holding almost equal numbers in the House, and the situation was even worse in the Senate, with nine Protectionists out of thirty-six members, making effective political rule almost impossible. It seems significant that Deakin was then reading and thinking about Stoicism, especially the philosophy of Epictetus. He told an A.N.A. banquet that his ministry planned to go 'straight on' with its programme, effectively throwing down a gauntlet.[65] During the recess Labor caucus had reaffirmed its decision to push for the inclusion of State employees in the Arbitration Bill, after the ruthless suppression of the railway strike the previous year by the Irvine government in Victoria. It was an amendment which Deakin and his colleagues believed to be both unconstitutional and anti-federal. Unimpressed by lectures on 'the might and majesty of the Federal principle', and eager to gain office, Labor took up the challenge.[66] His stoical attitude to this imminent collapse amazed his assistant Atlee Hunt, who confided to his diary that, although Deakin had told him there would be a new government within a week, he went on 'just as usual keen and careful for the future as if he was to be in office always. For a nervous excitable man he betrays few signs of being much troubled.'[67] To Tom Roberts, completing his epic 'Big Picture' in London, Deakin wrote in February, 'Politically we hang on by our eyelids but mine are not heavy with regret.'[68] This same mood, markedly retrospective and almost fatalistic, is evident also in his prayers, like one inscribed in January 1904, where Deakin recalled:

> the marvellous way in which even in my sight & under my observation our political life has been guided so that with an 'accumulation of faith' I may stand firm myself & hopefully [sic] in my work grateful, trustful, unafraid . . .[69]

With the opening of the 1904 Parliamentary session, the end was near. His diary spoke of 'Intrigues [at] fever heat'.[70] On 19 April Labor moved the Arbitration Bill amendment which Deakin had made a matter of confidence, leading to sure defeat. He left office on 22 April with dignity in a speech expressing his gratitude to his colleagues and to the Parliament, and the first Labor government in the world came into being.[71]

Though Deakin's personal God could never be equated with the impersonal Deity of Stoicism, a prayer penned just two days after his political defeat expresses thankfulness, and his present mood of stoical detachment:

> XVI. ... gratitude & praise be Thine O Father for the gift of political power, for what it has enabled me to do & for the manner in which I am able to relinquish it with joy. It has been a heavy but not a painful burden & has had many happinesses attached to it. Trials, innumerable vexations, anxieties have belonged to it at every step, but these are now forgotten, & only the beginnings I was permitted & empowered to make remain to encourage me in the hope that they will not all fade away unfruitfully.[72]

These words, addressed to the Infinite Source, could not be mere platitudes to a man of Deakin's religious sensibilities. Sincere in the conviction that he had been thus 'empowered', still he never seeks to explain the role of Lyne, of Labor, even of George Reid, in any Divine Plan. And he added a rider, that prime ministerial office 'has taught me much & left me I believe a better instrument if it be necessary to use me'.[73] The faintly martial tone of a soldier in reserve probably owes something to the influence of General Booth, founder of the Salvation Army, whom Deakin greatly admired since they became acquainted during his frequent visits to promote the Antipodes as a home for English paupers. Despite this tone of finality, Deakin was again politically active within a month, negotiating an agreement with Reid on the tariff. Over the next few months, an indecisive Deakin would record in some detail an existential confrontation, as he searched within himself for an answer as to where his Duty now lay.

Power was always more important to Alfred Deakin than he would admit even to himself. In April 1904, having resigned on an issue of principle, he reflected the growing disillusionment that followed the brief elation of Federation. Ministries worked with slim majorities in a Parliament where provincial and sectarian hostilities had been merely translated to the national sphere. Frustrations with the tariff, then the watering down of vital legislation such as the Judiciary and Arbitration Bills, had taken a toll on Deakin's morale and his health. Moreover the ascendancy first of the 'disciplined hordes' of Labor, then of his old foe George Reid, must have confused somewhat Deakin's sense of a Divine Providence guiding human affairs. In his inner life, he was feeling increasingly aloof and isolated. That familiar struggle in his nature between his highest aspiration, the life of meditation, writing and reflection, and his lower ambitions, represented by politics and power, intensified further. It is characteristic of Deakin that such tensions should once again yield a massive volume of deeply introspective prose.

Hence this first period out of federal office between April 1904 and July 1905 precipitated an enormous volume of religious writing. In a virtual explosion of some 400 handwritten pages, three further journals and another 'Gospel' were inaugurated, along with his usual prayers, 'Clues', devotional poetry and other writings.[74] Among these is a small notebook on the Koran and the *Bhagavadgita*, with a long alpha index of topic headings ranging from 'Alms' to 'Wine & Games', with appropriate Sura or Bible references, which he then commenced to fill out. In a manner reminiscent of medieval illuminated manuscripts, it begins with the word: '*God* in the K[oran] is nowhere defined or described.' This is the first of twenty-three headings extending over twenty pages, followed by a similar exegesis on the *Bhagavadgita*. The pre-Federation gospels had been in the main commentaries on Spiritism and Idealism. With the productions of this fourteen-month hiatus, a new function emerges for private writing, as testaments of faith and as psychological documents during a period of tremendous angst. We have seen how the urge for 'utterance', which had made Deakin among the most gifted orators of his generation, found muted expression through his private prose and verse. Early doubts as to his creative capacities increased as politics swallowed him up, and as he convinced himself that his true calling was to Divine secular service in the cause of Federation. Dreams of real creative work were virtually abandoned, until now when circumstances seemed to make his 'heart's desire' again, if only fleetingly, seem a possibility.

In considering this period, Professor La Nauze concluded that these fourteen months were only an interregnum in Deakin's federal career, and that his desire to quit politics was a fanciful dream born of disillusionment, fatigue and frustration, though sincere enough in its expression of religious feeling.[75] I cannot agree. The writings of this period suggest severe mental strain exacerbated by failing health, when Deakin was forced to make perhaps the major decision of his life. Their tone and structure differs from previous writings, even previous gospels, though his prayers, formulaic as they were, remained still the nearest expression of his feelings, failings, and aspiration to his God.

One feature already noted is what I have called a blurring of genres, the abandonment of distinctions, so that journal becomes gospel, and prayers merge into 'Clues', and vice versa. As Deakin put it years later, the productions of this tense period were efforts to arrive at the 'fundamentals' in his belief.[76] When he made this comment to himself in 1913 Deakin was engaged in the destruction of much of his private writing, and it seems significant that these efforts were spared, as though he wished posterity to witness his personal struggles. Their poignant and sincere tone, as well as their sheer volume, bear witness to an internal conflict of formidable intensity.

Out of office in June 1904 and writing to the former Governor-General Lord Tennyson, Deakin returned to a theme in their earlier correspondence. He could accept neither the present political situation of three parties, nor Labor's programme or 'their exclusive organisation with its class basis'. In order to 'get rid of the personal equation' he had declined to take office with either side.[77] Whatever Deakin meant here—a strike at fair play, a recognition of his own personal popularity, or his admitted respect for Watson and distrust of Reid—the same expression, pluralised, appears the following year as title for a searching analysis of his belief. Its use here may have prompted Deakin, given to such ruminations, to think about its spiritual implications. By mid-June Deakin had even more cause to be unhappy with the political situation, with the imminent fall of Labor and the ascendancy of George Reid which he had feared since Federation. Deakin did negotiate with Reid in May a 'truce' that would defer the issue of the tariff for a further two years. As Professor La Nauze noted, it was Deakin's 'deep-rooted distrust of Reid' that had guided his determination to 'retain personal freedom of action while supporting an alliance as the most practicable solution to the parliamentary impasse'.[78] His opposition to the 'pledge' which made a mockery of representative government precluded an alliance with Labor, while his personal animus would never allow him to join with Reid in a coalition, so that the compact on the tariff bought time until the issue was resolved by a future Parliament. It is possible that Deakin was at the same time opening the way for younger leadership in the Liberal ranks.

In April 1904 Deakin had apparently closed his political life with a blessing and a prayer. Two months later, another prayer introduces a new vocabulary of community and of pastoral concern:

> Merciful Father what I crave is a new life—not new by change, increase or advantage except in godliness & usefulness which are one. [but] A new life & a true life, truer to the higher needs of those whom I can reach & for that end to the higher in myself.[79]

To be of use, to attain the higher in himself so as to minister to those with whom he could find common ground in spiritual enquiry—this is what in middle age Deakin 'craved'. This significant prayer is perhaps the earliest sign of a new direction. Seeing himself as a man of faith with a storehouse of experience, in touch to some degree with a higher level of Self cultivated through study prayer and meditation, he desired to impart to others the 'lessons of the Soul' for which he believed life had fitted him. Neither was he seeking 'love novelty wealth or reputation', and although in the past he had 'imagined & even purposed so many vain things & fruitless fears', he now prayed directly for: 'clearness & certainty as to my powers & the necessities to which I can make them minister in Thy service'.[80] Another inscription on his forty-eighth birthday, not in a prayer book but in another journal, probably the first at hand, is in stark contrast to this new theme of pastoral concern in its mood of alienation and isolation:

> The presence of God in my life makes for self-reliance. Few people, so far as I can judge, are more receptive of influence—yet there has been none upon whom I could lean nor have leant for years in public affairs or even in private—All have failed me, or I have had to withdraw from them—... I act alone, live alone, & think alone—...[81]

He could still be 'reached', but only 'momentarily or by sympathy'. God had become his bulwark against the world, and in his growing aloofness he confessed:

> my salvation & inspiration come from philosophy a little, & religion a great deal, especially from the mystics ancient & modern Theosophical—with them, my load is lifted, & I regain peace, courage, faith—Praised is the God of Jesus, of Plato, of Epictetus, of St Francis, of Tauler, of Swedenborg, of St Paul.[82]

An aloofness built up over a whole career was prudent armament in the ruthless world of politics. But for all the heroic stoicism, a ready cause can be adduced for such feelings on this special day. Deakin's relations with his ageing mentor David Syme had become more distant the further he strayed from the influence of the *Age*. A few days before, they had discussed a speech he was to give at Ballarat. When he read the *Age* leader written by Syme attacking the speech, a heated correspondence ensued. He had been attacked before by the *Age*, Deakin complained, but this was the first time they had come into personal conflict. Syme, as always arguing for a 'vigorous protectionist policy' and trying to prevent a breach of the tariff 'truce', had called for a 'capable' Liberal leader.[83] He was scathing in his criticisms of Deakin, accusing him of 'losing himself in the clouds among politico-philosophical questions' like the 'tyranny' of Labor's pledge, and of giving the party no leadership 'only a series of windy speeches'.[84] In a furious exchange of letters over the next few days Deakin demanded the return of his original letter, and threatened to publish their correspondence. He was clearly hurt by what he regarded as an act of treachery, when, having endorsed every point in private, Syme had then publicly 'treated it with derision'. Deakin felt he had been the victim of 'newspaper machine politics'.[85] His tone is uncharacteristically heated and defensive, and there is more than a trace of wounded vanity. Early in his career Syme had been something of a father figure, and Deakin was clearly hurt as much by what he considered a personal betrayal as by the call for new leadership. For a year or so Syme's letters were addressed to 'Dear Mr Deakin' instead of, as before, 'Dear Deakin'. Perhaps too, with Reid about to assume power, Syme's personal attack made Deakin feel more acutely the slip of the political reins, which set him meditating more seriously a new course.

It was probably then that the topic of a change of career came up in earnest in family discussion. The suggestion seems to have come from his daughter Ivy and her fiancé Herbert Brookes, with whom Deakin shared increasingly close ties. A mysterious letter written on 7 September to Richard Hodgson in Boston may also have had some bearing. Hodgson's reply alluded to a request; he would be 'most delighted to take the matter in hand for you and shall consider it a pleasure'.[86] The nature of Deakin's request is not known, nor whether it related to personal or to political matters, although it was written on the same day that Reid announced his programme. We can only assume it had something to do with gaining an 'extra hint' via the psychic channels to which he believed Hodgson, as a professional psychical researcher, was privy. In his current perplexity and inner turmoil, he turned to a trusted friend and professional in order to solicit assistance from invisible regions.

Five days later, clearly frustrated by the announcement of the Reid–McLean programme—he informed Tom Roberts that 'Reid exudes self-satisfaction at every pore'—Deakin inaugurated a new journal.[87] The first seven-page entry in 'Materials' was dashed off on 12 September. I have called it a journal, but as distinctions were becoming blurred, the sole entry on that side of the journal (he turned it over for his next entry five days later) bears the mark of personal testimonial more akin to prayers than to 'Clues'. 'Materials' opens with a commentary on a pamphlet written by an English politician, Auberon Herbert, entitled 'A Politician in Trouble about His Soul'. Deakin had first read it in 1887, and seems to have sought it out in his shelves for just this occasion.[88] While he commended the title, he criticised the author's intent of justifying his theory that politics furthers religion by its contribution to civilisation and order. If this seems strange comment from one who was only recently offering up prayers to the Providence he discerned in political events, it is another index to Deakin's extreme disgust with the current political situation.

Indeed politics ought to be an expression of 'our deepest life & highest ideals'; but in fact it was the 'selfish competitive ruthless life of commerce' which actually operated, while the public interest was dealt with only in a 'casual & uncertain' way by those whose constant aims were 'wealth pleasure & notoriety'. Was Deakin, with uncharacteristic bitterness, referring to the new Prime Minister, the odious George Reid? The interests of this low type of politician were confined to 'commerce', grasping and cupidity. Following these veiled observations, the voice assumes suddenly a more reflexive tone: 'This is perhaps the true starting point for me.'[89] This shift in the authorial voice is a distinctive characteristic of Deakin's private writing from this point onward, sometimes effected by parenthetical comments.

The true starting point was to be a definition of religion and its significance to his own life. Religion deals with both the infinite without, and 'another sphere within us'. Not as in the old Methodist phrase 'a thing to be got', it is in essence the response of the individual to 'the profoundest thoughts, most exalted aims, noblest passions & most generous sentiments of the Soul'. Hence the quality of one's aspiration, the response of the individual to the Ideal, depends upon the level of one's spiritual evolution, extending from 'a savage zero to the perfect life love & worship of Christ', as Deakin expresses it in one dramatic phrase.[90]

A hidden agenda in these ruminations now becomes apparent. Deakin clearly distanced himself from 'priesthoods', those who expound tradition, the meanings of scriptures, and the authority of churchmen to whom, he added with faint sarcasm 'all these very important matters may properly be left'. The true authority of religion abides in neither theology nor churchmen, but in experience, especially what he called 'individual' experience, Deakin's own term. Though he spoke only in the abstract he clearly meant experience of an unusual, immediate, or transcendent kind, such as he had coveted always, and had tasted briefly and directly at least once in October 1899, and perhaps in the numerous reveries of his youth. Through these cherished experiences Deakin felt that, like Wordsworth, he saw at times into the heart of Nature. They were also—how he never makes clear—signs of salvation, and clearly Deakin considered them his most important 'qualifications' in religious matters. On this September day in his forty-eighth year, with no training save that of experience, and speaking as a 'plain man', Deakin put his trust in experience. The clergy could neither 'exclude the plain man' (and clearly he meant himself) from having a religious life, nor, he added, with another significant shift in the authorial voice, from 'offering it to others in case it may stimulate encourage or help them as it has the heart into which it has flowed.'[91]

He was setting the stage for a change, arguing forcibly for the authority of the individual, by which he meant the authority of the soul. His 'qualification' in religion—Deakin's purpose was as yet unspecified—derived from this deeper stratum of experience, whatever its source, that in the sufficiently purified person might yield prophecy, aesthetic and mystical experience, and the higher inspiration of the Divine Influx. Unlike science, which requires objective training, religion was subjective, hence 'individual' experience might have 'immensely more value to his hearers if they can enter into or make use of his testimony'.[92] Here for the first time Deakin referred to others as 'hearers'. The essay concludes with a flourish, appealing to:

> the uncanonised unconsecrated unconventional untrammeled minds [who] store up experiences actual, present, & sometimes all powerful over them which they are moved to share with others.[93]

The title signifies a new starting point, a reevaluation of his life, employing the 'materials' of his faith, ideals and experience. It is never explained how Deakin proposed to share these things with others, but he implied that they qualified him over the clerics to speak on Divine matters. To an introspective man like Deakin an assessment of his Duty was a constant labour. Now this self-evaluation was becoming more frequent, more intense and ritualised. To understand his destiny and that of his race, to give expression to his personal spiritual ideal—this was to be the 'new life' he envisioned.

Probably this inaugural entry, with its rounded argument and platform-style conclusion, was a first attempt at a public sermon never delivered. It is a further indication of Deakin's resolve to go out into the world and preach his personal gospel. Five days later, on 17 September, Deakin turned the journal over and commenced on the other side with a short and conventional essay on giving up 'life'—the folly of putting aside the real treasure of 'life eternal & infinite' for the temporary illusions of earth life.[94] Subsequent entries in the twelve-month life of 'Materials' spoke frequently of the transiency of earthly existence, and they expressed a new vocabulary of community. In October for instance, there is a reflection on the Divine presence in life, descending 'upon the altar of the pure heart content & happy even rapturous to see itself consumed for the sake of its brethren.'[95] The dramatic language though familiar seems bombastic, and new concepts, with pastoral overtones like 'brethren' and 'hearers', introduce a more public and emotive dimension. This new yet old direction brought also a closer identification with Jesus, as in an October prayer:

> By this path O Father I shall begin to follow the footsteps of Thy son Jesus as the soul reveals him through the haze of legend. Dwelling upon his ascent towards human perfection we can see him becoming more & more divine, independent of the sorrows & failures with which his course was clouded to mortal eyes ...[96]

Deakin maintained 'Materials' until 10 September 1905, a very important date as we shall see. The remaining entries inscribed on average weekly, resemble the 'Clues' in the melange of comments drawn from reading and observations about life, but they differ in their almost exclusive focus upon religion, God, the Bible and the soul.

On 19 October 1904 Herbert Brookes received Deakin's consent to marry Ivy, now twenty. It was a joyous occasion.[97] Deakin's success in counselling Brookes after Jennie's death had probably set him thinking about expanding his newly found pastoral duty. There was in Deakin's household real concern about the strains of federal office beginning in subtle ways to have their effects, signs of the 'brain fag' that within five years would finish him as an effective political leader. Hence the influence of Herbert and Ivy, and of others like General Booth, together with mounting frustration in his efforts to put his political ideas into operation, attest to a conscious effort, rather than the wistful daydream of former years, to embark upon a new career. His youthful hope of literary fame was now replaced by an urge to apply his deep religious faith and his formidable oratory in the more direct service of God. In January 1905 he had 'glimpses of the new path, the new duty, the new message—Search me & try me that I may search & try myself & my fitness for so great a change.'[98] For the first and only time in his life Deakin seemed ready to take the plunge into that religious life where his inner sensibilities naturally gravitated, that 'quieter & holier way'.

The question of why Deakin hid his spiritual light for so long is directly relevant to both his political career and his wishes to change that career in mid-life. Psychologists insist that the mid-life crisis or 'male climacteric' is a real phenomenon, especially among the highly strung and the gifted. And the compelling idea of a preacher bursting out of the secular shell of the parliamentarian gains force from his own comments from time to time, as when he warned Brookes in 1903 not to 'encourage my preaching tendencies, marked enough already.'[99] It is therefore consistent with both his highly strung personality and demanding responsibilities that, at mid-life in his forty-eighth year, Alfred Deakin seriously contemplated a new career as a preacher of his own particular kind of gospel, that Gospel which he had been already writing and thinking about for over two decades.

At the end of 1904 Deakin bought seven acres at Point Lonsdale where he built 'Ballara' (local Aboriginal for 'place of rest'), his haven for the remainder of his life. Christmas was spent there with the family and Herbert, Deakin happily supervising the building and fencing and planning the garden, his special province. During January he was not well. On 20 February, after a restless night when he was up at 3.30 and again at 4.30 a.m., he crossed by ferry to Melbourne, thence to Adam Street where Herbert called. The topic of discussion appears in Deakin's diary note 'Maddern & Reformed Church'.[100] Four days later in a letter Brookes proposed what must have been a topic of discussion for some time—the prospect of Deakin leaving politics. Brookes had written after having lunch with a Mr Maddern, whom he described as a commercial traveller and Methodist lay preacher. It is not clear whether Deakin and Maddern ever met, although he was a resident of Ballarat and it is evident that he had observed Deakin the politician closely. It was Brookes who brought up the issue, and who pursued it with Maddern at the subsequent lunch. Maddern it appears, had arrived at a conviction that Deakin was the man for the role of preacher in a Freethought-style church:

All his knowledge of you as a public man, politician and statesman had led him to believe in a man who must have a profound spiritual background, otherwise to him your public acts and personal relations with public men, the tone of your speeches, your reception of criticism, your attitude toward your enemies political etc., are wholly unaccountable unless behind them all there lies a serene faith in God and deep love for humanity.[101]

Like most of Brookes' letters to Deakin, this shows great deference and some flattery. It is not clear which were Maddern's and which Brookes' opinions, nor why Maddern did not approach Deakin directly. His work as commercial traveller had brought him into close contact with a variety of persons, which had convinced him of 'a need spiritual that has not been supplied by any Australian preacher'. Assuming a faintly conspiratorial tone Brookes wrote that within his own Methodist body Maddern was one of a number of 'liberal minded thoughtful men and women' who were 'trying to do something', and they needed a leader 'who would really lead and live the life and voice their highest aspirations'. There was none amongst the Churches who could do it—'He believes you can.' Winding up his appeal, Brookes continued:

I have long known you are the *one man* myself. I have often said I would like to see you in the pulpit ... I am deeply delighted to think you are beginning to think of crowning your life career with such a possible Act.[102]

Federal politics, he exclaimed 'is not *your* element great as has been your success—religion is', and he felt privileged to be discussing the matter 'with the leader while it is still in embryo'. Finally, with an allusion to Deakin's political defeat the previous year, he posed a challenge:

Politics suddenly turns you out of doors with all your magnificent powers magnificently trained for her service. Religion pure and undefiled would not act thus to *you* but might kill you with its great needs.[103]

This appeal, laudatory in the extreme, brought no result, since Deakin did not take Mr Maddern's offer any further. It did, however, serve as catalyst for a burst of intense and concentrated introspection.

A change was foreshadowed elsewhere, as in a current prayer where, at first with a certain indirectness, Deakin set out an Ideal, his 'dream of a possible future':

To be sincere, simple, studious & passionately devoted to the ideal without badge or credo to impose on others—to combine heat & light—tolerance illimitable with faith unshaken & able to justify itself by reason ... sublimating knowledge into wisdom & checking intuitions by induction & deduction—To teach without preaching, speak without artifice, appeal without undue emotionalism & argue without harshness dryness temper or rigour—[104]

Writing again to the sympathetic Lord Tennyson on 21 March, Deakin declared that unless there was a change he was 'inclined to leave public life altogether'.[105] A fortnight later, in response to John Forrest's letter seeking advice on the present political situation, he urged a return to Western Australian politics, since he could not 'think more gloomily' about the federal outlook than he did himself.[106] At issue was the congenital problem of Commonwealth political alliances—the 'three elevens'. Despite all their efforts, Federation seemed in danger from several fronts. The 'socialist wave' was upon them with its centralising mania, while on the other side, Reid and his Freetraders sought to destroy Protectionism. The 'States' righters' too were a growing problem.

On this same day, 5 April 1905, after composing that depressing letter to Forrest, Deakin inaugurated 'Personal Equations'. The fervent outpourings during this crucial month of April 1905 are equally instructive for their form and structure as for their content. Self-analysis melts frequently into political reflections, and a number of asides which are particularly illuminating; these emotive pages could have been produced only by a person experiencing great inner turmoil. By April also he could see an end to the Reid–McLean government and at this crucial moment of decision Deakin sought to assess in himself the 'fundamentals', the nature and depth of his belief, in the manner he knew best—by writing down his thoughts, since he could always see ideas better in black and white. If he took the radical step of walking away from a brilliant career that had already bestowed its highest encomium in the office of Prime Minister, what might he have to offer to the 'plain man' whom he sought to serve? Through these somewhat disjointed, overscored and heavily annotated pages, we witness the outlines of a process of earnest, not to say anxious, deliberation.

After responding to Forrest, we can imagine Deakin opening his new journal and inscribing his first entry. Across the top of the first page appears an outline plan of seven headings, probably jotted down later; only the first two, 'Personal Equations' and 'Personal Authority', were executed.[107] Above the first heading, a short preamble begins: 'Come to the gist of it—Speak plain', trying perhaps to capture the unadorned language of revivalism. Salvation must be 'an entire change of heart & mind from religious motives' beyond intellectual conviction, which is good but insufficient. One has to be saved, to have something to give, and one cannot be saved 'until knowledge takes hold & conquers', that knowledge being the 'truth about the Soul, its possibilities, necessities, & responsibilities'.[108] A week later Deakin returned to this short inaugural entry with a critical marginal commentary: 'This will not do ... the first thing is not theory.' It had become merely 'an essay turned into an address'. There was nothing in it for 'average people'. It was suitable only for the 'thoughtful', by which he meant those who could be reached through the intellect alone. Clearly Deakin was struggling with the idea of the nature of faith, inspired by the personal example of General Booth, then in Australia on one of his frequent lecture tours. 'Light, heat, leading' were absent, and to be worth doing at all, this 'dilettante appeal to dilettantes' would have to go. To reach the 'plain man' one must first 'dig into one's heart & life if one is to reach the life & heart of others'.[109]

Dissatisfied with the tone of his inaugural sermon–essay, Deakin resolved that he must first examine the substance of his belief before attempting to preach it. It was probably then that the plan with seven headings was jotted down. The change of structure—the sudden disjunction between the 'preamble', an intellectual discussion on salvation, the 'bridging' commentary, and the searching self-analysis that follows—clearly indicates a change of intention. During that second week in April Deakin commenced his announced task of digging into his own heart, recording both the process and the outcome in the ensuing pages. As historical document and personal testament, it bears faint comparison with Augustine's own inner struggles when he left the Manichee, labouring to realise Christ, by which it may well have been inspired, and we recall how that struggle led also to a massive volume of deeply introspective writing.

The revised venture opens with a bold profession of faith. We are entitled to have faith in proportion with 'just what Truth we have & no more.' He was not afraid of stating what is true and right, nor was he bound to any creed 'an instant longer than judgement & conscience warrant', feeling free 'to unsay as well as to say'.[110] From this manifesto of freethought, Deakin proceeds to make a second marginal comment, where again there is a shift from the declarative to a personal and introspective tone. It begins with notes to himself about the next section, which suggest an introductory manifesto to his future 'hearers', or perhaps a book. 'Expect to commence with a few words of personal character—As few as possible & not to be repeated.' The pronoun 'I' would be used only to 'warn' when he was taking sole responsibility for his utterances. Then, in a shorthand form of notes under the first major heading 'Personal Equations', he wrote:

> Free speech exercised public affairs now employed other & deeper problems. Dissatisfied with politics because depend absolutely upon causes, forces, & motives, that politicians hardly touch. Wider sphere now men as men irrespective of parties, elections, legislative machinery. Irrespective of personal gain [or whether?] Paid for saying things [,] [irrespective?] Of reputation future, [or?] Of reputation past so far as it might trammel complete utterance.[111]

In this testimony to Self, Deakin's personal equation was weighed up succinctly: on one side there was the constraining and mendacious world of politics; on the other an opportunity to reach a wider field, with no thought of personal gain or reputation, where he would be free to speak the truth as he saw it. A fundamental challenge for religion was in confronting what he believed was a coming great world crisis. In these thoughts Deakin mirrored current concerns about 'national efficiency'. With the recent successes of the Japanese over the Russians, and the threat of 'inferior' races which Pearson's *National Life and Character* had warned against a decade before, Deakin sensed with many others the end of the Pax Britannica. Thus his concerns about the 'socialist wave' and personal salvation, about pastoral care of the individual and society, about illumination and service, in brief his own political and spiritual concerns, come together in this journal. A bifurcation is proclaimed by the overall structure. In the back part of the journal two sermons, 'Eclecticism' and 'What is Faith?', were attempted over the next four days.[112] So that the fore part of the journal, after the first aborted and overly intellectual sermon, was reserved for self-analysis and self-criticism, while the latter part was given over to trial sermons. Deakin was trying to break through his tendency to intellectualise.

The presence of the venerable General Booth had a catalytic effect on Deakin in this present conflict. During that crucial week between 5 and 11 April Deakin seemed in both sections of 'Personal Equations', sermon and analysis, to be emulating the old Evangelist preacher. He chaired Booth's address on the 11th, and his diary for that day notes he had two interviews (at 4 and 6 p.m.), probably before and after chairing Booth's address. He recorded a precis of the interviews in a journal the following day, regarding them both as 'interesting & important'.[113] Some evidence suggests that Deakin may have even briefly considered joining the Salvation Army in a lay capacity; but the real influence of the old Evangelist was as role model, for his indomitable faith and dedication to service, qualities

Deakin greatly admired.[114] This influence, observed already in the preamble, is further exhibited in notes on his interviews with Booth, which began as commentary and developed into a sermon.

Deakin had earnestly sought out the old preacher, and his subsequent notes were transformed, under the fire of inspiration, into another attempted sermon. Booth did not discuss religion *per se*, but Deakin notes that he had 'providentially' made a great deal plain to him. As the old Salvationist leader 'rambled on with his anecdotes' Deakin came to see the futility of merely intellectual religion, of religion 'not finding constant expression in works'.[115] We are presented with the engaging image of the venerable leader of a great movement for social amelioration, who might have become a populist leader, together with the reforming politician who might have become a preacher, the former chatting amiably, the latter puzzled and respectful, drinking in his every word, perhaps reading too much into it. In any case, the resulting sermon 'What is Faith?' emphasises Salvationist concepts like 'Saving Truth' and 'Saving Grace', and it is prefaced by the directional comment: 'The first address should strike a keynote—What we need is *Saving Truth*—Truth that *saves*—'.[116] Probably it was then, talking with Booth, that Deakin was most fired to his new calling. Through the crowded pages of this bifurcated journal, he continued the process of an examination of his private faith, with parallel attempts on the obverse side to express that faith in public sermons.

It was at this point that Deakin first spoke in vague terms of what he called the 'undertaking' which he, and presumably Brookes, Maddern and others had in mind. They would gather together 'for mutual help for particular ends'. For his part he was anxious to share, but had no 'miraculous efficacy' to offer. The success of the enterprise would be 'consolation & stimulus, leading to individual, independent living', and the greatest mark of success according to Deakin would be his 'supersession' once his hearers would 'know what I know, see & feel all I see & feel'. Then would he be free to 'Go back to silence & my other tasks, Happy in this happiest ending.'[117] It is fascinating to speculate what was envisaged for this undertaking, and what his role might have been. Deakin went on in this half-mysterious, half-humble vein for some length. There is a certain awkwardness in this new language of community, emanating from an aloof and elitist Deakin, which seems forced, and one senses a real tension between the proposed role of leader of a fledgling movement and a spiritual discipline of 'erasing the self'.

In essence the movement was to have been founded on the simple, if not vain or simplistic, faith that like-minded seekers coming together would have some undefined influence on society, by virtue of their corporate efforts to 'find, spread, or serve truth & righteousness'. It appears that Deakin's was to be the role of initial consolidator and preceptor, rather than permanent leader. He might or might not join this enterprise, he averred, which must be self supporting 'morally, mentally, & financially'. He hoped that it would always be 'elastically framed for expansion, amendment, & re-formation'. At this point the journal breaks again into lengthy personal and systematic assessment. One or two extracts will render its mood:

> Effort to speak thoughts & feelings long accumulated which have found no speech. Fifty years of life only title to address; Thirty years of reading & meditation. Prepared for apparent success or failure—If no response—no listeners—it will cease—No complaint to make.[118]

Another shorthand addendum inscribed on the same date in the back part of the journal continues in similar tone, only at first with a public voice. In another attempted address, perhaps fleshing out the thoughts just recorded in the front part, he wished to 'speak my thoughts & emotions in the hope of mingling with yours', but he was neither 'priest or parson', nor Deakin insisted, did he have any ambition to become or be mistaken for them. 'Time comes when theory has to be exchanged for practice'; devoted to theory for years, he now desired 'entering the world & put to test', not with the aim of earning a living, but 'of living & enabling others to live'.[119] The final section of this lengthy address turns abruptly once more to the political career he believed to be ending. At this point, it is no longer clear whether Deakin was still composing an intended address, or lapsing into further reflection. The retrospective tone grew, as he cast his mind back to 1879 and his bid for the pulpit of the Unitarian Church before he had even entered public life: 'If I had followed my own heart I should have taken this step many years ago':

> So long as I could feel sufficiently useful to justify my continuing a political career that seemed to most to be marvellously successful I remained in politics—When I did not seem sufficiently useful I retired.[120]

We see that Deakin's moral benchmark was still Swedenborg's Doctrine of Uses rather than the Christian Ideal of unquestioning service. He had begun here in the hope of 'being useful in another way'; if he failed, he would endeavour to 'find some opening for service elsewhere'. Yet, frustratingly, for all this verbiage—and there is considerably more—Deakin specifies neither the object of this undertaking, nor the nature of the gospel he now desired to share. He strongly believed that 'the conclusions reached may help others unsaved', but what he understood by salvation is unclear, unless it be inferred from his comments elsewhere that 'individual' experiences were somehow signs of salvation. As for his 'hearers', seeking neither to proselytise nor to be paid, he would afterwards 'send them to their own faith with more earnestness & zest'. The status and affiliation of the organisation are left in some doubt; probably he envisaged it having a loose connection with the Australian Church, of which he was still a nominal member. Perhaps the closest we come to Deakin's personal gospel is in the following passage:

> Look life & destiny in the face—Calmly, confidently, serenely, but searchingly—Consider together life's meanings—now—Light from the past—Light on the future—Interest first & last here & now—One world at a time—The world as its highest & in its lowest—In its essence & in its reality—As far as possible as one whole.[121]

To extrapolate the basic elements of Deakin's message: it was to be an eclectic and holistic approach to religion whose first watchword would be 'Liberty, the second Liberty, & the third Liberty'.[122] Its teaching would encompass the operation of Providence in human affairs, as well as social and political issues, the possibility of prophecy, inspiration and Influx, Duty and the Ideal—in short, Deakin's own deepest concerns.

Deakin's ideas about this venture drew on the notion of a common Christianity as much as ideas about race and fears of a coming world crisis. The race was far from ideal 'gross, sensuous, coarse, harsh, frivolous & even base in money worship'; 'yet', he added, almost as an afterthought, 'we rule'.[123] In the forthcoming world crisis, they would reach out to the 'hearts & minds & souls' of men and women so as to think out 'our condition & future as citizens of the world'. By these means, Deakin the perennial optimist believed the individual might transform the world. As this lengthy testament proceeds the language becomes more obscure, evoking a private mysticism whose elements were racial as well as religious.

> Whoever is able to enlarge or multiply ideas—to elevate & fructify ideals—to extend the reign of wisdom of reason of justice—to make men better acquainted with themselves & each other—with their origin & future as units of one race—to vivify & purify their thoughts & emotions kindle new or rekindle old aspirations—in a word to humanise & to divinise—is dealing with the primal & fundamental forces of society & of humanity—[124]

As always, Deakin was determined to have a mysterious universe. Yet like Socrates, he shows a surprisingly naive view of the transformational possibilities of the life of righteousness, as he had five years before in defending the 'improving' value for young minds of an exposure to the world's scriptures. In the end, and despite his earlier caveat, Deakin the brilliant orator could not help making this intense self-examination sound like an address. Though he never approached the bedrock of his belief—whatever that might mean—he did in his own way work through the gospel he felt was his, and eventually decided against the pulpit.

There are few entries in 'Personal Equations' after this flood of prose in April 1905, beyond a few comparisons of the gospels of the great revealers Jesus, Buddha, Socrates, and Mohammed. Yet even during this soul-wrenching month Deakin was keeping one eye on the political situation. On the same day as he penned the sermon 'What is Faith?', after a meeting with Syme he privately assessed the situation as 'Politically impossible'.[125] From the end of May Providence in the course of events again seemed to point the way. On his return from Western Australia at the end of May, he received 'out of the blue' a plea to take the initiative against the Freetraders in an impassioned letter from E. W. O'Sullivan, an early ally in factory reform, now a radical State parliamentarian and one of the few Liberal Protectionists in New South Wales politics. Deakin responded that 'action would be possible in a few weeks' time'.[126] From this point his thoughts were again turning to his public career.

It appears that 30 May 1905 was the date on which Deakin made his decision to re-enter politics, when turning to 'Personal Equations' after responding to O'Sullivan's letter, he reconsecrated himself to the Ideal:

> *The best* idea of *the best* God expressing the Divine in *the best* i.e. divinest way through *the best* of all his *best* offspring whose treasures on earth are *the best* thoughts words & deeds in the service of *the best* causes. This the best creed—The *best* religion in this religion of *the best*.[127]

This passage with its excessive underscoring of the words 'the best', at least fourteen times, constitutes a sacred act—a rededication to the Ideal of Service upon receiving a 'sign'. It emphatically proclaims a religious decision to render the best service. Furthermore, given its inscription on the same date as his response to O'Sullivan, it seems to abandon preaching forever.

From 31 May Deakin was again active politically. He warned Reid not to seek a dissolution, and the next day he gave the same warning to George Turner, who was a member of Reid's ministry. With his Ballarat 'warning speech' three weeks later on 24 June, Deakin sounded his clearest warning, serving notice to Reid not to seek a dissolution as a means of avoiding a decision on the tariff by May 1906, as their compact had stipulated. The speech began on a rare personal note with a veiled allusion to his recent private struggles: 'After the last session', he told his electors, 'I was more occupied with the question whether in the circumstances I might not best seek release from public life altogether rather than expose myself once more to the heart sickening experience of the last year or two in the Commonwealth.'[128] His electors chorused: 'no, no,' but one Ballarat resident, Richard Maddern, if he were in the audience, would have understood the statement, and been disappointed at the choice Deakin had made. Writing to Griffith in July Deakin complained that 'Providence ... [has been] harsh to me in rushing me into the responsibilities for which I had no yearning.'[129]

Was then Alfred Deakin's reascension to political power on 5 July 1905 providential, or was it cleverly contrived? It is hard to say. There would be a certain aesthetic satisfaction in stating that Deakin's re-entry into ministerial politics was spurred as in 1900 by a conviction of Mission, rather than a naked grab for power. This would be too pat, for although Deakin feared for Federalism from the combined evils of a centralising Labor and the 'heresy' of Freetrade, and though his stature among the Liberals compelled him to take the reins once more, it can never be proven that this move was made from the highest motives, the analytic and self-critical writing notwithstanding.

From one perspective his actions fit the model of deviousness Reid urged, of a ruthless politician who seized power by breaking an accord at the first opportunity. But what Reid could not have seen was the anguishing in those journals. Perhaps, as Deakin insisted, he had simply 'publicly held Mr Reid to his compact' and did not yearn for leadership. After self-analysis, and a couple of written sermons, Deakin may really have decided that he was not fit to preach. And perhaps meditating on the Divine will manifest in the course of events he realised that the Reid ministry could not last, and O'Sullivan's letter finally precipitated action. I think this is what happened: that Deakin could only reconcile the dichotomy between his ideals and his ambition by bringing them together in a divinised secular Mission, as when he had dedicated himself to the cause of Federation almost twenty years before. What seems most important is that when the chance he had prayed for was actually given for change, Deakin did not take advantage of it.

This fourteen-month period saw other projects half completed, and a mass of devotional poetry. Suffice it to say that finding himself idle for the first time in many years, Deakin filled his time and his thoughts in private writing. One of these manuscripts, another curious allegory, provides an illuminating postscript to this tense period; it is an oblique literary testament to Deakin's current inner struggles which points to the manner of its resolution, and confirms again the potent authority of the voice he had heard some five years before.

'Ten Letters' is an unique, not to say bizarre, narrative, ostensibly an explication of the ideas of Epictetus and Plato written some time after June 1904. Curiously, it was left undated, and the most reliable evidence is provided by the surface on which these 'letters' were written, which a frugal Deakin turned over and inscribed on the back.[130] From one perspective it was Deakin's final gospel of great men; yet understood in relation to the 'telephone' voice and the interregnum period, it discloses other levels of meaning. These self-consciously gothic 'letters', with complex strands and several philosophic digressions, constitute also a morality play having obvious connections to his experience of counselling Brookes. More revealing yet is their allegorical dimension, where the relations between Deakin's public career and his private meditations during his recent existential dilemma are given a fresh perspective.

The letters, which run to over 250 handwritten pages, purport to be advice given by and through an unnamed writer to 'I', a young professional man living in London who had recently lost his young wife under unspecified tragic circumstances. Besides 'I', their recipient, and the writer, there are two other characters in this tale: the shadowy and mysterious 'P.S.' for whom the writer serves as amanuensis, and 'E. Price Morgan' the editor, who introduces the actors and appears again at the end to explain that these letters had been passed on to him many years later by their recipient. Briefly put, the plot is as follows: 'I' seeks out the writer, an old school friend and now a devotee of 'P.S.' living with him in Italy, to gain advice in his bereavement. After some preliminaries, 'P.S.' recommends through the writer firstly the 'gospel of imperturbability' of Epictetus the Stoic slave. Once having regained his equilibrium, 'I' is led on to the ideas of Plato and his commentators like Emerson. Then, 'trying Plato by Kant', the young man has a personal transcendent experience. Subsequent letters tell of 'I''s new found zest and faith, induced we are led to believe firstly by the 'plain living & high thinking' prescribed, then by his momentary liberation. Yet, significantly, instead of building on this 'partial enlightenment' 'I' decides to remarry and to return to the world of professional affairs.

Like much of Deakin's imaginative writing, 'Ten Letters' seem a composite of his own experiences and those of the few persons allowed near his sacrosanct inner belief, leavened by his own literary imagination, all strangely juxtaposed and worked into the narrative. We note how a writer takes material from life and recasts it in a new expression, and for other purposes. They probably began as a facsimile of Deakin's experience in counselling Brookes, possibly after his proposal to Ivy; then, seeing the allegorical possibilities, Deakin employed these 'letters', perhaps unconsciously at first, as meditative or abreactive vehicles in deliberating whether to leave politics for the pulpit.[131]

Who was 'P.S.'? The writer had lived with him first in Egypt, then in Italy. There is a sense of the Platonic symbolism of 'wisdom' in the former, and 'beauty' in the other, and by extension, London perhaps representing 'power'; but more importantly, though a disciple, the writer states that he had himself met 'P.S.' only once, and then briefly. This is where the allegorical dimension of the story becomes transparent, for if 'I' be the mundane self, and 'P.S.' signifies something like 'Permanent Self' or 'Primordial Self', the statement by the writer (mind?) can easily be taken as an oblique comment on Deakin's own sole and brief 'meeting' to date with the higher or permanent aspect of his own Being, in the experience he had described by a telephone analogy.

'I' was then introduced to the ideas of Plato whose 'superior range of mental vision ... endowed him with sound knowledge of rare spheres'. Epictetus had been prescribed for the 'styptics' and the 'anodyne' his ideas offered to the young man in his grief. Once overcome, the struggle turned against 'lusts passions & enmities', for when these have been vanquished 'we find ourselves at last in the presence of the soul.'[132]

In the seventh letter we learn that 'I', confined to his bed by illness, had suddenly experienced a momentary transcendence. Breaking into invisible spheres, he described 'an endless landscape of living light & illimitable promise'. The writer congratulates 'I', and explains that these heights might indeed be reached through aspiration and the 'opening of new senses capable of interpreting' this region;[133] then he alluded to a similar experience of his own, where we discern momentarily the unmistakably personal voice of Deakin, reminiscent of the 'film unrolling before his eyes'[134] of the 'M.S.' narrative:

> I have never been privileged beyond the momentary attainment of states of exultation when the cosmos or some of its problems have seemed to become unrolled before me until I understood or part felt that this was on the road to an understanding of the whole & revelled in the new life which appeared to be poured into me from a beneficent source in which nothing but my own weakness prevented me from dwelling eternally—[135]

It was a mystical experience the writer believed to be the natural result of a life of self-control, which together with a continuous elevation of character sometimes brought as with Carlyle a 'blessedness'.[136] But he advised 'I' not to stay bathed therein, except 'for a short time or at intervals'.[137]

There is ample precedent throughout Deakin's writing, beginning with his youthful addendum to the work of the most famous writer of Christian moral allegory, to support an allegorical reading of this tale. The letters move toward a liberation of the essential Self from the prison of earth life, as in Plato's Allegory of the Cave. In the last letter the writer learns of 'I''s intention to go back to his new life—his remarriage and return to his profession, instead of building on his spiritual breakthrough. He promises more teaching later when 'I' should 'crave rarer food', when his 'appetite shall have surfeited itself upon its present viands'.[138]

Thus like the Buddhist *bodhisattva*, liberation is unselfishly laid aside by 'I' for a 'Higher' end. Once having tasted, however briefly, the sweets of the higher life, 'I' returns via a 'remarriage', to the 'world'. The final moral seems to be that our partial knowledge of the beyond must subserve practical service in this world, that we should be content to see 'in part' until at last we are 'enabled to discern a vague outline of purpose & catch a hint of the general character of the scheme of Providence'.[139]

That 'partial enlightenment' therefore was an analogue of Deakin's own 1899 audition, just as the 'remarriage' and return to public affairs mirrors Deakin's decision to return to politics. In a beautiful passage at the end the writer holds up these Ideals for 'I' who could now dispense with 'recondite' magic, 'abstruse' philosophy or 'mysterious' theology, for he knew already how to begin to 'find the Soul':

> Everything which subjects the lower to the higher, which makes your life wise pure useful & unselfish, which makes your home a centre of harmony & kindness & affection, which makes your calling subservient to the public welfare & the minister of your private honour, which renders your heart more pitiful, sympathetic, modest & faithful; which lifts your mind above idleness, vanity, resentment or animosities[,] which sets steadily before you & yours the Christ ideal of Love to God & love to man [,] all this feeds the Soul & clothes it & makes ready for it a Kingdom whereunto it shall enter by & by—[140]

As for Brookes, there is no indication whatever that he experienced any sort of mystical transport.[141] We have seen in early correspondence how he gently repudiated or laid aside some of Deakin's more esoteric ideas. His response to the letter of October 1899 is unknown, but for his mentor Deakin, who had long coveted an immediate experience of this kind, that 'voice' was clearly of such enduring significance that five years later when he was considering a preaching career, it formed the substance of these 'Ten Letters', which he employed as a kind of allegorical psychodrama in reaching his political decision. Beyond further evidence of an afterlife, or a glimpse however paltry, of a transcendental reality, the 'voice' signified most in its moral utility; the Ideal was above all a moral imperative.

The last entry in 'Personal Equations' was recorded on 10 September 1905. Deakin, once again Prime Minister of Australia, was clearing up other loose ends in the various journals, and here he wrote:

> Nota Bene—This is another long stride—another mistake avoided—'Sermons never convince' but are useful in an explanatory way—Talking at people from a pulpit saves only a very few ...[142]

Having avoided the mistake of entering the pulpit, he had come full circle. Sermons, he now knew, were only good 'as drag nets & advertisements for the multitude'. The true religious life must begin in private faith expressed through works, prayer and aspiration, rather than by public preaching. What was needed, what the people wanted, was 'yourself your heart & life torn out of your self & given them in love in sincerity'.[143] With another shift in voice and this potent image of sacrifice, Deakin closed one possible avenue of service and reopened another.

Notes

1 For a discussion of the 'liminal zone' see Edmund Leach, *Culture and Communication: The Logic by which Symbols are Connected*, London, 1976.

2 They were married on 27 October 1897, and Jennie Strong Brookes died in April 1899. Brookes and Ivy were later involved with the Progressive Liberal Party and the newspaper *Battlecry*: La Nauze, *Alfred Deakin*, vol. 2, p. 548.

3 Deakin to Tom Roberts, 28 January 1903, 16 January 1904; Deakin to Dr Charles Strong, 8 May 1902; the only instance when Barton employed the heading was in a letter returning Deakin's resignation, which he tendered in April 1902 in protest against overseas borrowing and increases in 'members' allowances', that is, salaries. See Deakin to Edmund Barton, Barton to Deakin, 24 April 1902.

4 Deakin to Herbert Brookes, 11 July 1901, 25 July 1902.

5 Ibid., 23 November 1899.

6 Ibid., 30 August 1899.

7 Autobiographical Notes, 3/300, typescript, 3 August 1904.

8 Deakin to Herbert Brookes, 28 October 1899.

9 Ibid., 30 August, 3 September 1899.

10 Diary, 25 August 1899.

11 Herbert Brookes to Deakin, 29 August 1899; see R. Rivett, *Australian Citizen: Herbert Brookes 1869–1963*, Melbourne, 1965.

12 W. T. Stead, *Letters from Julia*, London, 1897, were communications alleged to come via automatic writing to Stead from Julia Ames, an American journalist he had once met briefly; J. Oppenheim, *The Other World* ..., p. 33.

13 Herbert Brookes to Deakin, 28 September 1899.

14 Deakin to Herbert Brookes, 1 October 1899.

15 'Medley', 3/296, 'Clue' no. 725, 21 July 1897.

16 'Boke ...', 5/878, prayer CXXXIV, 7 May 1892.

17 'Medley', 3/296, 'Clue' no. 753, 19 October 1899.

18 La Nauze, *Alfred Deakin*, vol. 1, p. 228.

19 Diary, 9 May 1901.

20 *Commonwealth Parliamentary Debates* (*C.P.D.*), vol. I, 10 May 1901, p. 32.

21 'Medley', 3/296, 'Clue' no. 771, 3 April 1901.

22 This comprised notes on recent events, which began with 26 September 1900, in a private memorandum to Barton suggesting the structure of the first ministry, and proceeding to the end of the year. These rough notes mostly record his conversations with Barton, especially his dilatoriness in making decisions: 14/519, 12 February 1901; see letter from Richard Jebb, 29 May 1907, quoted in La Nauze, *Alfred Deakin*, vol. 2, p. 353.

23 J. A. La Nauze, 'Alfred Deakin and the *Morning Post*', *Historical Studies*, vol. 6, no. 24, May 1955.

24 *Catholic Press*, 5 October 1901. His most serious illness during 1901 was an attack of English cholera, a type of dysentery, which he may have contracted in India.

25 Book of Prayers, 5/966–7, prayer CCXXXVIII, 3 August 1901.

26 Ibid., 5/967, prayer CCXXXIX, 4 August 1901.

27 Ibid., 5/968, prayer CCXLI, 12 August 1901.

28 'Medley', 3/296, 'Clue' no. 782, 17 November 1901.

29 H. P. Blavatsky, *Isis Unveiled*, vol. 1, 'Before the Veil', pp. xv–xvi; on the differing views of Socrates in Plato and Xenophon, see Micheline Sauvage, *Socrates and the Conscience of Man*, London, 1960.

30 Diary, 8 May 1902.

31 Diary, 3 September 1902.

32 London *Morning Post*, 12 May 1902.

33 Diary, 3 September 1902; *C.P.D.*, vol. XII, 3 September 1902, pp. 15676–82; Quick and Garran, *Annotated Constitution* ..., p. 172.

34 London *Morning Post*, 23 October 1902; Diary, 10 October 1902.

35 Diary, 24 October 1902.

36 Diary, 30 December 1902.

37 Book of Prayers, 5/979, prayer LVIII, 26 March 1903; Deakin visited Gillies on 20 March 1903, who died on 12 September 1903: 'Crude Index ...' in 'Medley', 3/296.

38 Diary, 7 July 1903.

39 Diary, 31 July 1903; Deakin to Herbert Brookes, 31 July 1903.

40 Book of Prayers, 5/1458, where on 29 November 1903, he recommenced the numbering with Prayer no. I.; Lady White Notebook I, p. 28 ff., copy in La Nauze papers, series 5248, N.L.A.

41 Book of Prayers, 5/983, prayer LXVII, 19 July 1903.

42 Ibid., 5/985, prayer LXXII, 30 August 1903.

43 La Nauze, *Alfred Deakin*, vol. 1, p. 290.

44 Diary, 25 June and 28 August 1903; La Nauze, *Alfred Deakin*, vol. 1, pp. 293–4.

45 London *Morning Post*, 16 November 1903.

46 On a proposed 'Monroe Doctrine' for Australia, see N. K. Meaney, *Search for Security in the Pacific*, 3 vols, Sydney, 1976, vol. 1, pp. 192–4, and T. B. Millar, *Australia in Peace and War*, Canberra, 1978, pp. 72, 107.

47 La Nauze, *Alfred Deakin*, vol. 1, p. 298; Diary, 23 July 1903.

48 Diary, 4 September 1903.

49 Diary, 5 September 1903.

50 Diary, 7 September 1903.

51 The tendency in some modern biography is to 'explain' a person through unconscious motivations. I have avoided the psychobiographical approach, partly because I find Freud's critique of man unconvincing. When applied to a human life in the abstract, it tends to explain in an *a priori* fashion phenomena not necessarily fitting the desired model, normal or pathological. The result can be a forced analysis, as in Erikson's *Young Man Luther*. This is not to deny the importance of unconscious or half-conscious themes, but in examining a life via religious belief and philosophic constructions, patterns which emerge from the text, not always conscious but evident to the pan-perspective of historical analysis need not, it seems to me, be packaged in a particular theory of the unconscious. E. H. Erikson, *Young Man Luther*, London, 1959; also Miles F. Shore, 'Biography in the 1980s—A Psychoanalytic Perspective', *Journal of Interdisciplinary History*, XII:I, Summer 1981, pp. 89–113.

52 Deakin, *The Federal Story*, p. 34; for a comprehensive discussion of phrenology in mid-Victorian culture see G. Nadel, *Australia's Colonial Culture*, Melbourne, 1957, pp. 130–41.

53 Diary, 14 September 1903.

54 La Nauze, *Alfred Deakin*, vol. 1, p. 308.

55 Deakin to Edmund Barton, 17 September 1903, Barton papers, N.L.A.

56 Book of Prayers, 5/986, prayer LXXIV, 20 September 1903.

57 Ibid., 5/986, prayer LXXV, 24 September 1903.

58 Ceci Hume to Deakin, 25 September 1903.

59 Deakin to Ceci Hume, 26 September 1903.

60 Christopher Crisp to Deakin, 26 September 1903.

61 Charles Strong to Deakin, 26 September 1903.

62 Henry Bannister to Deakin, 2 November 1903; Hudson Tuttle, *Religion of Man and Ethics of Science*, New York, 1890.

63 Book of Prayers, 5/988, prayer LXXX, 27 November 1903.

64 Book of Prayers, typescript, 5/966, Prayer III, 5 December 1903; Diary, 3 December 1903 reads: 'Not so well—decided for Tasmania'; the first part of the note, scratched out, initially read: 'weak'.

65 La Nauze, *Alfred Deakin*, vol. 2, p. 363.

66 J. Rickard, *Class and Politics*, Canberra, 1976, p. 208.

67 Atlee Hunt, Diary, 15 April 1904, La Nauze papers, series 5248, N.L.A.

68 Deakin to Tom Roberts, 16 February 1904.

69 The quoted reference is to the sermons of the American preacher Phillips Brooks: Book of Prayers, 5/993, prayer X, 24 January 1904.

70 Diary, 2 March 1904.

71 Except for the two-day ministry of Dawson in Queensland in 1899: La Nauze, *Alfred Deakin*, vol. 2, p. 365.

72 Book of Prayers, 5/995, prayer XVI, 24 April 1904.

73 Ibid.

74 Lady White Notebook I, copy in La Nauze papers, series 5248, N.L.A.

75 La Nauze, Alfred Deakin, vol. 2, pp. 381–2.

76 Counsel Fees, 3/290, 19 October 1913.

77 Deakin to Lord Tennyson, 2 June 1904.

78 La Nauze, *Alfred Deakin*, vol. 2, p. 371. Deakin's uncharacteristically jaundiced opinions of Reid are given in *The Federal Story*, pp. 55–7, 176. See also La Nauze, *The Making* ..., pp. 100, 193, and *Alfred Deakin*, vol. 1, pp. 162–3.

79 Book of Prayers, 5/999, prayer XXV, 16 June 1904.

80 Ibid.

81 Autobiographical Notes, typescript, 3/300, 3 August 1904.

82 Ibid.

83 La Nauze, Alfred Deakin, vol. 2, pp. 375–6.

84 *Age*, 3 August 1904; Diary, 4, 5 and 8 August 1904.

85 See letters, Deakin to David Syme, 4, 5 and 9 August 1904.

86 Diary, 7 September 1904; Richard Hodgson to Deakin, 18 October 1904.

87 Deakin to Tom Roberts, 31 October 1904.

88 Travelling Diary, 1887; 'Materials', 5/1459, 12 September 1904, p. 2.

89 Ibid.

90 Ibid., p. 4.

91 Ibid.

92 Ibid., p. 6. After Federation Deakin read widely in Idealism and on the psychology of the unconscious. Several current meditations concerned psychological aspects of religion, and in particular the sources of inspiration. 'Ten Letters', also from this period, discusses the 'two oracles of the soul': Ten Letters', 5/544, Letter IX, p. 35; see also Book of Prayers, 5/1007, 18 January 1903.

93 'Materials', 5/1459, p. 4.

94 Ibid. [back], 17 September 1904, p. 1.

95 Ibid., 9 October 1904, p. 2.

96 Book of Prayers, 5/1003, prayer XXXIV, 2 October 1904.

97 Diary, 19 October 1904.

98 Book of Prayers, 5/1458, prayer XXXVII, 29 January 1905.

99 Deakin to Herbert Brookes, 28 December 1903. For discussion of a 'male climacteric', see E. Jacques, 'Death and the Mid-Life Crisis', *International Journal of Psychoanalysis*, vol. 46, 1965.

100 Diary, 20 February 1905.

101 Herbert Brookes to Deakin, 24 February 1905. There is a Richard Maddern listed as a lay representative from Lydiard Street, Ballarat, to the Annual Conference of the Methodist Church in 1905 and 1906: *Minutes of the Annual Conference of the Methodist Church of Australasia (Victoria and Tasmania)*, 1905; 1906.

102 Herbert Brookes to Deakin, 24 February 1905.

103 Ibid.

104 Book of Prayers, 5/1458, prayer XXXVIII, 19 March 1905.

105 Deakin to Lord Tennyson, 21 March 1905.

106 Deakin to John Forrest, 5 April 1905.

107 I have called the first passage a preamble, since that became its status within the total piece, and allows for the possibility that the headings were added later: 'Personal Equations', typescript, 5/1462–1499, 5 April 1905. The seven headings were: Personal Equations, Personal Authority, Personal Supercession, The Methods, The Appeal, The Creed, The Aims; 5/1462. The phrase appears first in the 'Gospel According to Swedenborg', where, speaking of the spirit sphere, Deakin wrote that: 'The personal equation is an enormous factor in all spiritual perception': 5/1173, vol. 1, p. 131.

108 'Personal Equations', 5/1462.

109 Ibid.; this marginal comment is enclosed in quotations, and at the bottom is the notation: 'Gen. Booth after W. A. Brooks on Preaching'. It may have been a quotation, but I have not been able to trace the source.

110 Ibid., 5/1463.

111 Ibid., 5/1464, April 1905.

112 'Personal Equations' [back], 'Eclecticism', 5/1490–5, 7–9 April 1905; 'What is Faith?', 5/1496–7, 12–14 April 1905; on Australian reactions to the Japanese defeat of the Russians, see H. McQueen, *A New Britannia*, Ringwood, 1970, p. 69.

113 'Crude Index ...', in 'Medley', 3/296, 11 April 1905.

114 See Diary 9–11–12–13 and 16 June 1905, when Deakin had several private discussions with Booth.

115 'Personal Equations', 5/1484–5, 12 April 1905.

116 Ibid. [front], 5/1485, 10 April 1905.

117 Ibid., 5/1464–5.

118 Ibid., 5/1466.

119 Ibid. [back], 5/1483, 10 April 1905.

120 Ibid., 5/1484.

121 Ibid. [front], 5/1469-70.

122 Ibid., 5/1467.

123 Ibid., 5/1479.

124 Ibid., 5/1483.

125 Diary, 14 April 1905.

126 Deakin to E. W. O'Sullivan, 30 May 1905.

127 'Personal Equations', 5/1489, 30 May 1905.

128 Alfred Deakin, Presessional speech, Alfred Hall, Ballarat, 24 June 1905.

129 Deakin to Samuel Griffith, 10 July 1905, quoted in La Nauze, *Alfred Deakin*, vol. 2, p. 385.

130 'Ten Letters', 5/201-610; one is a letter from David Syme dated 8 June 1904.

131 Like 'Personal Equations', penned around the same time, there is a strong suggestion that this Bunyanesque allegory may have served also as applied therapy, so that these ideal typifications were employed for Deakin's own purposes of catharsis, which is defined as 'an outlet of emotion afforded by drama', or abreaction, 'the free expression or release of a previously repressed emotion'.

132 Ibid., 5/356, Letter V, p. 13.

133 Ibid., 5/421, Letter VII, p. 6.

134 'The M.S.', in 'Medley', 3/296, 'Clue' no. 818, 10-13 April 1904.

135 'Ten Letters', 5/479, Letter VIII, p. 8.

136 Ibid., 5/506, Letter VIII, p. 35.

137 Ibid., 5/429, Letter VII, p. 14.

138 Ibid., 5/596, Letter X, p. 29.

139 Ibid., 5/520, Letter IX, p. 9.

140 Ibid., 5/608-9, Letter X, pp. 41-2.

141 With the exception of this obscure reference in his 1912 journal: 'This day is one of our own dear dead days which Ivy and I have marked in our Calendar of Saints and one on which we hold special communion with the blessed dead. But this is our own affair': Herbert Brookes, Diary, 27 October 1912, La Nauze papers, series 5248, N.L.A.

142 'Personal Equations', 5/1489, 10 September 1905.

143 Ibid.

8

'Finish Your Job and Turn In'

*'On ne travaille pas, on écoute,
c'est comme un inconnu qui vous parle à l'oreille.'*

De Musset

After his torturous moment of indecision in 1905, Alfred Deakin went on to produce his most significant political work. With Labor's help, the second Deakin ministry achieved an impressive record of progressive legislation. On the domestic front the catchcry was 'New Protection', a Deakinite improvisation designed to win the support of the Labor party, without offending against either the letter or spirit of Federalism. It was a stupendously simple piece of social legislation, which established a direct linkage between tariff protection for employers and their provision of a fair and reasonable wage. Though it was judged unconstitutional and thus became a 'dead end' in Australian history, its importance, especially in the Harvester judgment, was symbolic, for the determination of the 'family wage' then arrived at by Justice Higgins became the standard until after the Great War. Its source may perhaps be traced in Deakin's notes to 1893, in the 'Social Justice Association' he was meditating in that dark year, to be like the Charity Organisation Society to which he had recently donated the proceeds of *Temple and Tomb in India*:

> It would have a hard fight with wealth, monopoly, greed & the general lawlessness ... It would reverse the methods of the Boycott—denounce no one—but announce those traders, dealers & employers who ought to be supported because they pay wages that enable their employees to live decently ...[1]

In foreign policy such as a limited sovereignty permitted, the government's aims were Imperial Federation and preferential trade with Great Britain. But the election in 1906 of Campbell-Bannerman and the radical Liberals, committed anti-Imperialists, ensured that the Imperial Conference which went ahead anyway the following year would be a failure, although with the recent Russian defeat by the Japanese defence was still an important topic of discussion. Deakin was the most enthusiastic of the advocates for the new Empire ideology of Joseph Chamberlain, Leo Maxse and the Liberal Unionists. He was even offered a seat in the Commons and the leadership of the party, which he declined.

Waking most days between 4 and 5 a.m., Deakin would turn to his journals or write his 'English letter'. The gruelling pace of politics, and the resultant strain of his second ministry are indicated by constant diary notations of fatigue, exhaustion and insomnia.[2] In February 1907 as he completed preparations to leave for the Imperial Conference, an unusual diary entry noted that he was 'Too tired for Books'.[3] Four days before his departure, enacting a familiar ritual on an important occasion, on 3 March Deakin prayed with true stoicism for the success of the conference. From 'Our Father, Father of Jesus Christ & of all souls' he asked first for protection and guidance for his children. Then:

> For myself, as ruler of all destinies & nations, let me prove honest, capable enough & sincere to see the truth & speak it, discern the right & do it, seek nothing for myself & all for my country, effacing myself & all in me that is obstructive to Thy will & its advance.[4]

The prayer closes with the hope that he might fulfil his duty to 'God who hast given me by ways & means most mysterious this apparently great & arduous opportunity'.[5]

Deakin's efforts at the conference would indeed prove arduous, if largely ineffectual.[6] His only assistant was Atlee Hunt, and he worked hard even on the ship voyage over. They reached London on 9 April to an 'avalanche' of callers and letters, not to let up for the five weeks of the visit. To make matters worse, Deakin immediately contracted ptomaine poisoning. As the 'physical cyclone' hit him on 11 April he vomited and purged all night. The next day he ate arrowroot, saw more callers, endured lunch with the Agents-General, and after dinner at Lady Loch's he was understandably 'Bad again'.[7] Despite this ominous start, he repeated that familiar pattern as with his 1887 and 1900 visits of intense lobbying in the advocacy of his cause. L. S. Amery, who along with Leo Maxse was trying to retain him for the British Parliament, wrote that for 'sheer fervid, sustained emotional and intellectual flow of eloquence' he had not heard Deakin's equal; and Lord Milner expressed 'blank amazement' at Deakin's capacity for work, on whose shoulders the main defence of the imperial views had fallen. Apart from the work at the conference, there were some 50 lunches and formal dinners, which Deakin always loathed, and at most of which he spoke. Writing to A. G. Stephens on the trip back, he likened this episode which he called his 'London nightmare' to that of 'the man who has lived through an insurrection—a night attack—a battle in a fog & has been carried off stunned from the fields of action'.[8] Yet even in his exhausted state, unable to remain idle long, on the return voyage Deakin gave an address and answered questions about Australia. It must have been a surprised group of third-class passengers who found themselves addressed by the Prime Minister of the Commonwealth on 11 June.[9]

Pattie wrote that Deakin was ill for the whole of the return ship journey, and that after 1907, he was 'never the same man again', after working from 5 a.m. to 1 a.m. nearly every day of his visit.[10] For two months afterwards, suffering more acutely from giddiness, Deakin could do little work, and he spent time at Point Lonsdale and three weeks from mid-August on a tour of Queensland, ostensibly for a rest. The strain of trying to push through a foredoomed Preferential Trade agreement in London had taxed an already frail constitution beyond its limits, and those strenuous performances in clubs and on the conference floor that had come so easily in the vigour of youth and the flush of Revelation, now took a disastrous toll.

Walter Murdoch remembered especially about Deakin after the Imperial Conference 'the distress with which he found himself sometimes unable to recall a fact or a name or a word'. To most, lapses of memory are common, but to Deakin it was an 'appalling experience when that hitherto flawless instrument played him false'.[11] It is crucial to understand that in his prime Deakin was not merely possessed of a retentive memory; it approached the 'photographic', and its gradual extinction had a profoundly depressive effect on the ageing statesman.

   Private reflections, musings and prayers, though hardly less plentiful, now focused upon narrower themes. From around 1905 until well after his retirement, when a degeneration in memory and inability to concentrate made him largely abandon the journals, Deakin's private writings dealt largely with two principal themes: reminiscences on his life, at least four between 1909 and 1915,[12] a phenomenon which it has been suggested was related to his complicated medical condition; and reflections on the nature of inspiration and its source(s).[13] Deakin's 'brain fag' as he called it, was devastating to one who could once effortlessly recite from his favourite poets, a condition all the more macabre for its gradualness, and the false hope brought by the occasional remissions. These periods may be identified in journals, when a rambling soliloquy suddenly resumes a clear line of reasoning, and that somewhat florid yet engaging journalistic style that was Deakin at his literary best. Frequently such passages were followed by Deakin's commentary on their lucidity and whether they indicated an improvement in his condition. It may even be speculated that his late compulsion with psychological phenomena was related to his concerns about the state of his own mind.[14] A short 'Clue' in November 1907 made the frank and wistful admission that: 'Probably these moods marked by notes, prayers, etc. *represent*, taken together, the greatest sum of happiness I have known.'[15]

   In January 1908, on holiday by the sea but still convalescing, Deakin continued a periodic reflection on the Lord's Prayer. Its essence, he concluded, was that 'Thy Kingdom come on Earth.'[16] Turning then to his book of prayers he continued this thought, which confirms again his abiding sense of Mission:

XLVIII ... Commonwealth, Empire & this civilisation out of which they spring are precious as means only. May I never forget their provisional & transitional character when labouring in & for them in order to reach the wider humanitarian, deeper spiritual & higher eternal ends for which they are the scaffolding ...[for] the coming of Thy Kingdom which Jesus foreshadowed & for which he prayed.[17]

   The diaries over the rest of the year, when Deakin's longest-serving ministry of three years and four months came to an end, and into 1909 when he resumed office with the 'Fusion', spoke of countless intrigues. Plots and counterplots were hatched as the Conservative forces attempted to fell the Fisher Labor government. At the centre of these intrigues were Forrest and his Liberal 'Corner', and Reid's former lieutenant the Freetrader Joe Cook, with whom in June 1909 Deakin formed an alliance, as he had twenty years before in Victoria with another Conservative, Duncan Gillies, although for the first time he took no ministerial portfolio. As this moment of decision approached, 'Clues' and prayers assumed a function not unlike that of 'Personal Equations' four years before, yet somehow without the same angst. They were still employed as solicitations of guidance, but now also as something like political confessionals, in laying out the political situation as he saw it, and in some detail, to a Higher region (of his own being?), seeking at the same time an answer to his perplexities.

Was it as his old friend Alkemade had unflatteringly if perceptively observed, that politicians were like actresses, and not even a wealthy marriage could make them abandon the stage?[18] In early 1909, debating with himself once more whether to resume office, he weighed up in one journal over three days the situation for and against such a move. Professor La Nauze referred to this new mode of political reflection as sounding 'like an apologia, addressed to an historian or biographer'.[19] He added that what Deakin was not admitting to himself however was the further move to the political right by the Liberals such an alliance would entail.

There was much to commend a Fusion of the anti-Labor forces, while on the negative side he listed the strain, the modifications of programme necessary, a further curtailing of family life and leisure for reading '& for the literary work upon which I desire to enter before leaving this life'. He would have preferred to leave at the end of the next Parliamentary session, 'but for my obligations to face the special rush of great problems in 1910–12 & complete my political task'. With this coalition, he would have a strong party with a long lease of official life, enabling him to advance 'a large number of my ideas', to attend the next Imperial Conference and to do some 'permanently good work' for Australia; and he added 'incidentally earning appreciation for myself . . .'.[20]

Deakin left it ambiguous, but part of that task was the imperative of securing a new tariff for the Commonwealth when after ten years, the Braddon Clause expired. As the events during 1903 have shown, Deakin regarded it as crucial to a true federal system that the Commonwealth should be financially independent (the tariff was renegotiated with the Premiers the next year, the States to receive funding of 25 shillings per capita). In another, and yet more subjective retrospective on his whole career extending over a week, Deakin listed similar political choices he had made in the past: the clear implication is that he had reluctantly accepted power from 1880, when his compromise vote had saved the Reform Bill, in 1900 when he 'defeated Lyne & placed Barton in power', twice in 1903 and 1908 when he had supported Lyne and now, when he had just offered to go to South Africa and on a world tour in the interest of imperial union, presumably rescinding the leadership.[21] The note ends abruptly with: 'But sufficient egotism'; and throughout these pages there is an unusual self-centredness, a fulsome quality to Deakin's prose, as though he were seeking to prove a case to himself about which he was no longer confident, that belies a colossal ambition for power, while indicating a mounting personal despair. The pretext for bringing down Fisher, which Professor La Nauze judged as 'hasty and opportunist', came with the 'Dreadnought' scare.[22] On 2 June 1909, to the fury of Lyne who cursed him as a 'Judas!', Deakin took office as Prime Minister for a third time.

The 'Fusion' of 1909 was a watershed in Australian history, a divide between colonial politics and the current two-party system Deakin had been trying to effect for a decade.[23] The complex reasons behind an alliance with the Conservatives have been analysed by Professor La Nauze and others, and they relate essentially to current fears of the growing power and solidarity of Labor. For Deakin the political situation was exacerbated also, as in 1903, by a narrow Victorian electoral base, so that an alliance with Cook of New South Wales which would not sink protection was desirable even if, as he insisted, only as 'a last resort'. This co-operation became possible firstly with Reid's resignation, forced upon him by his erstwhile followers, and secondly, to Deakin's surprise, by the ready assent of Cook to a policy that was essentially Deakin's. But the difficulties with such a move were formidable. Not only did it necessitate a movement to the right, especially in the implementation of Liberal industrial legislation but, even more unpalatable to the radical Liberals, it required an unholy marriage with the former enemy, the Freetraders. Despite its unpleasant ramifications, which included a loss of trust by many Liberals in Deakin's integrity, he may well have rationalised the Fusion as being the (Divine?) instrument for forcing that political cleavage into two parties crucial to the effective working of the Westminster system.

With the gradual extinction of that private mental discourse he had carried on during most of his life, Deakin's tendency toward aloofness was augmenting. Almost in compensation, the journals became even longer. Increasingly also there was depression, but of a different sort to the customary self-castigation of the prayers, and no doubt exacerbated by constant drugging.[24] Nothing could hold back the mental degeneration, which he continued to cover up. A retrospective 'Clue' on professional life as barrister in January 1909 is headed 'Vestigia nulla retrorsum'—there were no clues left behind, as with advancing illness, the memories of a rich and varied life slowly, inexorably retreated.[25] A journal entry dated 5 February 1910 draws the gloomy conclusion that not only was he 'poor & trivial & barren' in himself, but he had little confidence that the world as a whole had noticeably matured during his life in the management of its affairs. Turning his bitterness on himself, he could only regard with contempt 'the creature I have made of myself despite all the sunshine & happiness & opportunities with which I have been endowed'. He then alluded to a speech he was preparing; it too would be poverty-stricken, 'a mere catalogue of lame ambition after ephemeral reforms—such is the public end of AD.'[26]

Notwithstanding this gloom and despite failing health, during the electoral campaign in March and April 1910, and in expectation of a great victory for the Fusion, Deakin toured over eight thousand miles.[27] His oratory was now not so riveting—one journalist who had known him in earlier days recalled that his speeches seemed 'contrived and outmoded', and he was assailed everywhere with cries of 'Judas' and 'Traitor' by Liberal opponents of the coalition.[28] He suffered interruptions. At Bundaberg 'Tipsy men' disturbed his address, in his old constituency of Essendon he had a rowdy meeting, and in Brunswick he was even refused a hearing.[29] It is clear that Deakin and his colleagues had underestimated the groundswell of feeling against the Fusion, and they were routed by a triumphant Labor.

The journals over the rest of 1910, following his bad political judgment and crushing defeat, reveal a significant pattern: first a delayed shock at the size of the Fusion defeat, then morbid depression, and finally a dramatic and 'occult' resolution to the impasse in his public life. On 6 May, only three weeks after the spectacular defeat of his ministry, Deakin wrote stoically of the 'merciful deliverance' it had brought, that from a public point of view he could only 'bitterly regret', while he could 'most heartily welcome' it privately. It was true that he had expected a sweeping victory at the polls, but '[i]nstead of being crushed I am relieved'.[30] And at the end of May he declared that 'When Christian's pack fell from his back, he did not go upon his way more lightly or more rejoicing than I'.[31] This largely autobiographical entry, which touched on a number of topics, also extended over a week. Its tone shows both unusual stridency and a certain romanticism. Life was 'one long perilous & reckless adventure' he insisted, tolerable only 'if it be regarded as a necessary experience divinely ordained'.[32] Identifying again with his 'tribe of the nervous sensitives', at three different places in the journal he stated that 'my temperament is that of an improvisatore', by which he meant 'sanguine, spontaneous, irregular, rapid'.[33] In September Deakin drew up a new will, after discussing it with Brookes. He was becoming preoccupied with the past, almost as if he were thereby rejecting an invidious present.

For all the diaries and indexes he kept, the mass of material he collected, and the great bulk of notes he prepared, Deakin appears to have made only one attempt at the Victorian two-decker, in 1903 when he wrote a rough introduction for a projected autobiography. These overscored and severely edited two pages witness the rapid stream of his inspiration, but they are an early indication also of the effects of severe stress that became all too evident in later years. 'Clue' 808 quickly gets lost in verbiage and failed syntax:

> Should you chance to lie in the sward in the evening with your ear trustingly upon mother earth[;] at that level the grass however short will become magnified with a miniature forest sometimes deserted, some times full of life & of fragrance ... In the full blaze of daylight it could scarcely retain an attention which [would?] be witched away to the trees, the sky, the hills or other objects of interest—At this moment & for those past the pride & ambitions of youth & the critical rivalries of maturity [yet] old enough to feel the sentiment of the evening of [their?] days[,] this commonplace complex of stem & blade of growth & decay ... appeals by its very commonness & the wonder it begets in spite of it—[34]

From this he develops a laboured simile:

> So the events & opinions here to be discovered make no pretension to the extraordinary & if they have any merit owe it to that fact & to the simplicity with which the plain material afforded by the facts of experience are regarded—They are confessedly magnified as the grass is because the beholding eye is laid close to them & all sense of proportion or importance frankly put aside—It is a piece of turf taken at random, except to the observer out of an immense field; not singled out because it possesses even a mole hill nor any but a remote view of those miracles of nature & models of art we call flowers [,] but merely because that is where the eye happened to come— The light that transfigures & makes it beautiful to that eye is all borrowed from the literature in which it was shaped—This 'light that never was on sea or land' in no other sense belongs to the spot which its magic translates & may not be visible there to any one else here[,] though[invited to look ... at least over his shoulder[.]

This obviously hurried exercise, in the rush to get the idea down, if it is not a model of clear writing has at least an internal coherence; it illustrates the abstractions to which Deakin quickly escaped in what might be called his public metaphysical prose. We see the straining to hide yet reveal the secret side of his life, already something of the decline in the lack of economy of expression, in the overcrowded metaphors, and the brittle and tenuous remnants of a vigorous literary style. The bitter irony would not have escaped Deakin, that now when he had the leisure to tell his own story, the capacity to do so was rapidly diminishing.

It is debatable whether in 1910, Deakin would have remembered making that false start at autobiography. Still, further notes on his childhood and other details about his life continued to appear over the next few months. He had been looking forward to rereading and destroying nine-tenths of his accumulated notes and manuscripts so as to 'put the other 10th into shape, coupling this with any gleamings in the shape of notes upon Australian politics & politicians (as I have known them) which might be of service to future students of my time'. But with the present 'brain fag' alas his 'one hope' of useful employment in his remaining years 'has gone, all gone, I am not fit to write, I am not capable.'[35] It is a lament that appears frequently in Deakin's ruminations from this point onward. He was clearly losing his grasp. In October 1910 Deakin was preparing 'Books and A Boy' to read before the Browning Society, spending weeks on a task he could once have satisfied strictly extempore. The result was a crowded and rambling, at times a cloying reminiscence on his early reading which focuses inordinately on Bunyan, Defoe and Swift.

In his continuing chore of retrospective house-clearing, Deakin wrote precis of most of his early works before committing them to the flames; some of these exceed the original in length, and they contain numerous lengthy extracts and parenthetical asides as to their merits or otherwise, and on his mental faculties. It was here that he quoted his first inexplicable impulse to write verse, a little ballad of 1872 which begins:

> How haunting is the mystic ancient legend of the sea
> with the dust of ages in it waning dim & shadowy
> of the ghostly flying dutchman in his sad eternal quest
> how he wanders o'er the pathless sea forever without rest ...[36]

The remainder was, perhaps mercifully, lost forever.

Hence prayers, 'Clues' and other journals were partly the products of an enforced leisure after losing political power, but when viewed as a whole, they were becoming far more. The remainder of 1910 saw a characteristic outpouring of writing, tantamount to an extended reflection from varying perspectives—religious, personal, and political—on his life, that frequently develop into commentaries on the theme of his 'aloofness' contrasted against his 'egoism'. Some of it seems morbid, or at least gravely detached in tone, and the mood changes were undoubtedly related to his augmenting illness. In a September prayer he spoke of taking 'the last lap' of life in his stride, before getting into 'the tunnel yonder to emerge Heaven knows where "on the other side" conscious or unconscious'. This new detached perspective gave him a 'queer angle of vision' since he felt already like 'a man dead & translated, talking to the living'.[37]

The gradual degeneration of Deakin's memory and health renders his current fixation on the mind comprehensible. A measure of desperation is evident along with, as we have seen, lapses in syntax; another new feature was the practice of parenthetical commentary. A May 1910 journal is bizarre. It describes first and in some detail a sensation he knew to be common to 'mediums', one he had shared himself intermittently during what he called his 'dabblings in the seventies'. Lately this sensation had been revived occasionally, at times 'with some force':

It is a sensation in the fore part of the brain as if it were being breathed through—literally an 'in-spiration' usually above the forehead but centered in the front half of the head & as if at least 1½ to 2 inches from the surface—[38]

He reported its general nature as an 'impulse' or a sense of 'approbation' accompanying a thought or conviction. Its probable physiological origin is indicated, however, by his observation that it came after reading or 'when thinking upon some abstract or large question', that is, when exercising the brain. Words failed to describe it, but he was convinced that 'it is "inside" as clearly as it appears to have come from "outside" '.[39] There is much more, but this was the essence of his interpretation, which seems strained. At the back of his mind were ideas like Newman's 'personal assent' arising from an Illative sense, defined as: 'the faculty of judging from given facts by processes outside the limits of strict logic' in reaching religious certitude, and 'occult' ideas regarding this region of the head as the locus of the 'third eye' from which clairvoyance emanates. Two weeks later, returning to this already crowded page in the journal, he interposed a parenthetical afterthought: '(Does it imply a cessation of the public active life & the return to the inner & to writing as of old?)'; and jammed in again at the top of the same page two months later with an entry dated 28 July, he noted: '(It has died away again & all but disappeared i.e. in its "objectiveness" if that word ever applied to a brain tremor—)'.[40]

Deakin was clearly searching, desperate for an answer to his metaphysical uncertainties, and for an alternative, even an 'occult' explanation for those queer sensations. Beyond perceived links to past experience, especially his early spiritism, what seems of particular significance is the nebulous question he posed at the end. Why should this phenomenon, which had been rare for many years, occur again; he added: 'its return almost immediately after I am freed from official responsibilities again revives my curiosity as to its cause & meaning.'[41] We can only speculate what these were, but Deakin's interpretation of what to an outsider seem clear physiological symptoms gives a strong indication of an augmenting personal despair, a grasping at straws for answers.

In this protracted mood of gloom, Deakin observed in a journal on 4 November that the 'best' usually seems 'very bad':

> that only partially & very rarely does it seem even decently satisfactory, & that no proof is possible of 'the working together of all things for good'—far from it. I had once thought our Federation a distinct illustration of a real & great victory won against hopeless conditions—Now I am not so sure. But I remain consistently sanguine & so consistently contented.[42]

It is a startling admission, yet I think more a product of gloom coloured by wretched health and the unsettled current Parliamentary situation than a disavowal of Providence, since earlier in the same lengthy journal he declared: 'it has been in my public life that I have most relied upon the unseen in a spirit of faith at times indistinguishable from fatalism.'[43]

I have argued that these copious and somewhat disjointed outbursts begin to make sense when viewed as a process of review, made increasingly difficult by depressive health and diminished capacity, culminating in a dramatic resolution with a profoundly significant 'answer'. The response to the question which he had indirectly been posing through his journals over the seven months since his resounding political defeat in April, once again whether to quit politics, came to him through a voice heard on an early morning in November.

Awakening as dawn broke over Point Lonsdale in the early hours of Saturday 12 November 1910, Alfred Deakin heard a voice. He had returned from Melbourne late, and after a poor night's sleep he now began his day as customary when he could escape politics to his beloved Ballara by the sea, with an entry in one of his journals:

> No sooner returned from town last night & escaping the strain of active life (preoccupied, weary, & with a programme of labours to come) than I awake here free & peaceful, & *myself* once more.[44]

On this morning, however, there was a special excitement in this familiar discipline. As his hurried scrawl raced across the pages Deakin forgot his weariness, for in that twilight world between sleep and waking he had just received a 'monition', a message whose full weight of meaning he now feverishly tried to preserve:

> Then there drifts into my mind a whispered monition from my subconscious self (gravely earnest & yet with suggestions of whimsical ease so that it is in no sense even mandatory but joyously floats to the surface from unplumbed depths of intuition inheritance & foresight). It comes simply & in slangy phrase. It wells up lightly tho' embodying the profound judgment & conclusion arrived at deep down within me repeating again with friendly forcefulness & airy pleasantry the conviction that flows in upon me always now when I come here.[45]

After reassuring himself that this outbreak was not a result of conscious deliberation: '(... since I arrived and during the night I had not even touched upon the subject consciously)', he related the experience itself:

> Again by way of warning, counsel, & encouragement it found me saying to myself & from myself as if to remind me of my aim & destiny henceforward *'Finish your job & turn in'*.[46]

Whatever its source, the monition clearly held great authority for Deakin. He believed that the message was intentionally conveyed in slangy phrase, and that it pointed to 'patient meditation within me':

> I pay great attention to these admonitions—Many would attribute them to an independent, dictatorial external agent—I do not—If I did it would probably have less weight with me than it does while it represents to me principally the ripe results of my own unconscious meditations conducted in a cell so to speak more sacred, more independent of my ordinary self, less biassed by external influences or worldly aims, in a word the cream of one's conscience & the best fruits of one's judgment blended together—Of course this does not mean that it is infallible nor that it is solely self prompted or self known nor that it is the voice of God apart from my human sonship, (whatever that may be).[47]

The context suggests previous experiences of this kind. This was far from Deakin's final opinion about the message's meaning or its origin; before a bath and breakfast, he had completed seven quarto pages, and he continued his reflection intermittently over the next two weeks. The next day he lodged two further entries, and with the interruption of a trip to his constituency of Ballarat, he returned to the subject on 27 November with another six pages.[48]

In effect, this journal developed into a seventeen-page meditation once more on the question of whether or not to quit politics. The message was regarded as confirmation of an already formulated decision to resign, a decision Deakin would delay putting into effect for another two years. Beyond a discussion of his political future however, it provided a departure point over the next few months for reflection on a number of related topics.

Increasingly from the 1890s, ideas about the unconscious were in the forefront in art and literature, in the 'Natural' influences of the Art Nouveau styles, and especially in the budding science of psychology. Freud's *The Interpretation of Dreams* was published in 1899, and William James' *Varieties of Religious Experience*, the first Gifford lectures by an American, and very controversial when given at Edinburgh in 1901-2, relied as much on his psychological theories and the work of the Societies for Psychical Research as on his Pragmatist philosophy. Deakin read both James and the work that greatly influenced it, F. W. H. Myers' massive *Human Personality and Its Survival of Bodily Death* in 1903, the year when both were published. The importance of these authors to the present discussion lies in their conception of a 'subliminal self', a term first coined by Myers to account theoretically for phenomena like hypnotism and mental telepathy (another term he invented). Ambiguous enough to fit many moulds, this theory became an important interpretative concept for many Edwardian thinkers throughout the Western world, and in many fields.[49]

After an early positivist phase of Comte and Spencer, Deakin read widely in the major anti-positivist literature of his day. From Hegel and Kant, he had derived a keen sense of the Ideal, and of the distance from the noumenal that immersion in the material world brings. Later, through Swedenborg and Tauler, and Jacob Boehme, he located his own early experiences within a larger tradition of mystical experience. In 1903 Deakin's reading included not only James and Myers, but also Podmore on *Modern Spiritualism* and the Theosophist Leadbeater's *The Other Side of Death*. He was thinking, as always, about the sources of morality. In one 'Clue', we see him trying to reconcile thinkers as diverse as Spencer and Newman, and attempting to place them in a context of modern depth psychology. After reading Newman he wondered whether the response to moral conflict, which seemed to come like a verdict 'as if uttered from antenatal depths with a priori certitude', arose from 'inherited bias', or whether it was 'the judicial outcome of the whole subconscious mental life', or again 'merely the outcome, as essence, of our whole experience'.[50]

The older Deakin found solace in German Idealism, and in its lineage of Bergson, James and Eucken, closely related to the New Idealism that from the 1890s was creating a new paradigm in social thought with the deeper exploration of the human unconscious. Psychical research was an important part of a broader process which 'displaced the axis of social thought from the apparent and objectively verifiable to the only partially conscious area of unexplained motivation'. In a memorable passage H. S. Hughes captures the enthusiasm of the new intellectual concerns of the 1890s:

Psychological process had replaced external reality as the most pressing topic for investigation. It was no longer what actually existed that seemed most important: it was what men thought existed. And what they felt on the unconscious level had become rather more interesting than what they had consciously rationalized. Or ... since it had apparently been proved impossible to arrive at any sure knowledge of human behavior—if one must rely on flashes of subjective intuition or on the creation of convenient fictions—then the mind had indeed been freed from the bonds of positivist method: it was at liberty to speculate, to imagine, to create. At one stroke, the realm of human understanding had been drastically reduced and immensely broadened.[51]

Recent scholarship has confirmed the importance of the Societies for Psychical Research to the discipline of psychology before World War I.[52] Those who gathered around Henry Sidgwick at Cambridge and William James at Harvard were 'rejecting the grim conclusions concerning human life and universal order' toward which positivistic science seemed inexorably directed.[53] Their ideas about time, persons, ethics and religion were closely related to their involvement with the Societies for Psychical Research, of which James in the United States and Myers and Sidgwick in Britain were leading members. The theory of the subliminal consciousness arose out of the work of Myers and Edmund Gurney on telepathy and hypnotic memory. Like James, they were inspired by the ideas of Henri Bergson concerning time and intuition. In a frequently quoted passage from the 1892 *S.P.R. Proceedings*, Myers argued that the waking self represents but a small portion of the individual:

> the stream of consciousness in which we habitually live is not the only consciousness which exists in connection with our organism. Our habitual or empirical consciousness may consist of a mere selection from a multitude of thoughts and sensations, of which some at least are equally conscious with those that we empirically know.[54]

Myers originated the neutral terms 'subliminal' and 'supraliminal' consciousness, in preference to 'unconscious', which denied them consciousness, or 'secondary self', which gave implicit superiority to the empirical self. He advanced the idea that unusual phenomena were neither freaks nor miracles, but that they represent a continuous set of gradations between ordinary phenomena and the para-normal. Thus events like post-hypnotic suggestion, trance speaking, automatic writing, telepathy, hallucinations—visual and auditory—and crystal gazing were understood within a matrix of unusual facts about human personality shading off from 'normal' to paranormal.[55] Positing a subliminal self enabled an overarching theory, where the supraliminal consciousness might receive 'messages' from the subliminal, which allowed the accommodation of all manner of phenomena as a discrete series.[56]

It is easy to forget how up to date Deakin was in his reading, especially in the general field of religion. His voracious eclecticism made him familiar with literature of all kinds. But Deakin's links with the major currents of wider social thought concerning the unconscious were more direct, particularly to the American Branch of the Society, through James' Harvard colleague Josiah Royce, the Idealist philosopher with whom he had maintained an intermittent correspondence, and Dr Richard Hodgson, secretary of the American Society, who collaborated with Royce and James, as in his 'experiments' on the medium Mrs Piper. James' *Varieties*... explored mysticism, conversion, and other religious experiences based on a paradigm of religion as 'personal experience pure and simple'.[57] Deakin, like James, shared the current assumption that there is a common religious experience available to humankind, whose intensity varies with one's capacity for 'religious feeling' (hence the singular religious 'Experience' in the title of James' book). To James this transmarginal region was the source of our dreams, of mystical experience, of 'automatisms', and it was also 'the fountainhead of much that feeds our religion'.[58] James linked this idea philosophically to a Pragmatic justification, in terms of its social value. The utility of religion lay in the projected good that a community of saints might have on society in contrast to a community of sinners. In persons 'deep in the religious life', the door to this region seems 'unusually wide open'. But James did not reduce such experiences to mere epiphenomena, for:

> if there be higher spiritual agencies that can directly touch us, the psychological condition of their doing so might be our possession of a subconscious region which alone should yield access to them—The hubbub of the waking life might close a door which in the dreamy Subliminal might remain ajar or open.[59]

James was one source for Deakin's conception of the relation of a subliminal region of Self to the religious life, through aspiration. It was an idea that Deakin embraced enthusiastically. The analogy with a sort of permeable membrane conditioned by a purity of life through which 'higher' forces and influences might gain entry, is irresistible. The essence of religion was conceived as a personal quest, arising from the feeling that 'there is something wrong about us as we stand', whose resolution comes with a sense that 'we are saved from this wrongness by making proper connection with the higher powers.'[60] At best Myers' complicated theory was replete with tensions and contradictions, at worst its nebulous quality undermined the very spirit survival theory it sought to affirm, and even fragmented the notion of personality.[61] Yet the theory of the subliminal consciousness greatly influenced Edwardian psychology, especially James' work on an 'horizon' and 'stream of consciousness' as a continuous flux of mental activity.[62] James, unlike Myers and Hodgson (and Deakin), was never convinced of personal immortality, and perhaps reverting to his early Swedenborgian monism, he came to believe that the individual consciousness figures as a 'beam filtered out from the universal consciousness by our brains'.[63] We can however understand its pull on Deakin, since it allowed him to retain cherished fundamental conceptions like Inspiration and Influx, while applying the modern ideas of psychology and psychical research to his eclectic personal religion.

Through our opaque historical camera we have witnessed subtle changes in the function of private writing during the post-Federation era, first in a blurring of genres, then in a narrowing of focus. After the Imperial Conference in 1907, the journals began to serve as something like political confessionals, and as the conjunction between political gloom and Deakin's personal despair over his health augmented, they grew inordinately concerned with the past. Finally, with the massive defeat of the Fusion, their focus became even more narrow. From this perspective, the monition may be regarded as cathartic, the culmination of a process resolved as before through writing out ideas, but now more intensely concentrated on an external, or at least a Higher, authority for his decisions.

In a reflexive way, the whispered monition was a reward for and a confirmation of his inner efforts. Deakin's reflections on the monition discloses a complex system of relations between personal and transpersonal regions of the self, foreshadowing in some ways Jung's archetypes, with the usual traces of Herbert Spencer and the positivists, as where he speaks of 'unplumbed depths of intuition, inheritance & foresight', suggesting a transpersonal 'inheritance' of race and kind.[64]

The extended reflection through the ensuing pages, even more intense since the audition, continued intermittently for at least a year, and probably longer.[65] Over the first two weeks following its reception, Deakin turned over every nuance of meaning of this pregnant phrase, as a warning of an untimely death, an exhortation to 'turn within' to more spiritual concerns, or to quit politics for that 'quieter and holier way' he had been dreaming of since his young manhood. He explored every possibility as to its origin. The monition was not to be equated with intellect, he averred, for it sees beyond reason and intellect, so that the mind and its rational faculties (located somewhere between the physical and the spiritual regions of Self) seems to exist apart from this essential Self. If it is difficult to understand an entity communicating from one part to another of itself and still remaining the same being—an external conscience, even a guiding spirit might be more comprehensible—Deakin insists that this 'inward monitor', 'subconscious', 'superconscious', or 'vaticination' as he variously terms it, originates in some manner from within himself. He accepted the idea that the monition came from his 'best' Self, defined parenthetically as '(my most receptive & reflective & mature self moral & intellectual self)'; but he was certain also that:

> ... it sees further & deeper than itself & is to some extent either recipient of an or in touch with higher truth than anyone—perhaps higher than human—influences compounds of mortal with immortal—& that thus I have what if not a 'direction' is a very great support to me in my life decisions & attitudes.[66]

With characteristic ambiguity, and awkward syntax which confirms a continuing decline, Deakin cherishes the possibility of obtaining an 'extra hint' via the Higher Self either from itself, or from what he calls 'the wider & purer regions in which it moves or with which it communicates'.[67] 'Human' in this context includes spiritualised humans after death, and the 'higher than human' truth, as in the 'vision of judgment' fifteen years before, suggests Divine knowledge above the ken even of departed spirits, what Swedenborg had termed the celestial world. Hence the source of the monition may be external, but its reception depends fundamentally upon the moral worthiness of the aspirant. Deakin's 'Best', summed up in the principle of Unselfish Love, was the sum and product of his aspiration, his efforts at moral and intellectual improvement, become a subliminal channel for inspiration and prophecy.

Probably the clearest expression anywhere of Deakin's belief in an immanent and immortal Self is found in his verse. Some time around Federation Deakin commenced a complex round of devotional poetry, in three cycles. The following passage, from Cycle I, 'The Script', expresses the essence of his ontological belief better than the reams of speculation he produced over nearly a half century:

> *There in the mirror that we term 'within'*
> *The inward inlook of the consciousness*
> *The Self!*
> *A medley ever changing in its flow*
> *Sensitive & receptive & expressive*
> *Attracted & repelled disturbed then calm*
> *The waves of feeling floating it along*
> *Flashes of thought & glow of meditation*
> *Turning, returning so, evolving slowly*
> *A multitudinous incessant throng*
> *Perceptions & conceptions & ideals*
> *Passions eructions & volitions blended*
> *Around a centre undiscoverable*
> *Knit in a unity we style the Self.*[68]

The source of the monition, whatever its nature, Deakin with tortured punctuation termed: ' "my best" (however "bad") & "my highest" (however "low")'.[69] From this point, the reflection develops into something more than a confirmation of moral authority in a period of existential doubt, for having identified his political career and his religious quest almost totally, Deakin needed the approbation of this voice of admonition. Perhaps by placing responsibility on something effectively or putatively outside himself to justify his decision to quit politics, he wished to abrogate his duty to a region and persona beyond his conscious influence; it was a corollary to his sense of Duty and Mission to require Divine approval to rescind it. When he returned to his meditation the next day, 13 November 1910, Deakin advanced two causes for these 'babblings': to compensate for a loss of memory, and secondly as 'aids to judgment in the important decisions I have soon to make'.[70]

Hence Deakin accepted the message as a charter to 'finish' the political job, and approval to 'turn in' after its completion. In this light, his actions seem propitiatory, invoking a Higher part of himself to guide his judgment. In passing, an ancillary function is disclosed, as a salve for his ego after the resounding defeat of his Fusion forces eight months before; he declared again that he had 'risen from outer failure undepressed' and speaking of the 'imputations' that his resignation might bring, he insisted that he was not inwardly affected by them 'when one knows them to be false by knowledge of one's self & sentiments as no one else can'.[71] Deakin frequently employed the formal pronoun 'one' when referring to his Higher nature.

The political battler was turning from the outer world in his 'aloofness', measuring himself by the Swedenborgian and Kantian principle of intention as the standard of moral credit, by 'knowledge of one's self & sentiments'. Writing his third journal when he returned from Ballarat a fortnight later, he declared that he had 'done more' than his duty, and 'fought the good fight with sincerity'.[72]

We have observed through these journals how the ground was prepared for what Deakin believed to be a Higher Inspiration, and by an ongoing dialogue with the source(s) of the monition how he laboured to elaborate its full meaning, and to obtain continuing assistance from it in order to finish his 'job'. It is likely that this process of written deliberation had made his present Duty clear. In his declared aim to 'do something to retrieve the political situation in the public interest'[73] was the germ of a resolve that would impel him to lead his last political fight the next year to defeat Labor's referenda. They were opposed by Deakin from the conviction that they would have changed the precarious balance demanded by a true Federalism, for a more centralised system. Hence with regard to one agendum of this study, the consideration of the importance of private experience to his wider public life as discerned through the opaque medium of secret reflection, we see that as at previous junctures in his career, Deakin looked to a Higher moral authority for the direction of his public exertions. Even if such an abiding conviction were proven to have been fantasy or empty rationalisation, it can still be argued that this monition experience had an inordinate influence on Australia's federal history. These referenda were defeated in 1911 and again in 1913, though Deakin had retired before the second referendum. The spiritual basis for Deakin's political resolve is found in these private reflections, in the supplication to an ambivalent yet potent Higher authority, which inspired a tired Deakin to fight the good fight one last time, so as to ensure a workable federal union.

Reversing his usual practice of an end-of-year summary, Deakin inaugurated the rough diary for 1911 with a prefatory comment: 'Nearing the end—a critical year public & private—perhaps the critical year for my future short or long.'[74] Then, as he always did on 1 January, he composed a birthday poem for Pattie. The crisis Deakin envisaged related to Labor's proposed referenda to give the federal government greater powers over trade and commerce, monopolies and industrial matters. Deakin and the Liberals objected that this would destroy Federation by reducing the States to 'junior sleeping partners' in an unitary form of government. On 2 March 1911 Deakin opened the anti-referendum campaign, and over the next two months, until 25 April the day before the poll, he campaigned vigorously, speaking in thirty towns and cities in all States except Western Australia. A typical diary entry dated Geelong 7 April, reads: 'Spoke one hour very tired—interruptions ... another crowd another speech—quiet—dead beat.'[75] A few days later he confessed: 'In myself, the sense of duty is gone ... at all events, my mainspring seems broken.' Yet girding himself to the Ideal, he would nevertheless remain. As he confided to his journal:

> It is only because my *inclinations* turn that way that I feel any doubt at all, so plain & clear is my inward monitor & my judgment too of my wisest course ... [the] firm admonition to 'finish my job' evidently meant finish with leadership.[76]

On 26 April 1911 Labor's referenda proposals were defeated. Deakin was elated with the result. 'So we have won', he congratulated himself in a journal, and this by the margin he had fixed before mentally.[77] One wonders how Deakin reconciled this present triumph with the humiliating defeat just twelve months before, though one can imagine him reasoning that in the scheme of Providence which knows no individuals but only the Divine pattern, both events were necessary. In a letter to Brookes he ventured:

> It seems almost a concerted design that brought Herbert & Ivy Pattie Katie & Vera all who lure [word unclear, 'were lured?'] into the fishing line each with a special piece of service to fulfil—[78]

This had happened before, but 'never so perfectly or so efficiently or in such an important matter.'[79] It appears then that Providence had brought them all together, under Deakin's leadership, to retain the federal compact divinely ordained. However the most compelling evidence for the transcendental authority of this final 'job' appears in a journal written a month later, when he observed on 2 June 1911:

> The mysterious admonition has not been renewed & probably there is no sufficient reason why it should—I should be glad if it did & have been listening anxiously ever since April 26 but in vain—It does not seem as if I had yet 'finished my job' & that therefore I must not 'turn in'.[80]

The date is crucial; it was on the same day that Labor's referenda were defeated. Deakin had therefore expected a recurrence of his mysterious 'Divine sign', presumably as to what he ought to do next. The clearest connection is drawn by this passage between the monition experience of November 1910 and the April 1911 referenda; it is among the most authoritative evidence for the continuing transcendental authority of a voice in Alfred Deakin's personal religion. Like Socrates, having 'heard' nothing more, Deakin believed his Duty was to remain at his post. He now added another thought about its meaning, to 'turn inward', conveying thereby nothing more than 'a cheery, friendly, far-seeing, philosophical counsel for myself to follow'. He added: 'I took it, of course, to indicate the Referendum but I had no inkling whether it went any farther ... though I am very ready indeed to "turn in" without more delay.'[81] Deakin was continuing to devote a good deal of his scant leisure and failing attention to the monition. Later in the year, in a dark mood brought on by still further mental deterioration, he would wonder whether it was a 'Banshee warning given in the most polite disguise, or a summons that it is my duty to obey'.[82]

Writing to comfort Walter Murdoch in August 1911 after his unsuccessful application for a Chair at the University of Melbourne, Deakin compared their situations. But, he added, 'the parallel is not complete, for my rejection came to a very tired man stubbornly finishing his task.'[83] Some sixteen months after the event Deakin was still musing on that massive defeat at the polls the previous year; and he did not believe his 'job' was yet finished. In his politically beleaguered and personally despairing frame of mind, a natural disposition to 'aloofness' intensified further. In October he wrote:

> The more the Parliamentary situation develops in this new session the less hopeful appear my prospects of escape from public life or of 'turning in' (except in the sense of 'turning within' of which I have just been reminded by a precious passage written here (have turned back searched twice thro' these notes & as usual cannot find it)— I have begun 'turning within' more steadily, more consciously, more persistently than ever before) ...[84]

Thus almost a year after hearing the monition, Deakin was still searching out its fullest significance, already revealed in part by his political successes against the referenda. The curious asides, parentheses within parentheses, are a peculiarity of Deakin's late writings, as are frequent references to forgetfulness in the most mundane matters. Current diaries often have blanks for the names of persons he had been speaking to just that day. In Tasmania he had set out to relearn Wordsworth's 'Ode'; the 'plodding pedestrian poet' as he called him, was a great comfort in his current state. It makes sad testimony to the debris of a once remarkable mentality that Deakin now found it beyond his capacity to manage even a few stanzas from one of his favourite poems. If this continued, he noted sadly, 'one of the pure lights of my life will have gone out in darkness.'[85]

By the end of 1911 Deakin knew that he was only going through the motions of being leader. He covered up, employing extensive notes for his speeches which he followed closely. 'The AD of 50 years', he confessed in a journal, 'journalist & politician, MLA & Minister ... is buried somewhere; he no longer lives in me, though I continue to act his old part for the time being.'[86] The next year brought even more rapid disintegration, both in his own health and in Pattie's. Journals spoke of 'the mental & moral stripping—the critical nudity' in which Deakin now found himself.[87] In probably his last attempted narrative in February 1912, his grave condition is indicated first by an unconscious allusion to his own wretched condition in the opening lines: 'Was it relapse some ten days ago since into the remote before birth of this planet?' The bizarre 'seeing eye' experience which he laboured to set down through several rambling pages was a pathetic attempt to compose again in the experiential mode, influenced by heavy medicinal drugging.

Deakin attempts to relate an experience in which unsuspected relations are disclosed among ordinary objects, where everything is 'strange, weird, grotesque, irrelevant & inexplicable', and ordinary men are revealed as 'ungainly forms housing temporarily crude sprouting intelligences'.[88] With its disjointed sentences, laboured images and at times almost incoherent syntax, it shows little of the confident style of the journalist or the cadences of the natural orator, and it bears only faint resemblance to the crisp and moving experience narratives of two decades before, which it seems to be imitating.

Incredibly, given his current state, in May Deakin had 'Another wave of doubt' regarding his retirement. He felt he could now rely only upon his 'faith in the summons' he had received through that voice.[89] But the final impetus for his retirement was forced upon Deakin finally in September 1912, when in a curiously detached tone, he recorded a horrendous breakdown:

> The last ten days has witnessed my first decisive breakdown in faculty & in health, in brain & digestion, in mental & physical energy, all at the same time. There is little doubt now of my early disqualification for permanent public office or work. Whatever the symptoms sprang from, they afforded clear evidences of nervous & mental collapse.[90]

Deakin could not retire until a new leader for the Fusion was elected. The contenders were John Forrest and the Freetrader Joseph Cook, who won on Deakin's casting vote in January 1913. Given his long-standing fears about Freetrade, it seems ironic and incongruous both politically and morally that it would leave Forrest, his long-time friend and supporter, with a bitter taste of treachery. His choice of Cook is puzzling, though he may have considered pragmatically that the support of New South Wales was more crucial to Federation than that of Western Australia, and Deakin weighed other factors like Forrest's age of sixty-five years, and his 'casual and neglectful' manner in the House. But in a letter to Forrest he insisted that Cook's loyal and hard-working service since he became deputy leader four years before 'made it my duty to support him'.[91]

On Deakin's retirement, a letter from Higgins expressed his own regret at his decision, and those in all parties who had seen how he had 'sweetened and ennobled politics'. Higgins could not have known how his kind and thoughtful closing comment, 'I suppose that in your retirement you will plunge more deeply than ever into your books',[92] must have greatly saddened its recipient. Casting a retrospective eye on his career, a newspaper editorial observed that his personal integrity had never been in question, for he was not in politics 'for the loaves and fishes'. Among his many strengths were modesty, a thorough commitment to democracy and an Australian patriotism. His weakness was hesitancy and 'a susceptibility to outside pressure that killed a political career which might have been historic'.[93]

There were periods of relative lucidity. An article he was reading in February on 'Freedom' prompted Deakin to contemplate an essay which would 'lay out the "concept" freedom open to serious challenge by writing a plain record of a few of the most striking & significant experiences of the occult which were mine in my youth & particularly of those prophetic in character'.[94] Sadly, Deakin had already forgotten that he had produced at least two lengthy and detailed records of these experiences, firstly in 'Personal Experiences ...', and again less than three years before, in a general account of his early life. Retrospectives on his public and literary life continued to appear in the journals, increasingly repetitive and halting, along with more reflections on his early spiritism, on parents, wife and sister, punctuated with frequent assessments of his 'brain fag', about which in February 1914 he wrote:

> flashes of restoration are neither frequent nor durable. Knowledge comes & goes, after I have seen the natural development of an argument or a situation perfectly clear [sic] before me most & sometimes all of it vanishes so quickly & as [sic] absolutely that I cannot retain or describe a single feature of all that was obvious & lucid a second before ...[95]

He had no suicidal tendencies, 'though for a moment of wrath & despair I often feel capable of any sacrifice rather than prolong my miserably inept & useless existence.'[96]

From this point onward Deakin's mental world was shrinking, and the darkness began rapidly to close. On 29 August 1914 war had just been declared, and as Deakin was laboriously writing a tract bemoaning the 'poor bare animal & vegetable growth that man is', he was interrupted by a telephone call from Cook, now Prime Minister, urging him to accept a post as member of the Food Supplies Commission. Deakin did not want to, and he doubted his strength, but would agree if Cook thought it essential: 'he does—that settles poor me.'[97] Deakin could not contribute very much to the commission, which had a short but busy tenure, and it was disbanded when Labor came to power at the end of the year.

A more painful episode arose from another appointment which Cook had urged successfully on Deakin before losing office, the presidency of the Australian Pavilion at the Panama Exhibition. There was some confusion over whether with war declared, the Exhibition should be terminated. The ruthless Hugh Mahon, the new Minister for External Affairs, sensing incorrectly on Deakin's part an attempt to subvert the authority of Cabinet, set about settling old scores at the expense of a confused but dignified Deakin, who indignantly denied culpability. A reply from Mahon smugly observed: 'The candor of your denial is superficially impressive, but I reflect that there is an intellectual process, known to theological casuistry as "mental reservation". Perchance you have had some fleeting familiarity with this branch of the dialectical art', he asked patronisingly. Mahon then twisted the knife: 'Nothing in your laboured apologia can obscure the outstanding fact that ... you resuscitated the cadaver by a coup, in keeping with your olden feats in another sphere.'[98] Pattie wrote of Mahon that 'no words can express the bitterness and meanness of his actions.'[99] If it is an unsavoury episode, it is further testimony to a sea change in the politics of the era. Prior to the Fusion, no politician would have felt such rancour against him, and it had been an unwritten rule in the early Commonwealth parliaments that Mr Deakin was exempt from the vitriol poured regularly on colleagues. Now another generation of Labor men, led by that master of political invective W. M. Hughes, had relegated Deakin to their populous outer darkness.

Following the Panama Exhibition debacle, Deakin resigned and came home. More aloof than ever he avoided company, and he continued to attempt to write and to assess his mental decline. In a journal written at the end of 1915 headed *'Notes to be kept in mind & gradually made clear'*, Deakin lamented: 'I learn nothing new that exists for me more than a few days—What I think I have learned soon dies away into a mere tag & tangle of words, words, words ...'.[100] In late 1916 Deakin sailed with Pattie for London and New York in a desperate attempt to find a cure among the leading medical specialists. It was to no avail. From this time Deakin virtually gave up writing, even in his diary. His last and heavily overscored diary entry was recorded on 19 January 1917. Once more expressing his disgust with his fragmented memory 'fleeting, partial, pretentious, self contradictory & self applauding', he admitted:

> ... Life has ended—in truth in fact & in judgment—None can know, not even my self ... what once I was capable of doing or did ... The bell has struck its last final warning— My memory is but a little fiction a chance return of the pitiful & a withering memorial of AD.[101]

He was too hard on himself. At his best, 'Deakin the Dreamer' would never have dwelt on these dark days of growing incoherence and depression. His true memorial rests in what he believed he, in concert with many others, had been allowed by the Grace of Providence to achieve for his countrymen. Except perhaps in those very last moments of what he termed his 'lapse into fatuity', that indomitable Faith had sustained his optimistic view of the unity of all life, and had borne glorious fruit in the practical legacy of stable government in a truly national union. The tender and lyrical soul of Deakin the perennial optimist celebrating an abiding Faith in life, in rejuvenation and renewal, in the profound conviction that 'all things come together for good' is expressed in the mood of a poem, perhaps his best, written 'impromptu' in May 1910, only a month following his crushing political defeat:

> *O bird song—can it be*
> *That I at last am free*
> *This mellow autumn morning time to muse and*
> *list to thee—*
>
> *Returning to my own,*
> *Myself, my life, alone—*
> *To privacy to liberty—to fresh seed to be sown*
>
> *Tho sunshine's misty gold*
> *Shows leafage yellowing mould—*
> *It floods my captive heart with youth*
> *When all seemed spent and old*
>
> *Yes! Tho so late—I sing,*
> *Race swallows on the wing*
> *Share their lightness and their brightness*
> *Speeding sunward to the Spring.*[102]

Notes

1   'Clues', vol. 4, 3/286, no. 609, 7 April 1893; on the significance of 'New Protection', the Harvester judgment, and the Fusion on Australian history, see J. Rickard, *Class and Politics, New South Wales, Victoria and the Commonwealth 1890-1910*, Canberra, 1976, pp. 204, 211 and *passim*.

2   In 1905 there were 57 such notations, nearly doubling the next year to 96. His 1907 diary records 65 notations of exhaustion, and Deakin was suffering frequently also from giddiness.

3   Diary, 15 February 1907.

4   'A Dreamers Diary', no. 64, 3 March 1907; Lady White Notebook I, copy in La Nauze papers, series 5248, N.L.A. This is the only prayer inscribed in this 'Clues' style journal.

5   Ibid.

6   Deakin's industry is all the more remarkable given the condition of his health. Lord Milner praised Deakin's 'extraordinary intellectual energy'; London *Times*, 17 May 1907. L. S. Amery wrote in his memoirs that he rated Deakin 'the greatest natural orator' of his day in English, as Briand was in French: quoted in La Nauze, *Alfred Deakin*, vol. 1, p. 245.

7   Diary, 12 April 1907.

8   Deakin to A. G. Stephens, undated, circa June 1907.

9   Diary, 11 June 1907.

10 Pattie Deakin, Reminiscences, 19/288, undated.

11 J. A. La Nauze and Elizabeth Nurser (eds), *Walter Murdoch and Alfred Deakin on Books and Men*, Melbourne, 1974, p. 73.

12 Among Deakin's retrospectives, see Foolscap A1 Notebook, 3/293, 5-9 June 1910; Foolscap A3 Notebook, 3/294, 6-14 May 1911; an especially lengthy account in Counsel Fees, 3/290, between August and November 1913, pp. 140-235; and less coherent attempts in 'A Ragged Re-Examination of the Ultimate', November-December 1915, pp. 65-75, and 3-4 January 1916; Lady White Notebook II, copy in La Nauze papers, series 5248, N.L.A.

13 Deakin's medical condition was indeed complex. He suffered heart attacks and cardio-vascular distress. His amnesia, according to a modern medical authority, is not uncommon, and was connected with blood pressure, and a degeneration of the brain tissue and the vascular system. It could be brought on or hastened by periods of intense strain. Such cases occur in excitable people, and often memories of childhood and distant events are clear, but not the recent past. It is a condition more likely to occur in men with big frames, and along with depressive symptoms and self-blame, it is accompanied by sleeplessness, and often by a consciousness of progressive degeneration: J. A. La Nauze, conversation with Professor R. D. Wright, 27 February 1957, transcript in La Nauze papers, series 5248, N.L.A. For Deakin's own account of the history of his breakdowns, see Red Spine Book, 3/281, 4 September 1913.

14 The degree of Deakin's absorption is evident in journals written during his conva-lescence upon his return from the Imperial Conference On 18 September 1907, labouring to express a thought concerning 'the way of salvation', he wrote five 'Clues' of varying lengths. Having completed no. 12, he marvelled in no. 15 at how, though he was tired, nos. 13 and 14 'at once follow as its completion'. In no. 16 he commented further: 'To get rid of a haunting thought is a marked relief & also an impetus. Sometimes I hardly know what the thought is when I commence to try to express

it & quite often as in this case it carries with [it] a concealed progeny ... the curious sense of doing what one wished to do without having known that one wished to do it is often notable'. 'Clues', vol. 5, 3/282, nos. 12–15, 18 September 1907. Deakin had inaugurated this final volume of 'Clues' on 30 July, upon returning from England, recommencing with no. 1.

15 Ibid., no. 44, 11 November 1907.

16 Ibid., no. 66, 5 January 1908.

17 Book of Prayers, 5/1044, prayer XLVIII, 5 January 1908.

18 Alkemade to Deakin, 25 November 1910.

19 La Nauze, *Alfred Deakin*, vol. 2, p. 540.

20 Autobiographical Notes, typescript, 3/300, 6 February 1909.

21 The world tour was to be funded by South African industrialist Abe Bailey: ibid., 13 February 1909.

22 La Nauze, *Alfred Deakin*, vol. 2, p. 556.

23 On the Fusion from the point of view of the conservative forces at State and federal level, see J. Rickard, *Class and Politics ...*, p. 254 ff.

24 Diaries from 1909 have frequent references not only to being 'exhausted' and poor sleep, but also to being 'very nervy', with regular entries regarding taking 'doses' of an unspecified medication, possibly laudanum. See Diary, 24 April 1909, 5 and 22 July 1909. In one journal he noted: '[Dr] Crivelli has patched me up & stimulated me': Red Spine Book, 3/281, 18 September 1912.

25 Autobiographical Notes, typescript, 3/300, 7 January 1909.

26 This is one of the rare instances of Deakin using his own initials, which has here an ironic tone: Autobiographical Notes, typescript 3/300, 5 February 1910.

27 'Under Australian Skies', in *Life*, 1 May 1910, p. 469.

28 The defeat of the 'Fusion' was monumental; Deakin made the sardonic observation that they had lost in every constituency in which he had spoken, and he was almost right; the only constituency they had won was his own, and that by only 443 votes in 20,000: M. H. Ellis, 'Deakin the Dreamer', *Bulletin*, 23 June 1962, p. 21.

29 Diary, 16 and 18 March 1910; 2–6 April 1910.

30 Autobiographical Notes, typescript, 3/300, 6 May 1910.

31 Red Spine Book, 3/281, 29 May 1910.

32 Ibid., 27 May 1910.

33 Ibid., 29 May 1910.

34 'Medley', 3/296, 'Clue' no. 808, 11 March 1903.

35 Red Spine Book, 3/281, 3 September 1910.

36 Foolscap A3 Notebook, 3/294, September 1910.

37 Ibid., 24 September 1910.

38 'Medley', 3/296, 'Clue' no. 848, 21 May 1910, pp. 64–6.

39 Ibid. p. 65.

40 Ibid., 3 June and 28 July 1910, p. 66.

41 Ibid., 21 May 1910, p. 66.

42 Red Spine Book, 3/281, XV, 4 November 1910.

43 Ibid.

44 Ibid., XVIII, 12 November 1910, p. 83.

45 Ibid.; the original rendering of this paragraph spoke of 'a whispered monition *of*'.

46 Ibid.

47 Ibid., p. 84.

48 Three pages were [completed?] at 6.45 a.m., and another page at 10.30 a.m.: ibid., XVIII and XIX, 13 November 1910, pp. 90–3; XX and XXI, 27 November 1910, pp. 94–9.

49 F. W. H. Myers, *Human Personality and its Survival of Bodily Death*, 2 vols, London, 1903; those associated with the societies included eminent persons in all fields. Among the literati were J. A. Symonds, poet and scholar of the Italian Renaissance, W. B. Yeats, Frederick Tennyson, Andrew Lang, 'Lewis Carroll' and Laurence Oliphant. Psychologists besides James included G. F. Stout, Liebault, Bernheim, McDougall, Janet, Flournoy, Richet, and Lombroso; even Dr Freud contributed a paper to the S.P.R. *Proceedings* in 1913. Among physicists there were William Crookes and Oliver Lodge, who became identified with Spiritualism, and J. J. Thomson, discoverer of the electron, and Lord Rayleigh, famous for his recalculation of the absolute units of electrical measurement, who remained strictly psychical researchers. The membership included a host of clergymen. Politicians were represented by W. Gladstone, and especially Arthur Balfour, who was the society's president in 1894, and his brother Gerard: Oppenheim, *The Other World* . . ., p. 245.

50 'Medley', 3/296, 'Clue' no. 802, 18 January 1903.

51 H. S. Hughes, *Consciousness and Society, the Reorientation of European Social Thought 1890–1930*, New York, 1977, p. 66.

52 Janet Oppenheim, *The Other World* . . ., surveys the contributions of psychical research to the theoretical studies of personality, telepathy and especially hypnotism; after World War I, with the trend to psychoanalysis, they became irrelevant.

53 Oppenheim, *The Other World* . . ., p. 200.

54 F. W. H. Myers, 'General Characteristics of Subliminal Messages', in *Proceedings of the Society for Psychical Research*, London, 1892; quoted in Oppenheim, *The Other World* . . ., p. 257.

55 A. Gauld, *The Founders of Psychical Research*, New York, 1968, p. 278.

56 Oppenheim, *The Other World* . . ., p. 263.

57 William James, *Varieties of Religious Experience, Being the Gifford Lectures on Natural Religion delivered at Edinburgh in 1901–02*, London, 1929, p. 29.

58 Ibid., p. 484.

59 Ibid., p. 242.

60 Ibid., p. 508.

61 Oppenheim, *The Other World* . . ., pp. 259–60; see: 'Myers & the Subliminal self', 'Medley', 3/296, 'Clue' no. 810, undated, circa March 1903, pp. 178–82; and 'Eucken & Co', Red Spine Book, 3/281, XLIV, begun on 23 March 1912 and 'finished hurriedly' on 19 October 1912, pp. 202–31.

62 See B. Wiltshire, *William James and Phenomenology*, Bloomington, 1968.

63 Oppenheim, *The Other World* ..., p. 265.

64 Red Spine Book, 3/281, XVIII, 12 November 1910, p. 83.

65 On 9 January 1913 Deakin recorded what was apparently another message received in the same manner: '... arising from the subconscious or descending from the superconscious realms within, there came, as I was waking, in the fanciful fashion occasionally experienced by me, two short sets of key words, which seemed to evoke or at least to express my inner mood, disclosed to me as I awoke an hour or so ago—the first was *"filmy"* which to me symbolized our merely surface knowledge of the inner self (not to speak of higher elements of the Unspeakable) ... [the next] *"flimsy"* which covered our human knowledge, philosophies ... and *"unfathomable"* a finger-post word pointing to the abyss, to the Infinite ...'. There is much more, but this passage strongly suggests a forced endeavour to repeat the November 1910 experience; Autobiographical Notes, typescript, 3/300, 9 January 1913.

66 Red Spine Book, 3/281, XVIII, 12 November 1910, p. 87.

67 Ibid., p. 88.

68 'The Script', 5/1455, stanza XXIII. The devotional poetry consists of three cycles each in 49 verses of varying lengths. These meditations upon a theme—Knowledge, Faith, the Soul, God—repetitious, employing much alliteration, and treating subjects as antinomies, are rhymed generally in couplets. Surprisingly they are mostly undated, but the occasional date places the middle of the work at around Federation. Cycle I 'The Script', Cycle II 'The Way', and Cycle III 'Pray', relate to the symbolism of seven in occultism, in what appears to have been a form of verse prayer. 5/1454-5, 2 vols, undated.

69 Red Spine Book, 3/281, XVIII, 12 November 1910, p. 83.

70 Ibid., XIX, 13 November 1910, p. 93.

71 Ibid., XXI, 27 November 1910, p. 97.

72 Ibid.

73 Ibid., XIX, 13 November 1910, p. 93.

74 Diary, 1 January 1911.

75 Diary, 7 April 1911.

76 Red Spine Book, 3/281, 14 April 1911.

77 Diary, 26 April 1911, called it: *'The Day'*; Red Spine Book, 3/281, 28 April 1911, p. 13.

78 Deakin to Herbert Brookes, 28 April 1911.

79 Ibid.

80 Red Spine Book, 3/281, 2 June 1911, p. 37.

81 Ibid.

82 Autobiographical Notes, typescript, 3/300, 10 December 1911.

83 Quoted in La Nauze and Nurser (eds), *Walter Murdoch and Alfred Deakin* ..., p. 58; Murdoch told La Nauze that after moving to Perth he had seen Deakin again on a visit to Melbourne: 'He was greeted with the old warmth and dignity, but it became evident that Deakin did not really recognise him': Ibid., p. 69.

84 Red Spine Book, 3/281, XXXI, 7 October 1911.

85 Ibid., X, 6 May 1911, p. 17.

86 Red Spine Book, 3/281, 25 November 1911.

87 Autobiographical Notes, typescript, 3/300, 3 January 1912.

88 Red Spine Book, 3/281, 10 February 1912, p. 190.

89 Ibid., XXI, 14 May 1912, p. 53.

90 Ibid., 18 September 1912, p. 57.

91 Deakin to John Forrest, 10 February 1913, La Nauze papers, series 5248, N.L.A.

92 H. B. Higgins to Deakin, 9 January 1913.

93 *Catholic Press*, 16 January 1913.

94 Red Spine Book, 3/281, XXXV, 20 February 1913, p. 77.

95 'Medley', 3/296, 26 February 1914, p. 116.

96 Ibid.

97 Literary Memoranda, typescript, 3/302, 29 August 1914.

98 H. Mahon to Deakin, 13 January 1915.

99 Pattie Deakin, Reminiscences, 19/289, undated.

100 Autobiographical Notes, typescript, 3/300, 30 December 1915.

101 Diary, 19 January 1917.

102 'Medley', 3/296, 14 May 1910, p. 62.

Conclusion

Professor La Nauze observed that Alfred Deakin was 'determined to have a mysterious universe';[1] Deakin would have insisted that he *found* himself in such a universe, a Kosmos of 'inexhaustible mysteries' made comprehensible, moreover, only by a spiritual interpretation. In examining the shifting patterns and textures of Deakin's eclectic personal religion, we have seen that a great deal of his energies were consumed in attempting to unravel some of these mysteries, especially those relating to his own being and destiny, and in applying these insights to his life and, with an augmenting commitment to secular service, to his political labours. That Alfred Deakin lived his life by an Inner Light is patent. His spiritual belief could be called Unitarian, and it had affinities with the Quaker faith. While he regarded himself as a follower of Jesus Christ, his pantheon of 'World Teachers' included also Buddha, Socrates, and Mohammed, and his conceptions had more in common with Judaism, Neo-Platonism and Gnosticism than the Anglican faith in which he was nominally reared. Yet while they testify to the breadth of his vision, these terms fall far short of an adequate description of Deakin's intense spiritual Faith.

It has been said frequently that the Victorian and Edwardian era was a time of religious doubt, as the triumphs of science undermined the authority of the Bible and opened religion to the private conscience. Historians of the period have generally considered the ructions caused in religion in terms of their social effects on the churches, which in consequence began to stake out a greater social role.[2] But the historical record has been weighted heavily against the vigorous heterodoxy of the era. Janet Oppenheim posed a challenge to historians with her observation that in their reaction to materialism the attitudes of those involved in Spiritualism and psychical research were 'far more representative of contemporary religious attitudes than the agnosticism embraced by the comparatively few intellectuals who have dominated the historical record of that crisis'.[3] Though her comments relate to the English scene, they apply with equal force to Australia.

Like Cardinal Newman, Arthur Balfour, Josiah Royce and other Idealist intellectuals of his time, Deakin was reacting against the current 'materialism' of his day in the manner and with the presuppositions at hand, being especially keen to defend immortality as the basis of true morality. His early spiritistic investigations had made him sanguine as to a continued existence beyond the grave, and they formed the basis of an enduring conviction of another Reality interpenetrating this world and having direct effects upon human life and society. In an era characterised by religious doubt, Deakin's heterodoxy was unusual neither in this interest in Theosophy and psychical research, which he shared with other Australian public men like Judge Windeyer, Inglis-Clark, W. D. C. Denovan, Dr Charles Strong and even David Syme, nor in a conviction of guidance.[4] At the turn of the century, an abiding interest in psychical research and its religious implications informed the inner life of leaders at both ends of the Empire, Arthur Balfour of Great Britain and his counterpart Deakin at the Antipodes, and with Smuts in South Africa Deakin shared not only a habit of private introspection, but something of a capacity for mystical rapture.[5] Psychical research was widely regarded as an experimental branch of psychology, and 'occult' interests were far more respectable than in our own era. When the Theosophical leader Colonel H. J. Olcott toured the colonies in 1891, his Sydney lecture was introduced by Edmund Barton; he shared the platform with Dr Garran, former editor of the *Sydney Morning Herald*, who moved a vote of thanks for his address, which Lady Jersey, the wife of the Governor, who was in the audience, judged as having 'excited considerable interest'.[6]

What marks Deakin out among the elite, political, professional and intellectual, in which he moved, beyond an abiding faith in Providence and in the role of prophecy, were his own remarkable private experiences, and the great authority they were to assume toward the end of his life. These peak experiences which were understood at various times as aesthetic reveries, mental mediumship, or Divine Influx conveyed through 'Subliminal' channels, were the cherished fruits of Deakin's inner strivings.[7] Neither the ecstatic reveries, when at times he was 'witched out' of himself by a vision of Beauty or Truth, nor the sedulous scrutiny of the course of events and the confidence in prophetic utterance, nor the intimate authority of those 'voices' heard in 1899 and again in 1910, bear parallels among his peers. It is thus on the level of experience, if anywhere, that Alfred Deakin must be considered a mystic.

Through the powerful metaphors of Self and Mission Deakin understood the essence and purpose of his life, which he expressed in his journals and prayer books as an Ideal of a life devoted to the pursuit of a Higher Truth, and service to a personal God, to humanity and especially to the Anglo-Saxon race. He would have been the first to confess that he constantly failed, but added that the Ideal is by definition unattainable. It was the sincerity of effort and the sublimity of moral intention, the aspiration nourished by occasional inspiration, that continued to give meaning and direction to his existence. What has engaged our attention is how Deakin perceived his role in this cosmic drama.

We have observed that central tension developing early in life, constantly represented to himself as a contrast between the 'higher' life of the poet, the mystic and the religious, and the 'lower' life, the 'cold dead level' of politics. Yet he remained a politician, gaining in stature as parliamentary leader and orator even while he privately prayed for that 'quieter & holier way'. Frequently, after a day of tense debate in Parliament and unable to sleep, Deakin would enter his intimate world of books and private writing, and that sacred region of prayer and meditation, sometimes working well into the night. There he continued in secret a literary discourse he felt unable to share with the world, though he was arguably one of the finest prose writers of his day. There too his faith was rejuvenated, when at times he received an answer to his perplexities, and he would communicate through the pen his gratitude for a 'sign' that had been vouchsafed to him. Clearly writing was a central activity to Deakin's inner life, one that *integrated* his experience, aspiration and belief into an unity he could recognise. All private writing does this to some extent, but like his public oratory, it was the intensity and sincerity of these performances to Self that made him an unusual person.

Reflection and introspection were constant activities, and we have seen through Deakin's private discourse with Self his changing conceptions of the Ideal. Hence just prior to the Grand Prophecy he concluded the year's diary with a 'Polycrates ring', a caveat to himself not to allow political power to blind him to his true Goal, or to let it become 'pleasing or even necessary' to him. Less than a week later he received that first important 'sign' in the Grand Prophecy, whose spiritual significance was to augment over the rest of his life. By the end of that first trip 'home' in 1887, after discussions with Hodgson and Bryce, Deakin proclaimed in his travelling diary his newly-found Mission, to 'awaken' the 'natives' to the urgent need to federate the Australian colonies, a task he laboured at for thirteen years. The *Federal Story*, the public narrative of the Federation struggle, at times against seemingly insurmountable obstacles, was an oblique testament to Divine authority for Australian nationhood. With the remarkable audition of October 1899 there came a sea change in Deakin's paradigm of Inspiration, illustrated in the later 'out of body' experience narratives. A crisis of Duty in 1905 was characteristically debated with himself in special journals like 'Materials' and 'Personal Equations', and allegorised in that curious final gospel 'Ten Letters'. We have observed finally through his agonising in late journals how, having identified his inner life almost completely with his political career, Deakin obeyed an instruction to 'turn in', completing in the process a final 'job' with the defeat of the 1911 Labor referenda he believed would have meant the demise of Federalism.

Though articulated only indirectly even in intimate prayer, the manifest destiny of the Anglo-Saxon race was a living Ideal to Deakin, and as his strenuous ritual performances in London suggest, the idea of a self-sustaining outpost of the race in the Antipodes was intimately related to his sense of Mission. Belief in supernatural guidance has accompanied political power at least since the Pharaohs, providing a rationale for a Savonarola to burn heretical books as readily as it could fire Florence Nightingale, through an early vision of Christ, to work for 'sanitation'.[8] For Deakin the conviction of a political Mission evolved slowly, though from the first there was a strong sense of being a 'man apart'. Gradually he came to believe that along with countless others, he was engaged for his own time and place, however imperfectly and despite all the 'littlenesses' a career in politics required, in executing this larger Purpose. Though its outlines remained opaque, and he might have considered it rank presumption to look too far behind the veil, the fulfilment of that Purpose 'long locked within us' became the fundamental Ideal in Alfred Deakin's life, the engine of all his endeavours, public and private.

There was another powerful and enduring aspect of Deakin's belief, that his good fortune signified that Providence would in time require payment, through the sacrifice of self in some form of service. It was the other side of being conspicuously blessed with a happy family life, a meteoric rise in politics and countless opportunities. A sense of undeserved blessings and personal failings complete the equation, in a pattern of insufficiency common to the religious minded, especially the Christian. But its special role in Deakin's inner life was the imperative it spelled, and the manner in which he felt he neither deserved his bounty, nor had made fruitful use of what was given. It is a pattern discerned also in Deakin's public life, as on the three occasions when he was called to London as 'tribune' of the people.

In arguing for colonial autonomy in 1887, in defending the Constitution in 1900, and again in labouring for closer imperial ties in 1907, Deakin came curiously full circle, but he also followed a familiar and significant pattern. On each occasion, an energetic populist appeal to the British public through its press was accompanied by a separate appeal to the political and social elite of England through banqueting and speech-making, together with strenuous lobbying and oratorical performances in conference. On each of these occasions he placed a greater burden on his health, and it is this fact that more than hints at the potent symbolism of 'Sacrifice' in Alfred Deakin's inner life. Seeking always to apply his religion of 'the Best', he exacted a heavy personal toll, and after 1907, he never recovered fully. This aspect of Sacrifice was a powerful moulding force for his religious world view culminating in strenuous labour and broken health, but accomplishing much in the process.

In his Ideal of personal illumination, through his cherished 'individual' experiences, Deakin achieved what he might have considered moderate success. What links them in the texts, beyond vague, general or 'literary' references, are the two auditory experiences of 1899 and 1910. Deakin's success however was considerable, so far as a person living in the real world can succeed, in his efforts to live according to his moral Ideal of Unselfish Love. Through the higher phenomena of prophecy and inspiration, the Ideal was broadened constantly. If Deakin's quest for illumination was only a qualified and sporadic success, even a failure, measured by the insights it brought concerning the 'invisible', his sincere desire to serve was a glorious triumph in the tangible results rendered to posterity, though even here Deakin was clearly not so sure in those later muddled years. Perhaps we can only speculate, with the strong indication provided by the subtext of his final allegory, that greater spiritual credit derives from greater sacrifice. If he was a failure in his quest for Truth, perhaps that was part of the price, and maybe too part of the reward. Like 'I' in 'Ten Letters', Deakin eschewed the 'sweets' of a higher illumination to return to the 'world'.

Alfred Deakin was a mystic if that term be defined by a heterodox world view, an explicit belief in personal guidance, and the operation of spiritual influences on this world. But most importantly, as I have endeavoured to show, his faith was sustained by prophecy and 'signs' and later, with 'a return upon Mystic sources of consolation',[9] by those remarkable private experiences. A lifelong dedication to Duty bore tangible results in what I have argued was *sui generis* a spiritual Mission. We have traced something of the texture and changing patterns in the inner life of an important Australian intellectual, a visionary whose 'practical' mysticism has left an enduring legacy in the institutions and the political processes of his beloved nation. This enduring faith, fed by aspiration, sustained by the occasional inspiration, melded to a moral Ideal of Unselfish Love, and understood within an intellectual framework that incorporated evolution and reincarnation, constituted the essence of Alfred Deakin's personal religion.

For beautiful simplicity and sincerity of intent, no words can express Alfred Deakin's vision better than his own. Part verdict on his existence and part aspiration for the future, they were written in late 1910 in that extended reflection following the monition:

> I should like to die used up in a practical sense, having
> *spent my all, given all, done all, and accepted all in peace.*[10]

Notes

1 La Nauze, *Alfred Deakin*, vol. 1, p. 65.

2 W. W. Phillips, *Defending 'A Christian Country'*, discusses the impact of this crisis in Australia, and the adaptability of the churchmen, especially to the challenges of modern science and the Higher Criticism; see chapter 10, 'The Legacy of the 1880s'.

3 J. Oppenheim, *The Other World* ..., p. 2. See also Jill Roe, *Beyond Belief* ..., p. 5, for comments on the break of the grip of rationalistic historiography, as with Frances Yates' study of *Giordano Bruno and the Hermetic Tradition*, London, 1964.

4 Diary, 30 January 1897, refers to 'Clark's gathering—Theosophy'; see also C. Badger, *The Reverend Charles Strong* ..., p. 232.

5 Deakin's contemporary as Prime Minister, Arthur Balfour, became convinced of a continued life in the hereafter from the remarkable 'cross-correspondences' of psychical research, rather than via any personal illumination. See J. Oppenheim, *The Other World* ...; W. K. Hancock, *Smuts*, 2 vols, Cambridge, 1962, vol. 1, p. 13.

6 See Jill Roe, *Beyond Belief* ..., pp. 65–8, for an account of Olcott's 1891 Australian tour; for Newman's attitudes to 'materialism', see Geoffrey Faber, *Oxford Apostles*, pp. 19, 415–20.

7 Abraham Maslow identifies a range of ego-transcending experiences sharing 25 common characteristics; among these are that the occasional reception of such experiences gives meaning to life, they are self-validating, there is an attenuated consciousness of time and space, and that peak experiences involve the emotions of wonder, awe, reverence, humility, surrender and worship: A. Maslow, *Religions, Values, and Peak Experiences*, Columbus, 1964, pp. 59–68.

8 F. B. Smith, *Florence Nightingale: Reputation and Power*, Canberra, 1982.

9 Red Spine Book, 3/281, no. 26, 3 October 1911, p. 127.

10 Ibid., 8 December 1910.

Index